The Million-Dollar Bugs

Other books by Michael Pearson

The
Million-Dollar
Bugs

by MICHAEL PEARSON

G. P. Putnam's Sons
New York

To Sue, who has had to cope, not only with the lengthy absences from home, but also with ethical drugs as a subject of conversation for a very long time

1

ON a warm September morning in 1961—in a large room on the third floor of New York's towering white Federal Courthouse—three men stood before a judge. One of them was exceptionally tall; at six feet three, he loomed above the other two. He was a man of fifty-six, with steel-rimmed glasses, dark hair that was graying, and he had a kind of quiet dignity that suggested that he was accustomed to authority. His name was Dr. Wilbur Malcolm.

"Have you read the indictment?" asked the judge.

"I have," answered Malcolm.

"And how do you plead?"

"Not guilty."

The prosecutor rose to his feet. "If it please your Honor," he said, "the government asks for bail to be fixed."

Surprise spread across the judge's face—not least because the issue of bail had already been agreed on in his chambers. Then his lips tightened. "I think," he said, dismissing the request, "that it's unlikely that the defendants will flee the country."

It was indeed unlikely. For Wilbur Malcolm was the antithesis of even the broadest concept of an alleged criminal.

He was rich. He was a man of power. He enjoyed high status and great respect—both as an executive and as a scientist—and his career was marked by unqualified achievement. As the $135,000-a-year chairman of the board of the American Cyanamid Company he bossed a multimillion-dollar corporation, long established in U.S. industry, with operations throughout the world.

More important, perhaps, he could claim what few other top American executives could claim. He had without question enriched the condition of man. During his rise to the supreme role in the corporation, he had provided the dynamic behind the discovery of a series of revolutionary new drugs that had saved millions of lives and helped transform major scourges into minor, easily curable diseases.

Why then, on this September morning, was he facing criminal charges for which, if proved, he could be sentenced to jail? [1] It was a query that could also be posed about the two men standing beside him. For John McKeen, president of Charles Pfizer and Company, and Frederic Schwartz, executive head of Bristol-Myers Company, were also responsible for the large-scale production of drugs worth millions of dollars every year.

Essentially, in the answer to the question lies the tortured story not merely of three industrialists, but of a whole industry racked between the conflicting forces of human welfare and the profit motive. Its fantastic record of achievement over the past thirty years has brought benefits to humanity that are completely without precedent. But ironically, these successes have been produced against—or even because of—a turbulent background that, at first sight, seems to have no place in the curing of disease: enormous profits; fierce competition; the violent conflict of giant corporations that, in certain cases, went far beyond the limits of aggressive promotion to encompass such techniques of private detection as bugging of competitors' telephone lines; industrial espionage financed by big foreign companies; the legal exploitation of the patent laws by teams of skillful lawyers; and, most important of all, a long and acrimonious battle that is still being punched out in Washington with a dedicated opposition lobby and the U.S. government.

The story of Cyanamid is the story of the drug industry itself; it intertwines all these elements. The company's executives pioneered some of the first and most important of what were known, before they became commonplace, as the wonder drugs. They fought competitors, they fought industrial spies, and they fought the government. Sometimes they won, and sometimes they lost. Either way, the spectacle can only astonish the lay witness and pose this question: Is this truly the best way for society to produce and distribute its panaceas?

The indictment of Wilbur Malcolm and the other two executives in 1961 was the first overt move in court in a ten-year struggle—the repercussions of which will reverberate through America for a long time—between the Justice Department and the makers of the $100,000,000 worth of tetracycline antibiotics that were then sold to the U.S. public every year. The charges accused them of rigging the market to protect big profits in the most important drug in this group—a product, commonly sold under trade names like Achromycin and Tetracyn in the form of round yellow pills that have been swallowed at times of illness by almost everybody in the United States.

If the directors of other drug companies sympathized with the three executives—and the evidence, which was mostly undisputed, contained little in the way of Machiavellian intrigue —it was because they operated their companies in much the same way as the men accused. They shared with them the same motivation, the same attitudes and the same fears. In fact, the prosecution came at a time when the whole industry was under cold and critical public scrutiny, when newspaper headlines often accused it of gross profiteering in human sickness. But the root cause of this hostility—and of Wilbur Malcolm's fight with the government—lay way back in the thirties. For it was only then that research—the key to the whole dilemma of the drug-makers—first began to appear as a sizable item in their balance sheets.

The age of the wonder drugs erupted, for all practical purposes, in 1938. Six years earlier, in the Bayer plant in Elber-field, Germany, Dr. Gerhard Domagk tested the healing effect of dyes on mice that had been infected with lethal doses of streptococci germs. But although most of these animals died from septicemia, he did make one important discovery. If he fed the mice the red dye Prontosil *before* infecting them with disease bacteria, they survived.

In February, 1935, Domagk's daughter, Hildegarde, acquired a poisoned finger. Despite surgery, she ran a high fever and displayed most of the symptoms that the chemist had seen in the mice he had infected with the same germs. As she deteriorated, it soon became clear to Domagk that, like his animals, his daughter was going to die. Desperately, he made her swallow a big dose of Prontosil.

Hildegarde recovered. The next year, in Queen Charlotte's Hospital in London, Dr. Leonard Colebrook decided to try Prontosil on some of his patients who were severely ill with puerperal fever—a disease that was often fatal following childbirth. He wrote in the *British Medical Journal*:

> At first we treated only the more severe cases, for which we had no promising therapy. The grave prognosis in such cases had become all too familiar to us. The death rate had ranged consistently between twenty and thirty per cent.
> Almost at once, with the new drug, there was a surprising

and most gratifying change. Signs of incipient peritonitis did not develop as we expected; positive blood cultures changed quickly to negative. . . . This was something we had never seen before in ten years' experience of the disease.

The case mortality in the first series of 64 patients . . . was 4.7%. In the previous five years before Prontosil it had ranged from 16.6 to 31.6% averaging about 25%.

Scientists at the Pasteur Institute in Paris showed that the active agent in Prontosil that attacked the streptococcal infection was a substance—discovered years before in 1908, but undeveloped—called sulfonamide.

It changed the whole direction of medicine. In 1936 two U.S. doctors attended a meeting in London where English physicians reported on their results. They were Perrin H. Long and Eleanor Bliss of Johns Hopkins University, Baltimore, and they conducted the first experiments with the sulfas in America—on a seven-year-old child suffering from erysipelas and a woman dangerously ill with puerperal fever. They reported vividly: "We witnessed quinsies melt away, the advance of erysipelas stopped in its tracks and running ears dry up in a short time. . . ."

But doctors like this were rare. The medical profession, accustomed as it was to quack remedies, was highly cynical of the claims for the new drugs, for the sulfonamides operated in a way that was outside its experience. Never before had doctors been able to destroy disease germs in the human body simply by prescribing a pill. When Franklin D. Roosevelt, Jr., was cured almost overnight of a raging strep infection, a reporter covering the story for a newsmagazine asked an eminent physician to check his article for accuracy. He was told his journal would look ridiculous if it printed such fantastic nonsense about miracle drugs.

Within a year the first of the miracle drugs was available

for general prescription by GP's. Now, if they chose, they could check a range of infections in a matter of hours. By current standards the scope was small, but it included one important scourge. Lobar pneumonia, which had previously killed one patient in four, was now transformed into an illness that was only slightly more serious than a bad attack of flu.

The medical men were not the only people to be overwhelmed by the sulfas. The new drugs, with their novel concepts, produced a traumatic effect in the boardrooms of the drug firms. For they flashed in front of them a tantalizing glimpse of both the discoveries and the fortunes that could result from successful research programs.

Until then few U.S. drug firms had spent much money on research. This was regarded as the province of universities and private institutions. But now, over the next few years, company after company decided to invest in laboratory exploration.

Inevitably, it changed the men who were running the drug houses. Those quiet, careful executives who for years had been running companies making small but steady earnings, who took few risks and concentrated their energies on production, were suddenly transformed into speculators on the grand scale. It is not strange that their attitudes to prices and profits were drastically altered along with everything else. Now that they were gamblers, they began to think like gamblers.

This is in no way a defense of men who have so often been attacked, for motivation does not provide an excuse. The drugmakers did not simply stake big sums in research that they might never recoup in the form of a commercial product. They did so knowing that even their successes could fast be rendered obsolete by competition. This was why the action in the marketplace often became rough. For against this background, it was clearly vital that a new breakthrough product must be exploited to the hilt, that competition must be held at bay for as long as possible, that prices must be geared as high as the public would stand for the short period that the drug had the edge on its competitors.

As a result, sales teams expanded fast. Promotion, which had previously been nonexistent, became a major spot in the annual accounts. The whole process of patent application was shaped into a highly skilled art conducted by seasoned professionals.

During the next two decades the big investment in research paid off in a spate of new drugs. Some, like penicillin, were developed from earlier work by university scientists; others, like the tetracyclines, were inventions within the industry; still more, like streptomycin, were the result of close cooperation between the two.

In total, they revolutionized medical practice: antibiotics, steroids, antihistamines, tranquilizers, synthetic vitamins and miraculous new vaccines. Many of the diseases that had previously maimed and killed—scourges like syphilis and polio and TB and diphtheria and malaria and typhoid and dysentery and meningitis—could now be cured with a course of tablets or prevented with the probe of a needle. Big strides had been made in palliating—if not curing—the major crippling complaints such as arthritis. In 1958 a report of the Federal Trade Commission stated that over ten years the annual death rate from only eight of the diseases responsive to antibiotics had been cut by 56.4 percent—a saving of more than 80,000 lives a year in America alone.

Inevitably, profits of the drug companies soared. On Wall Street their shares lost the dull look that had characterized them before the war and blossomed into glamor stocks. Their return was higher even than that of the automobile industry.

Strangely, sold as they were on their own public relations image as the white-haired benefactors of mankind, few of the drugmakers sensed the danger that they were creating. Some of their own scientists in their ever-growing research divisions could have told them that action is always followed by reaction. The pharmaceutical industry was not immune to the natural law. By the late 1950's politicians had become accustomed to the marvels of modern medicine and were growing critical of its high costs. The big buyers—who purchased the bulk needs of hospitals and the armed forces—began to resent the restrictions on their negotiating powers that were imposed by the patent system.

The opposition crystallized around the late Senator Estes Kefauver, chairman of the Senate Subcommittee on Antitrust and Monopoly. His highly publicized investigation into the industry ended the twenty golden years. At the end of the thirties the sulfas had changed the drugmakers into different men. Now, at the end of the fifties, Kefauver stopped them in their tracks. They were never the same again.

On a morning in September, 1939, a large Cadillac turned out of the gates of a drug plant set in the farm meadows of Pearl River—a little town in that part of New York State that juts across the Hudson into the belly of New Jersey—and moved swiftly along the road to New York City. It carried a party of executives of Lederle Laboratories to a meeting in the office of William B. Bell, president of American Cyanamid, on the fifteenth floor of the Rockefeller Plaza complex on Fifth Avenue.

Cyanamid was primarily in the heavy chemicals business. It had been founded in 1907 by an engineer, named Frank Sherman Washburn, who bought the North American rights to the world's first artificial fertilizer—a chemical discovered in Germany called calcium cyanamide. This product—which was to provide the base for a worldwide organization—gave Washburn the idea for the name of the corporation. In 1930, Cyanamid had purchased Lederle Laboratories as a natural move into a related industry. It was a drug house that was typical of many in the industry. It had no sales teams—at least not in the

modern sense—or research scientists or even staff patent lawyers. It made biological products such as vaccines. Its customers
were public authorities that controlled hospitals and distribu-
tors that supplied drugstores.

Wilbur Malcolm, a bacteriologist with the Massachusetts
Department of Health, had joined Lederle as assistant director
soon after Cyanamid had bought it. A well-built man of six feet
three, he was known to his colleagues as Weed—a taunt from
teen-age friends when he was a thin, fast-growing boy that he
had accepted eagerly as an alternative to the loathed name his
parents had given him.

Malcolm sensed early the new age that was dawning. In
1938 a Cyanamid chemical plant at Bound Brook, New Jersey, was producing sulfanilamide—the first of the sulfa drugs to
be available to the American public, although it was not, of
course, sold under a trade name. It was just supplied in bulk
to other companies. It meant the dismantling of Lederle's
"rabbit city" of 30,000 animals, used for making antipneumo-
coccal serums. Until then, the serums had been the best treatment for pneumonia. Now the sulfas had rendered them obsolete.

The same year Malcolm became lab director and, in his new
role, urged the Cyanamid president to allow them to invest in
exploratory research. For a public corporation in the 1930's, it
was a radical proposal that might need a lot of explaining to
stockholders. Inevitably, the return on the capital invested
would be long-term. Several years of draining expense would
have to be borne before any profit could be expected, and, even
then, it might not materialize.

It was a traumatic decision for a corporation president, but
at last, a year later, William Bell decided to back Malcolm.
The meeting to which he summoned the Lederle executives
on that morning in 1939 was, therefore, crucial. He announced
a drastic change in policy that he was prepared to finance with
Cyanamid's ample resources. From now on, he told them, he

wanted them to devote their main energies to studying the causes and searching for the cures for the principal ailments that afflict mankind. In other words, Lederle was to become research-orientated. This was more than a decision to spend money on research. It involved a complete change in operating philosophy. Lederle was to be geared to exploit the inventions of its scientists. It would market its drugs under its own trade names. This meant that it would need a sales force and promotion and public relations.

Malcolm has recalled Bell's words at that meeting. "It's a huge gamble," he told them. "You may come up with nothing, but if you discover a single drug that will conquer even one major disease, then the public will be well served and our company will prosper." Swiftly, Malcolm reorganized his laboratories to put the new policy into action and went out to find the men he needed—microbiologists and chemists and bacteriologists and lab technicians, who, for the first time, would be working in areas that did not necessarily have anything to do with the drugs in current production.

Construction gangs moved into the plant to erect the buildings that the new teams of scientists would need—one for penicillin research, another for the groups studying virus diseases, a third to house the big new organic chemistry laboratory.

Meanwhile, Stewart Smith—whose title of sales director had previously been something of an overstatement—started building the nucleus of a national team of detail men to replace the handful of Lederle representatives who had previously maintained contact with their bulk customers. Instruction classes were opened in the plant to teach the new recruits how to talk to doctors with confident knowledge about the products that would carry the Lederle trade name.

The salesmen had an easy ride with their first product, for it was sulfapyridine, developed in England under the brand of M & B 693, the earliest of the sulfa drugs to go into general use and fantastically effective against pneumonia.

Smith's team was promoting sulfapyridine under license. It would not be too long, however, before the emerging sales force would have products to talk to doctors about that had been developed by the new teams of researchers, with their microscopes and elaborate structures of glassware.

That first year, as more research laboratories were built onto the red-brick complex in the lush fields at Pearl River, Malcolm's scientists began their search for new medicines by the only route available to them: by discovering new knowledge about the human body through experimenting biologically with animals and chemically in the test tube.

They sought a cure for cancer that—unlike today when it stands starkly isolated as one of the two main human ravages —was then one of many killer scourges; they worked hard to develop a typhus vaccine; they mounted a concentrated study of TB. They set up a big research project into penicillin, which by that time had not become a practical medicine—it was just a substance that had interesting therapeutic prospects. Most important of all, in terms of Lederle's progress, they attacked the problems that surrounded sulfanilamide in a determined attempt to reduce its toxicity and to increase its potency.

By 1941 Malcolm's scientists had developed two new sulfas —sulfadiazine and sulfaguanidine. Both were superior to sulfapyridine because of slower absorption into the bloodstream and less toxicity. During World War II all GI's carried sulfadiazine tablets in their kits. Sulfaguanidine also had a special role—it was ideal for treating dysentery and bowel diseases.

However, these successes did not emerge until later when the results of the research started coming through. Meanwhile, Lederle's profit and loss account did not look too good. In 1939 Malcolm spent $300,000 on research, and William Bell, at the annual meeting of stockholders, had to report that Cyanamid's drug subsidiary had not contributed its usual small but reliable portion of the corporation's earnings. It had made a loss.

Undisturbed, Bell doubled the budget. Five years later Lederle was spending $2,500,000—modest by later standards —but more than the profits. But by then, apart from the other products like sulfaguanidine that were fast recouping the investment cost that had been plowed into their development, Malcolm knew that he had a good chance of justifying the new policy in the form that his president had directed: in a spectacular new drug that would put Lederle firmly in the top rank of the big league. The source of his optimism was in a round plastic petri dish in the research block at Pearl River. It was a bug, a microorganism, tawny-brown in color, that could be seen only with a very powerful microscope.

The sulfas had alerted the drugmakers to the potential fortunes to be made with their test tubes. Penicillin, however, opened up an entirely new avenue. For it was produced by a living organism.

The microbiologists in America and Britain who developed and made penicillin could be compared with dairy farmers operating on a microscopic scale. From the trillions of microorganisms that exist around us—in the air, in the soil, in water, or in a mold on a rotten melon in Peoria, Illinois, where, in fact, the best bug was found—they discovered a family that produced a substance that was lethal against certain disease germs. But at first the organisms did not make this incredible chemical in enough quantity for economic production— "There's more gold in the sea," as one scientist put it, "than there was antibiotic in the early penicillin fermentation broths"—or in a form that was sufficiently pure. In other words, they produced other materials at the same time.

The bugs, in fact, proved to be very temperamental. On certain diets and in particular environments they produced far better than they did when subjected to other conditions. So the scientists bred them like cattle, exploring by trial and error, building up their yields, achieving small successes by inspired hunches that were conceived against a growing background of knowledge. They isolated the big producers. They tested them with various nutrients. They worked out the temperatures they preferred. Ultimately, they discovered that they were most prolific when air was bubbled through the broth while they were fermenting.

As a concept, the whole idea of antibiotics was extraordinary; this may be one reason why society took so long to develop the original discovery in 1928 by Sir Alexander Fleming, who—working in the grime of Paddington in London—noticed that mold on a saucer had cleared a surrounding ring of bacteria. Even after Nobel Prizewinners Howard Florey and Ernest Chain had proved at Oxford University a decade later what penicillin could do in the human body, it still took years to develop the drug as a practical usable product—despite the massive support mobilized behind the project by a U.S. government engaged in a world war and the research groups of several drug firms, including Lederle.

In the early days of production, penicillin was made in milk bottles because no way had been found to ferment the organisms in larger vessels. This problem was solved in time. Deep-vat fermentation became practical with the discovery of the bugs' partiality for corn steep liquor. But Lederle was unfortunate. While some other companies were fitted out by the government with big fermentors that would have an important value in peacetime, the plant at Pearl River maintained production in milk bottles. The government wanted a hedge just in case unexpected problems arose with deep-vat fermentation.

But long before penicillin was being injected into soldiers and other sick people, the message of the drug had been absorbed by the drug firms. The U.S. Patent Office had declared that penicillin was not patentable because it was a "product of nature" in the same category as, for example, wool. Already, however, the patent attorneys were growing smart. The war would not go on forever. It could be argued—as it was—that although the product existed in nature, it was transient in character, had therapeutic qualities that were previously unknown, and anyway could not be injected into people without a great deal of development in the laboratory.

The drugmakers, already deep in speculation, gambled with their biggest throws yet that if they could find newer and better antibiotics than penicillin, they would be allowed to patent them. And, if they did, the rewards with which the sulfas had teased them would be infinitesimal by comparison with the killing that could be garnered from the right kind of microscopic bug.

The possibility was obvious that better organisms than those that made penicillin might exist in the world. And the race was on. From all over the world, samples of soil and dirt and mud and rot of many different kinds poured into the research laboratories of the U.S. fermentation drug houses—millions of organisms that were carefully tested and almost always discarded as useless.

Malcolm did not choose a bright young scientist to lead his screening team in its scavenging global investigation. At first sight, this might seem surprising, for a great deal depended on it. Instead, he asked a man who was seventy-one to take over control of the program. But what Dr. Benjamin Duggar lacked in youth he compensated for in experience and eminence. He had, in fact, joined Lederle as a consultant after giving up his appointment—at the retiring age of seventy—as professor of plant physiology and economic botany at the University of Wisconsin. He was one of America's leading experts on soil organisms and fungi.

Nevertheless, from his lab on the third floor of the research block at Pearl River, the professor directed his search more by instinct than by practical scientific knowledge. For how could anyone know what organisms could make an antibiotic that was valid to the human condition?

Since Sir Alexander Fleming's discovery that certain bugs could produce a substance that would destroy disease bacteria, the scientists had come a long way. In its simplest form, this antibiotic action explained why nutritious grass could grow on land that had been spattered with cattle excreta that was riddled with poisonous germs. The organisms in the soil killed the harmful bacteria.

The trouble—as the chemists working on the screening programs knew only too well—was that often the attackers were not selective in their toxicity. Some were just plain lethal. Others were indiscriminate in the character of the bacteria they assaulted. What was needed was a bug that made a product that was poisonous to harmful germs but that tolerated others.

Duggar, a genial old gentleman, with straight gray hair and light-blue eyes that smiled behind steel-rimmed spectacles, had a hunch that the bug the researchers were looking for would be found in soil that had lain undisturbed for years— such as old cemeteries, prairies, deserts, or the ground beside cross-country rail tracks. At his request, friends working for universities all over America sent him samples of soil that met this formula—each in a little bag that Duggar had supplied, carefully tagged with a label showing the origin.

Together with the other samples that were coming in from all over the world, these were screened by his staff under the supervision of his two girl lieutenants—Doris Dansby and Dorothy Evans. A few grains of the soil were shaken onto nutrient liquid in a round shallow petri dish. The organisms were allowed to multiply for a few days until the colonies—groups of mold—were visible to the human eye. Then they were dropped into a test tube containing liquid cloudy with disease bacteria. If the liquid cleared, it meant that the germs were dying, that the product of the test organism was an antibiotic. But was it selective? What else would it damage?

All around the antibiotics lab at Pearl River there were petri dishes on shelves containing growing colonies of cultures, as the biologists called the organisms, forming into various shapes in a range of different grays and browns.

Then, one afternoon in 1945—a year after Duggar had joined Lederle—one of his researchers walked into his lab and reported that they had found a bug that was different from all the others.

It came from soil sample A377, which had been sent to them by a friend of Duggar—Dr. William A. Albrecht, professor of soils at the University of Missouri. It had been gouged from the rough turf of an old timothy field that met Duggar's specification: It had not been dug for years.

By then about eighty antibiotics had been isolated by chemists throughout the world, although very few of them were therapeutically valuable. But this new bug that had arrived at Pearl River was phenomenal. The range of bacteria it destroyed and the speed with which it deployed its lethal power were on a scale that none of the team had witnessed before.

At that time, in 1945, the hopes of Duggar's staff had often been raised before only to be extinguished when previously hidden faults of a bug became apparent, when they walked into the lab the following morning to find the test rats cured of disease—but dead.

This time their experience was different. The organism—which, in colonies on the petri dish, looked at times like circles of bronze lace—excreted a substance that distinguished to some extent between good and bad. When it was first injected into mice, it performed as well as it had done in the test tube. The animals were cured of the diseases that had been induced in them, and they did not die—at least not until they were sacrificed by researchers. In the detailed autopsies the damage to their organs was found to be minimal.

The team was a long way from making a wonder drug that was both suitable to administer to people and economic to make. Lederle had only just started producing penicillin in quantities large enough for doctors to prescribe in general practice, despite the fact that four years had passed since a London policeman, hopelessly ill with septicemia, had recovered miraculously when injected with the small quantity of the drug that had been made by Florey and his team in his research laboratory at Oxford—only to die when the stock ran out and the disease germs mounted their counterattack.

In 1945, Duggar's new drug was as crude as oil when it gushes from a new well. It would have to be refined. It would have to be tested in an elaborate series of animal experiments. The bugs would have to be bred to yield far bigger quantities of this promising new antibiotic. The conditions they enjoyed most would have to be studied—factors like nutrients, temperature and aeration. Methods would have to be tailored to remove the other substances the bugs produced at the same time as the drug.

Weed Malcolm would often walk over from his big office on the fourth floor of the administration building to the research block to watch Duggar's team conducting the grueling series of experiments. Before they began the long haul of animal testing, they explored the drug's effect on fifty types of disease germ. Developing the bugs in petri dishes on agar—a gray, gelatinous substance that antibiotic organisms feed on—they watched them multiply. At first they could only see them through a microscope, but as they bred into millions, they were clearly visible on the assay plates as they changed their patterns and colors—an altering kaleidoscope of white lace at the early stages, changing over a week to a brownish gray, before turning darker.

Then they would squirt disease germs over the bug colony and study the result through a microscope—the natural battle as the antibiotic excreted by Duggar's bugs attacked their natural enemies.

Then followed the long tests in animals—mice, rats, guinea pigs, rabbits, cats and dogs—in an attempt to forecast the effect of the antibiotic in humans. They conducted long electrocardiographic studies to judge its effect on the heart rhythms. They mounted a whole range of tests on the blood of dogs that had been given high doses of the antibiotic to discover its action on pressure, clotting time and sugar content. They dyed the drug, then drew off blood at five-minute and thirty-minute intervals after dosing the animals so that they could study with photoelectric meters the length of time it remained in the bloodstream.

They injected the product into the skin of guinea pigs to see if it caused irritation and into conjunctival sacs in rabbits' eyes to examine its special effects. And they mounted a long program of toxicity studies in mice, dogs and cats, deliberately building up the dosages so they discovered at what point the drug made them ill and how much was needed to kill them.

Meanwhile, the chemists were working on production techniques—at first on a small scale with flasks in the lab, then in the pilot plant, which was designed as a small version of the main production equipment, so that the process engineers could help iron out the snags that inevitably emerge as the volume of production is raised.

For Duggar, however, his new antibiotic had one quality that made it especially exciting: the sheer range of disease germs it would attack effectively.

The Pearl River team was not, of course, the only group of scientists making progress in this area. Two years before, at Rutgers University, Dr. Selman A. Waksman—working in cooperation with the drug firms Merck and Squibb—had developed streptomycin, made by a bug found in a piece of California soil. What was particularly important about Waksman's discovery was that his drug was effective against a whole range of bacteria—including TB—that were resistant to penicillin.

The scientists divided the types of disease germ that responded to penicillin and streptomycin, which went into bulk production in 1946, into two groups that were named after the identification system: Gram Positive and Gram Negative.

What pleased Duggar at Pearl River, however, was the knowledge that his new bug made a substance that not only killed most of the bacteria in *both* groups, but was also lethal to rickettsiae—a group of germs that caused such mortal diseases as Rocky Mountain spotted fever and such unpleasant ailments as rickets—which resisted both penicillin and streptomycin.

Because of its effect against a broad spectrum of human diseases, it conjured up a prospect of single-pill medicine, which never materialized in practice because certain drugs have always been especially effective against specific diseases. Without question, however, it was revolutionary. Because of the gold color that characterized the drug made by his organism when it was crystallized to powder, Duggar named the bug after the Latin word for gold, *Streptomyces aureofaciens*. The trade name given to the drug it produced was consequently Aureomycin.

Duggar's team was only one of the many units in the research block. Others were working in other directions. One group was making a big attack in trying to develop a polio vaccine. Another was probing for treatments for heart disease. A third was making a sustained assault on diseases of the central nervous system. A fourth was researching cancer. But Aureomycin —because of its broad potential—was the star product under development in the research block.

By 1947, when Lederle applied for a patent in the drug, the giant fermentors—each as big as a house—were already installed. Through the fall of 1947 and most of 1948, Aureomycin was being tested on human beings in carefully controlled clinical trials in hospitals. The assistance of the Food and Drug Administration was sought in evaluating the new drug.

Then, in the summer, a team of doctors in the Baptist Hospital at Winston-Salem, North Carolina, subjected the new antibiotic to a crucial test in humans. Three patients had been carried into the hospital on stretchers—a farmer named Boss

Walsh, who had been out turtle hunting when he was bitten by a tick carrying Rocky Mountain spotted fever, and two children, Eddie Butler and Louise Moose. Although Eddie and Louise lived in different counties, they, too, had been bitten by the same kind of deadly tick.

By that July, 1948, there was no treatment for the disease in normal use. Patients just sweated it out and either survived or—in up to 40 percent of the cases—died. Dr. Duggar knew from tests on the organisms in the lab that Aureomycin destroyed Rocky Mountain rickettsiae. The big query now was: Would it do the same in the human body as it had done in a petri dish at Pearl River? It did. The fever subsided quickly. The three patients, who might have died, recovered fast.

Throughout that fall the plans for the launching of Aureomycin went into action. Teams of detail men—now operating under a new sales director, Henry Wendt—were calling on doctors throughout America to tell them about the new miracle drug: the first antibiotic that was truly effective against a broad spectrum of human diseases. Dr. Duggar was the star speaker at a symposium held in New York City in cooperation with the New York Academy of Sciences where many of the different scientists and doctors who had conducted trials reported their findings. The medical press published papers about the clinical tests in hospitals—such as the Rocky Mountain spotted fever experiment in North Carolina. Advertisements emphasized that the new antibiotic took over where penicillin failed.

Meanwhile, Aureomycin was in production at Pearl River, spreading an acrid pall across the plant as the launch stock was built up in all its different forms—liquid for injections, pills of various sizes, syrups for children. The clattering machines in the printshop were producing labels in the millions.

Occasionally, Weed Malcolm would go over to the fermentation area and talk to the engineers beside the big green vats and watch the yellow crystals—like powder in clear liquid—

swooshing through the glass pipes to be strained and purified and purified and purified. Often there were crises—as indeed there are today—for the production of a drug based on living organisms is very delicate. At these times a sample of fermentation mash would be tapped from one of the vats and rushed over to the research block for high-speed study. What was going wrong? Why had the yield of antibiotics suddenly dropped?

At last, on December 1, 1948, Aureomycin was launched. All over the country, trucks were delivering the product of Dr. Duggar's tawny bugs to drugstores. Doctors were prescribing it for patients.

The medical profession—now accustomed to the use of penicillin and streptomycin—had long become blasé since the distrust with which it greeted the sulfas. But Aureomycin was again in a different category because of its staggering range.

Doctors could prescribe it for more than 100 diseases. Furthermore, unlike streptomycin and penicillin, which they had to inject into patients, they could administer it in the form of pills—something that was to save them a great deal of time. But Aureomycin was to maintain its role of dominance for a very short period—and, for that matter, its price.

In the late fall, as the launch date for Aureomycin drew nearer, Malcolm presided at a management meeting in his office to decide the price at which Lederle was going to sell the drug. The discussion ranged wide over such issues as production and distribution costs but centered inevitably on what is known in the drug industry as payout time—the period between the launch date and the marketing of a better drug by another firm.

"You really should think of obsolescence," Malcolm said in 1967, "at the same time as you think of research. Obsolescence is a driving force for your researches and it is the dread of obsolescence that has resulted in the great progress that has been made in the last twenty years. . . . When we are estimating our future development in the drug industry in this country we say that any product that has been in existence for five years or longer . . . is an old product. In the chemical industry we say ten years."

In the decision that Malcolm now had to make lay the whole paradox of the system under which society at present produces its drugs—the same system that it employs to find its oil, manufacture its steel, or even provide its toothpaste.

In fact, the drugmakers have always seen their responsibilities to the public in terms of quality and hygiene and invention—not in price. For they are subjected by their stockholders to exactly the same pressures as the managers of other kinds of business. If challenged about their profits—as they have been regularly since 1959—they will retort that they are not philanthropists and they do not carry out the function of the public agencies concerned with welfare.

"Why is it," demanded one drug executive, "that we are expected to supply our product cheap to underdeveloped countries when no one demands that food firms should do the same? Yet starvation is a far bigger problem than illness."

Malcolm, in short, was in business. Furthermore, he had a miracle for sale. What was the right price tag for a miracle? There was a very rough rule-of-thumb pricing formula, but in fact, this was a guide that was entirely protective. You had to sell at four times your cost, so the theory went, to be certain— after paying overhead, research and promotion—of making an adequate profit.

But practical policy was not as simple as this. For example, some products—such as those with a small but vital demand for rare kinds of illness—were sold at a loss because the volume was just not adequate to maintain proper profit ratios. And if the drugmakers' claim that they bore this as a public service was regarded skeptically—even though it conformed with their philosophy based on the supply, rather than the price, of drugs—it was no more than what many businesses did. Certain loss lines often contribute to a general situation of profitability.

The same physicians who treated rare diseases also had patients with the common complaints.

In practice, despite the formulas, the price of new drugs—like the price of most new products in any area—was dictated more by market factors than anything else. Was the new drug better than competitive medicines that doctors were already prescribing? If so, it could stand a higher price.

Aureomycin, however, was more than just a new product. It was unique. Although other drugs were equal to it against certain diseases, none had its shotgun qualities for attack on a wide front. Without question, if economic factors were the sole criterion, it deserved a big premium. And economic factors had been central in its development. This was how a capitalist society obtained its miracles, and rightly or wrongly, it was how it paid for them.

Malcolm had played with big chips. From the moment that Dr. Benjamin Duggar had peered through a microscope at his new bug, four years—and millions of dollars of investment—had gone by. Now, for just a short while, Malcolm held a big lead over all his competitors.

He well knew that this period of superiority would be brief. For months, rumors had been permeating the industry that scientists at Parke, Davis and Company in Michigan had also been working successfully on a miraculous new broad-spectrum antibiotic. Even now, it was being tested in American hospitals on human patients. Clearly, the payout time for Aureomycin was going to be short.

After assessing all these aspects, Malcolm made a decision: The price of Aureomycin to the druggist would be $15 for a bottle of sixteen capsules. This meant that by the time the retail and wholesale profits had been added, the patient would be paying around $1.50 for each pill he swallowed.

Today, with the benefit of hindsight, this seems grossly exorbitant. Perhaps it always was. But at that time, when the whole concept was novel, most sick people did not complain too much about the expense of a pill that, if it would not exactly bring them instant health, produced an effect that seemed pretty close to it—at least by the standard of the 1940's.

In fact, Malcolm maintained the initial high price of Aureomycin for less than three months. In February, 1949, he slashed it by a third to $10. For now, he knew, it was truly threatened by Parke, Davis. Lederle had taken four years to develop its new drug from the discovery of *Streptomyces aureofaciens.* Its competitors moved far faster than this. It was in early 1948 that microbiologists at the Parke, Davis plant—who were working with scientists at Yale University—examined the remarkable behavior of a bug they had isolated from a piece of soil that had been sent to them from Venezuela. Eighteen months later, in June, 1949, the drug it made—Chloromycetin—was available to doctors as an alternative to Aureomycin for the treatment of many diseases. In particular, it was sensationally effective against typhus, and even before it was launched as a product for general prescription, it had stamped out an epidemic in Mexico.

Meanwhile, Charles Pfizer—a company that had been founded in New York exactly 100 years before—had just acquired a new president: a tough, imaginative and fiercely aggressive Brooklyn-born character named John McKeen, who was the complete opposite of most executives in the industry, still colored as it was by its low-key origins.

Even though he was a chemical engineer by training, McKeen, by temperament, was a man of the marketplace—a brilliant entrepreneur who would undoubtedly have made as big a fortune in advertising as he did in drugs. As long ago as 1957 his salary from Pfizer was reported as $200,000 a year. His stock in the company was valued at $3,000,000.

Like Cyanamid, Pfizer was in the chemical business, its specialist line being citric acid—a basic constituent of fruits used, after fermentation, in the manufacture of soft drinks. In 1936 the company moved by natural progression into the drug business. It began to make vitamin C—a product closely related to citric acid. Five years later—since it was in the fermentation business—it plunged into penicillin.

Like Cyanamid's Lederle, before President William Bell had revolutionized its policy in 1939, Pfizer did not sell directly to drugstores. It marketed no products under its own trade names. It just produced in bulk for other companies.

It had done well in penicillin, but by 1947 the inexorable laws of a free economy had begun to come into force. The drug, having been in short supply for years, was now being produced in quantities that were greater than the demand. As a result, prices began to drop. In addition, several of Pfizer's major customers had started to make their own.

In fact, the history of the unpatented and therefore unprotected penicillin did much to shape the attitudes of the drugmakers during the later years, when the pace grew hot. Without question, it deeply affected McKeen. In 1943 the plant price of the drug had been $20 for 100,000 units. By 1950 the figure had dropped to 4.5 cents. "If you want to lose your shirt in a hurry," commented McKeen to a party visiting the Pfizer plant in Brooklyn, "start making penicillin and streptomycin."

Streptomycin was in a similar category to, though it was not as extreme as, that of penicillin. Although at one stage Merck held a patent, it relinquished it voluntarily at the request of Rutgers University and was merely one of eight makers licensed to produce the drug. But again, overproduction had sent the price diving to levels that were considered uneconomic.

By the time McKeen became Pfizer president in 1949, with his penicillin sales at their lowest levels, he had learned the lesson that was being flaunted in front of him by Cyanamid with its Aureomycin. What Pfizer needed was a wonder drug of its own that it controlled by patent so that—although its market position might be attacked by other products that were better—it could not be rendered uneconomic by other firms making too much.

Pfizer's success with the development of its first broad-spectrum antibiotic astonished the drugmakers. Like Malcolm six years before, McKeen mounted a worldwide screening program for molds, though Pfizer's search, inspired by its penicillin situation, was far more urgent and concentrated than Cyanamid's had been. Travelers, airline pilots, missionaries, prospectors—any contacts in other parts of the world—were commissioned to send in soil samples that were systematically analyzed by a team of only eleven persons.

The fates were with McKeen. Within weeks, his screening group reported it had found a promising organism—in a handful of dirt from a patch of ground near Pfizer's new plant at Terre Haute, Indiana. In the development and tests that followed, it was clear that Terramycin—as the Pfizer scientists called their new drug—was far superior to Aureomycin. It was more potent and less toxic, both elements being connected. For all drugs are poisonous to a degree. The larger the quantity a patient needs to take, the more liable he will be to unpleasant side effects—headaches, nausea, depression. The fact that Terramycin was more potent meant that doctors could prescribe less. Its lower toxicity gave it an additional plus.

As soon as McKeen learned the built-in qualities of his new drug, he realized that this was his opportunity to do what Cyanamid had done in 1939—to switch to distributing drugs under his own trade name. The speed with which he achieved this was phenomenal.

A company distributing ethical pharmaceuticals on a national scale needs a large sales force. Cyanamid maintains 800 detail men—controlled by regional offices—to call on doctors. Pfizer's army of representatives rose later to 1,300. But on February 9, 1950—when the board made the final decision to change its traditional policy and sell Terramycin as a Pfizer brand—the entire promotional staff consisted of 10 men. McKeen did not wait to train more representatives. Time, as he saw it, was short. He planned to launch his drug by using his skeleton force where it would have maximum impact—and to compensate for his lack of men with advertising. He mounted the biggest promotion campaign that had ever boosted an ethical drug. In two years he spent $7,500,000 on advertising.

In February, however, his range of action was limited. The Food and Drug Administration had not yet stamped Terramycin with its approval. And, without FDA authority, the drug could not be sold—or even advertised in the *Journal of the American Medical Association,* which, since this was read by all doctors and senior hospital staff, was a vital medium for any new pharmaceutical product.

So McKeen mounted his campaign by stealth, running a series of advertisements in issue after issue that did not even mention the word "Terramycin." Superficially, the ads appeared to constitute a prestige campaign promoting Pfizer as an organization. But the pitch of the copy was on the word "Terra" —"Terra firma," "Terra bona," "Terra fertilis" until eventually, after the FDA had passed the drug, Pfizer could print the word "Terramycin."

One day in March, McKeen gave orders for telegrams to be sent to all wholesalers, advising them that Terramycin would be released for sale as soon as it was cleared in Washington, and he had a special telephone switchboard set up so that his tiny team of salesmen could promote the new product to drugstores by telephone. Then, carrying elaborate demonstration kits, they made a concentrated attack on the wholesalers, visiting every firm in the country. By working nights and weekends, they covered the wholesale network of America in two weeks.

Simultaneously, mailing shots were dispatched more than once every week to the 200,000 GP's in the United States. Because personal calls were clearly impractical for the small Pfizer team, they set up displays in hospital staff rooms, where the reps could describe the new drug to several medical men at a time.

"The Terramycin Blitz," as *Fortune* magazine described it later, was an enormous success. Within a year, Pfizer had won 25 percent of the broad-spectrum antibiotics market, cutting Cyanamid's share to 48 percent and the Parke, Davis holding with Chloromycetin to less than a third.

Preparing for the imminent competition from Terramycin, Malcolm had cut the price of Aureomycin to $8 for sixteen capsules—nearly half the price two years before, but still fantastic by modern standards. Immediately, Parke, Davis had dropped the price of Chloromycetin to the same figure.

In view of this, McKeen's decision on the pricing of Terramycin was intriguing. He overruled his sales director, who wanted to match the competition, and insisted that the Pfizer drug should carry a premium. "I thought it was a drug that had a certain superiority," he has said, "and I thought by pricing it higher, we would create this impression in the doctors' minds."

Terramycin was launched at $8.40—but only for a few weeks. When, in May, Parke, Davis cut Chloromycetin to $6, Pfizer dropped promptly to meet the rival firm all the way.

"We found the sales department was correct," conceded McKeen. "This premium did hinder us in the marketplace."

Inevitably, Malcolm met the competition. Aureomycin, too, came down to $6.

Just over a year later, in the fall of 1951, Pfizer suddenly cut its prices again by 90 cents. Immediately, the other two matched it. And that was where the price stayed for a long, long time.

At Pearl River, Weed Malcolm and the Lederle executives, trained in the traditional ways of a conservative industry, had watched Pfizer's aggressive promotion of Terramycin with some distaste—qualified, perhaps, by a degree of reluctant admiration. But even if they did not like McKeen's methods, there was no doubt that they were successful. Since he was a competitor they were going to have to live with, clearly they would have to match his techniques if Lederle were to hold its dominant position as the leading producer of broad-spectrum antibiotics. Just what this role meant is revealed vividly by the fact that in 1950 the company's sales of Aureomycin alone— excluding all its other lines—stood at a sizzling $50,000,000 a year.

Terramycin's whirlwind arrival in the market did not reduce the sale of Aureomycin. For the domestic demand for antibiotics in the United States, which was still rising fast, was joined by a sudden voracious need from overseas: On June 25, 1950, North Korean troops crossed the thirty-eighth parallel, and the U.S. Army was once more committed to battle.

Temporarily, as the casualties mounted up, the fortunes of the penicillin producers changed. Suddenly, there was not enough of the drug to satisfy the demand, and the prices moved up from their all-time low. The new situation meant that one hard-pressed company in Syracuse, New York, could breathe again: In 1949 the ethical drug division of the big Bristol-Myers Company had been in trouble. It had made a loss during six of the previous twelve months.

Although the company of which it was a branch was substantial, the division itself was a relatively small operation. Originally, it had been a small independent company called Cheplin Biological Laboratories, which Bristol had purchased. Cheplin had been a lot smaller than Pfizer and Lederle before they tailored themselves to the new age of the wonder drugs. Employing some fifty people in limited premises, it had made profits of only around $13,000 a year. However, it had been similar in character to what they had been—a steady, unremarkable little business making various kinds of chemical solutions for hospitals. During World War II, Bristol had turned it into a penicillin producer—a decision that brought adequate rewards at the time but contained the roots of problems for the future. For gradually, the company had discontinued its other lines until penicillin was virtually its only business.

In short, Cheplin—or Bristol Laboratories, as it was now called—was highly vulnerable. In an attempt to broaden its product range, Frederic Schwartz, President of Bristol Laboratories, had set up a research effort, though this was small by comparison with the projects of Cyanamid and Pfizer. By this time, however, Schwartz had fully realized that the future of his drug business depended entirely on the discoveries that could be made by his scientists.

The situation created by the Korean War boosted Bristol's business and gave Schwartz a brief respite to cover his flanks. It was not quite enough. In less than two years, penicillin production swamped even the excessive demand from the Orient. Prices dived once more. The losses of Schwartz's drug business soared near the million-dollar mark. It was clear that unless a miracle happened, the corporation would have to prune its ethical pharmaceutical division. Something like a miracle did occur, and in common with so many of the events in the industry at that time, its setting was the research laboratory.

As 1950 drew to a close with Bristol's small laboratory team working to find an antibiotic better even than the big three that doctors were already prescribing, the large research groups maintained by Lederle and Pfizer were racing each other to do the same.

It was the beginning of the most prolific, most profitable and most troublesome decade in the history of the drugmakers. During the last three years of the 1940's other wonder drugs had been presented to doctors along with the antibiotics. Among them were synthetic cortisone for treatment of rheumatoid arthritis, vitamin B_{12}—which transformed pernicious anemia from a mortal disease into a controllable complaint—and promethazine, the first of the new school of supertranquilizers.

Soon there were to be many more. But the profits of the drugmakers in the patented products that already existed rose steeply as they developed their techniques and discovered ways of cutting corners in production. At Pearl River—apart from his men searching for new products—Malcolm now maintained a large department of research scientists working solely to improve methods used in the plant to produce their drugs. His microbiologists were constantly breeding up the strains of the production microorganisms so that they became literally pedigree bugs—with yields of antibiotic that were anything up to 500 percent higher than they had been before.

The success of the researchers—and of the important role played by Aureomycin—was reflected in the profits, which leaped from 6.7 percent of Lederle's sales in 1948 to 19.4 percent in 1950. By 1951 the company was earning $18,000,000 a year.

But unseen below this picture of growing prosperity, alien forces were gathering. For one thing, these zooming profits depended on the superbugs that Lederle microbiologists were husbanding so cleverly—aristocrats that, though invisible to the naked eye, were each worth far more than any prize bull.

For a company could double its yield—and its profit—overnight with the help of an exceptionally good organism. Since Lederle's bugs were available to many people in the plant—and were easy to conceal—sooner or later theft was inevitable.

Strangely, in common with other drugmakers, Weed Malcolm took few measures to guard against this danger. Meanwhile, ironically, trouble was emerging from the very key to their soaring profits—the American patent system.

2

THE windows of the research block over-looked Lederle's ample parkland at Pearl River, which, in the last few weeks of 1952, was covered in deep snow. The north wind—bitterly cold even before it crossed the ice floes drifting down the Hudson—lashed the lab windows.

Behind the glass panes on the third floor on a day in December, a short, slim research chemist named Dr. Jim Boothe was conducting a routine experiment. Aureomycin was the trade name of a product known to the scientists as chlortetracycline —the first of four drugs that ultimately formed the tetracycline family.[2] Pfizer's Terramycin, known chemically as oxytetra-cycline, was a kind of first cousin within the group. Strangely until the summer of 1952, although the chemists had known what Aureomycin could do to a sick person, they did not know exactly what it was. They could not define its precise chemical makeup. It had, in fact, taken them four years of intensive study to establish the formula.

Once they knew the structure of the compound, they were in a position to experiment with it, to treat it with other chemicals to see what happened, to alter the makeup in the hope of improving it. On this December day, Boothe was trying to reduce it—to remove one of the elements that formed the drug. He had shaken some grains of a black powder containing palladium —a catalyst that would promote chemical change—into a flask of Aureomycin. Then he bubbled hydrogen through the liquid.

After only a few minutes, the chemist realized that something interesting was happening. He glanced at the gauge on his apparatus that measured the hydrogen content of the liquid. "Look," he said to his assistant, "the hydrogen's disappearing. It's being used up."

An hour later, he poured the liquid into a test tube and sent it to the assay section on the same floor for analysis. Later that afternoon the analyst called him. "Jim," he said, "the chlorine atom's off."

What Boothe had done was to change the fundamental structure of Aureomycin. The hydrogen had reacted with the chlorine and eliminated it. This had transformed chlortetracycline into tetracycline. This was not a complete surprise to Boothe, for logic—and a brief experiment carried out by one of his colleagues way back in 1948—had guided his decision to use hydrogen, which, in any case, was known to have an affinity for chlorine.

However, the truly significant question his experiment posed was: Would the compound in its altered form, without the chlorine, be a better drug than it had been before? Or, for that matter, would it be worse?

Boothe had it tested on disease bacteria in a test tube in the microbiology lab. When he saw the cloudy liquid clearing as the organisms were killed, he knew that his new substance was still a potent antibiotic. The report that followed more systematic trials on the bacteria in vitro, in the glassware, supported his optimism. Then he asked the biologists in the animal block to set up trials in vivo, in living mice.

Two days later he walked over to the experimental therapeutic building to find out the results. They were exciting. Tetracycline was less active than chlortetracycline, or Aureomycin, as an antibiotic. It did not destroy disease germs as fast. But this, in fact, was a scientific technicality. The new drug was completely adequate to cure disease. But what was vitally important about the tests was their revelation that the new drug was far more stable.

Aureomycin broke down very fast in body fluids and, in a very short while, lost its antibiotic potency. This meant that patients had to swallow many pills at frequent intervals to maintain the attack on the disease germs. But tetracycline retained its potency for far longer, so that fewer and smaller doses were necessary; this, in turn, inevitably decreased the liability to unpleasant side effects.

Side effects, in fact, had been causing the drugmakers a great deal of concern. Critical reports from hospital staffs and GP's were stripping the gloss from the antibiotics that had seemed so miraculous three years before. Most of these subsidiary complaints—such as nausea, headaches, stomachaches—that patients sometimes had to endure along with the cure were comparatively minor, but some were extremely severe. Because Chloromycetin—by far the best treatment for typhus—was suspected of causing aplastic anemia in a few rare cases, the FDA had even withdrawn its certificate and referred it to the National Research Council for study.

Aplastic anemia is a disease in which bone marrow stops carrying out its natural function as a producer of cells in the blood. As a result of the FDA's action, Parke, Davis was forced to suspend distribution of the drug until the council made recommendations on its future. Later the drug was allowed back on the market, although the company was ordered to print prominently on its labels the dangers inherent in its use.

Lederle did not face problems with Aureomycin that were anything as serious as those of Parke, Davis, but Malcolm was growing increasingly anxious about the adverse reports that were filtering in from the medical world—often through the Cyanamid detail men—about the side effects of his drug in the form of gastrointestinal complaints. McKeen, too, had heard the reports, and Pfizer was exploiting what it saw as a weakness in Cyanamid's armor. It made great play in its aggressive promotions of Terramycin, claiming that its product caused the fewest side effects. There were signs that the message was getting through to doctors. Sales of Aureomycin were easing.

Malcolm ordered a whole range of clinical studies in hospitals to establish the truth about Aureomycin—for the reports varied greatly—and urged his chemists to search for ways of reducing the danger of intestinal reactions.

Every two weeks he met the research chiefs to review general progress in the research program, but at the time, anxious as he was about Aureomycin, his top product, this was his prime concern. It was in March, at one of these meetings, that Dr. H. Williams, Lederle's research director, told his boss that Boothe had developed a new drug. "So far," he said, "it looks good. We've tested it out on animals, and it's a lot less toxic than Aureo. Dr. Carey's arranged clinical trials."

Dr. Benjamin Carey was the Lederle medical chief. By that meeting he had already asked hospital consultants in various states to explore the new drug's potential on human patients. One of the doctors was the eminent Dr. Maxwell Finland of Massachusetts General Hospital, who had been a great help in the early studies of Aureomycin.

During the next few weeks, while Dr. Carey waited impatiently for the reports from the hospitals, Malcolm stayed closely in touch with progress. Animal tests were still continuing. In the pilot plant in the research block the chemical engineers were running sample production runs to establish the problem areas and—with the help of the research chemists—to develop methods of solving them.

All the information flowing into Malcolm's big office on the fourth floor of the administration building convinced him that the new drug was going to be very important. By May he had not yet received the formal reports from the doctors conducting the clinical trials, but unofficial talks with them contributed to the general atmosphere of optimism that was pervading Pearl River.

At a meeting of the management committee on May 25, Malcolm decided to take a chance. He authorized his production director to tool up his plant to start manufacture, so that Lederle could begin building up the stock it would need for a nationwide launch of the drug.

He told sales director Henry Wendt to make plans for a campaign to introduce it to the medical profession, estimating cautiously that it might reduce Aureomycin's sales by 10 percent.

But by July, two months later, after he had read the reports of the clinical trials, Malcolm had changed his forecasts. Clearly, tetracycline was far superior to any of the antibiotics that were then being prescribed. It was more potent and more stable and less toxic even than Pfizer's Terramycin. He instructed Wendt to revise his promotion plans on the assumption that tetracycline would become Lederle's star product.

"In other words," said one executive at the meeting after listening to Malcolm's forecasts, "its sales will be eighty percent of Aureo's—not ten percent as we planned."

"It's going to be a hundred percent of the business," asserted Malcolm confidently.

The launch was planned for November—in four months' time. It was not long.

Apart from the stock that had to be made and packaged in various forms ranging from orange-yellow pills to injectable solutions, the promotion material had to be produced—hundreds of thousands of elaborate mailing shots for dispatch to America's doctors, hospital interns, officials of state and city medical authorities. Advertising had to be designed for the medical journals. The detail men would have to be carefully briefed. The support of influential specialists would have to be gained. Application to the Food and Drug Administration would be necessary.

The same heady mood of anticipation that had preceded the launch of Aureomycin at the end of 1948 was experienced once more by the Pearl River executives. The opening shots in the campaign were to be fired at the Antibiotics Symposium that was now held every year in the Mayflower Hotel in Washington, D.C., in the month of October. It was then, too, that Weed Malcolm's optimism that his new drug would herald another period of prosperity for his company—similar to that which Aureomycin had created—began to be clouded.

In March, seven months earlier, Jim Boothe and his coworker John Morton had sworn out an affidavit claiming the discovery of tetracycline, and Harvey Edelblute, one of Cyanamid's attorneys, had applied formally for patents in the drug. It was while the symposium was actually in progress that Edelblute received the first official warning that another company was competing for the patents—a formal letter notified him that a technicality, known as an interference, was shortly to be declared. In line with Patent Office rules, he was not told the identity of the other applicant. But it did not require much speculation to figure out which company was the most likely contender. Pfizer's scientists had published papers in the scientific journals indicating a high degree of success in research in this area. But the situation was not quite as simple as this. For within a few weeks there were no less than three competitors for the patent.

The purpose of the U.S. patent laws—which are founded on a clause in the Constitution—is to provide an incentive to invention in the form of a monopoly for seventeen years. This applies not only to products—which cannot be made, sold or even used without a license from the patent holder—but also to processes of manufacture.

Although product patents were more important because of the absolute control they provided, much of the skill deployed by the specialist attorneys was directed at process rights, for since each new manufacturing development carried a seventeen-year term, a company could keep extending its interest far beyond the life of the initial patent by updating the production techniques. These rights could also be framed in much broader terms. "If the Patent Office accepts your first application," commented one attorney cynically, "you know you haven't made it wide enough. You've left something for another guy."

Pfizer, of course, owned both product and process patents in Terramycin. It had a complete monopoly in the drug. No other company could make or sell it without a license, which John McKeen would be unlikely to grant. Furthermore, this situation applied throughout the world except in those countries where control was limited by law. Cyanamid had exactly the same powers over Aureomycin.

In the case of both these drugs, the patent applications had been uncontested. But tetracycline—Malcolm's new drug—was to be the subject of one of the fiercest patent battles that have ever been fought.

The symposium in October was an annual occasion that was barely tinged with the flavor of commercialism. As always, it was attended by most of the leading microbiologists and other scientists working in the antibiotics area at universities, drug firms and research institutions. Many of the speakers were eminent.

Malcolm had not yet announced publicly that he was to launch a new product in November, but at the symposium Dr. Jim Boothe and other scientists from Pearl River read papers about their new drug.

Among the listeners was Pfizer's John McKeen. He recognized the signs soon enough, despite the emphasis at the symposium on science rather than industry: Cyanamid was about to launch tetracycline as a line.

Immediately, the stocky blue-eyed Pfizer president became keenly alert. This was not solely due to the fact that tetracycline would clearly be a big competitor to Terramycin. The main reason for his concern was that two of his chemists had applied for exactly the same patents almost a year before—patents, not just in the hydrogen process that the Lederle experts were now busy explaining, but also in the drug, the product, itself. Furthermore, he was fairly certain that they had filed their application before Cyanamid.

In July, 1952, fifteen months before, one of his chemists had shown him a paper written by a Lederle research doctor in the *Journal of the American Chemical Society*. By then the Pfizer PhD's knew the chemical makeup of Aureomycin, but it was obvious that Pfizer was ahead of Pearl River. For the article suggested two possible formulas—and one of them was wrong. This meant that the Lederle men were still probing.

If the patents in tetracycline were issued to Pfizer, McKeen would control it. He would be able to stop Cyanamid, big though it was, from selling what was clearly going to be a major product. In this event, if Malcolm persisted, then McKeen would be able to sue—for he would be infringing Pfizer's legal rights.

What had happened, in fact, was a coincidence: Working independently, two groups of scientists had made the same discovery—a discovery on which billions of dollars ultimately depended. For Malcolm's forecast in July was dead accurate. Tetracycline came to dominate the antibiotics scene.[3]

Considering the immense potential of the new drug, the first moves in the battle for tetracycline were fairly muted and controlled. When McKeen returned to his office in Brooklyn after the symposium, there was a note on his desk informing him that—just as Cyanamid's Harvey Edelblute had been notified —the Patent Office was about to declare an interference.

McKeen summoned a management meeting to decide what action he should take. For although Pfizer was in a strong position in one sense, this was marred by an important flaw: The only way the Pfizer chemists knew how to make tetracycline was, like Jim Boothe, by bubbling hydrogen through Cyanamid's Aureomycin—and they could not do that without a license from Malcolm under his company's process patent.

This was why McKeen had taken little direct action about the discovery in his research labs. What he needed was a new process—a different technique for making tetra—that did not infringe Cyanamid's patents. And the most likely way that his scientists could achieve this aim would be to find a family of bugs that directly produced it, just as Duggar's *Streptomyces aureofaciens* made Aureomycin.

For months, the Pfizer microbiologists had been searching for this ideal microorganism. In special sterile compartments in their labs, they had been pounding Aureomycin-making bugs with ultraviolet rays in the hope of producing a mutant that met their specifications.

Just as human beings produce genetic throwbacks—such as a red-haired child born to black-haired parents—so do bugs. Mutation can take place naturally, or it can be drastically induced by exposure to ultraviolet radiation that kills more than 90 percent of the microorganisms that are bared to the deadly rays. But the few that survive the treatment are radically changed. They look different—and they often produce different substances.

Ultimately, the Pfizer scientists achieved their aim and developed a bug that made tetra. But they had not succeeded by the time McKeen called his meeting in late October. He knew from his own trials that it was a very good antibiotic that would inevitably affect Terramycin, which, at that moment in Pfizer's fortunes, accounted for annual sales of $39,000,-

ooo—more than a third of the company's total gross of $107,000,000.

Until then, there had been no great need for urgency. Unlike Malcolm, whose main product was waning, McKeen's Terramycin was gaining ground all the time. Why should he do anything at this particular time to attack his own highly successful drug?

Now the situation had changed. Malcolm's obvious intention to introduce tetracycline had forced McKeen's hand.

After consulting his executives, McKeen made up his mind. Little could be gained by a head-on battle with Cyanamid. The time had come to explore the possibilities of a deal. He called Weed Malcolm and suggested a meeting.

That decision, made by the Pfizer management in the Brooklyn plant—only just across the East River from the Federal Courthouse in Manhattan—was the first spark in the running fuse that exploded into the violent fight between the tetracycline makers and the U.S. government.

By background and personality, the two executives—thrown together by their mutual interest in a multimillion-dollar market—could hardly have had less in common. It was not strange that, according to associates, they did not appeal to each other.

McKeen, the brash entrepreneur, had blitzed the drugmakers into new concepts of how to sell ethical pharmaceuticals and forced on them methods that although they had to accept them as part of the changing pattern of the times, many found unsavory. He was the maverick of the industry.

By contrast, Malcolm had risen to corporate power in a very different environment. He was no whiz kid. Quiet and courteous, he had entered the industry from the rarified world of science in the Public Health Service and was now a vice-president in a very large and diverse organization—a multimillion-dollar hierarchy, controlled by committees that were fully conscious of its great resources and its strong market position in the world.

Normally, blue-chip companies of this size do not embark on major actions in a hurry. They move only after all aspects have been carefully evaluated by experts. It is rare for them to need the flexibility and capacity for fast maneuver that is often vital to smaller companies for their survival in a competitive market. In that fall of 1953, however, Malcolm was not in a normal situation. And without question, he was in a hurry. "McKeen had me over a barrel," he told the Kefauver Subcommittee later, "and I wanted to get off that barrel." What he meant was that the whole machinery at Pearl River was committed to the imminent launch of tetracycline under the Lederle trade name of Achromycin. He had already delegated Aureomycin, like an aging actress, to a minor role. If McKeen prevented him from making his new drug—which he could if he won the patent— then Lederle would suddenly be in a disastrous trading position.

When the two men met on November 5 in the Cyanamid office in Rockefeller Plaza, the plant at Pearl River was producing tetracycline at full capacity for the imminent launch. Trucks were traveling daily to the railheads as the regional warehouses were stocked.

Suspiciously, the rival executives faced each other across Malcolm's desk—only a few doors away from the room where, fourteen years before, William Bell had authorized Lederle to embark on a major research program.

To the Justice Department, that meeting was the beginning of a criminal conspiracy—even though the deal itself was not illegal and neither Pfizer nor Cyanamid has ever tried to keep it secret.

On that first occasion, only Malcolm and McKeen were present. McKeen did the propositioning. They were competing for the patents. If they left the decision to the Patent Office, it would involve years of legal wrangling. Would it not be in the interest of their companies for their attorneys to meet, to examine together the laboratory records of both firms, and to agree on which had invented the drug first? The company that conceded the priority could then withdraw the application at the Patent Office, and the winner of the patent would license the other to make and sell the drug.

Malcolm was noncommittal. He would discuss McKeen's proposal with his management. He still hoped to establish priority, but his research men had warned him that the Pfizer president was almost certainly negotiating from strength.

The following week the two executives met again—this time with their general counsel, their top house attorneys. In effect, Malcolm agreed to put Pfizer into the tetracycline business in competition with himself. Not only did he accept the cross-licensing proposal that McKeen had suggested to him, but he also undertook to sell his rival enough bulk Aureomycin for Pfizer to set up immediate production of the new drug—and to supply him with a license and the technical know-how to make it in future in the most economical way. The decision on which would concede priority for the tetracycline patent was left to their lawyers.

In January, 1954, Austin Phillips, one of Cyanamid's patent attorneys, wrote to Malcolm, who was then on a trip to the Far East, and told him that Pfizer's case for priority was overwhelming. It had clearly invented the drug first. In February, Cyanamid conceded the priority and formally withdrew its application for the tetracycline product patent.

Meanwhile, Cyanamid's sales director, Henry Wendt, stepped up his tetracycline promotion. "I wasn't very happy about having a competitor in the market," he told a New York court in 1967. "Initially, we thought we'd have it to ourselves and it wouldn't require such an expensive crash program. . . ."

Expensive it certainly was. In testimony Wendt listed the specifications: 17,000,000 pieces of direct mail to 100,000 physicians and a big advertising campaign in the medical journals. "We promoted it as heavily as we knew how," he said.

". . . We tried to make Achromycin a household word in medical circles. . . ."

It is interesting that by comparison, Pfizer—the hardest promoters in the business—was curiously restrained. As a result of McKeen's bulk deal with Malcolm, it was in the market with tetracycline by January. But in contrast with Lederle, it was pretty lukewarm about Tetracyn—the name under which it sold the new drug.

McKeen decided that the drug should be sold by a different sales force from that which was promoting Terramycin. He handed it to a subsidiary company, J. B. Roerig and Company. Three days before Christmas, Thomas G. Bradley, Pfizer Laboratories' general sales manager, briefed his detail men by letter about the attitude he expected them to adopt to the Roerig team.

"To date," he wrote, "we have no conclusive evidence that Tetracyn [tetracycline] is therapeutically equal to or better than Terramycin and therefore we must take the position that the burden of proof lies with those promoting this new product. . . . Under no circumstances is the present and future of Terramycin, our 'bread and butter' to be jeopardized. We do not suggest that anything should be done or said that will deter the Roerig boys in their attempt to get their product established. Rather, it may be suggested, you help them where you can— except where it would jeopardize your T.M. [Terramycin] volume. . . . Under no circumstances is the future of this seventy million dollar baby to be endangered. Let's use our heads—and get all the business."

This defensive posture to Terramycin, the "seventy-million-dollar baby," is probably the reason why, although the two tetracycline products are virtually identical, the sales of Pfizer's Tetracyn have never approached those of Cyanamid's Achromycin.

But although the two companies now had a somewhat uneasy

understanding, this had not solved all the problems that stood between Pfizer and the patent.

Within ten days of the meeting between Malcolm and McKeen, H. J. Lidoff—the examiner at the Patent Office who was dealing with the application—raised a disturbing issue with the Cyanamid attorney Harvey Edelblute. He, too, knew that it was possible that a bug could be found that would produce tetracycline directly—thus avoiding the cumbersome need to treat Aureomycin with hydrogen—for already in his files were two applications for patents from other firms making claims on this basis. Was it possible, Lidoff asked Edelblute, that the bugs that made Aureomycin also produced a little tetracycline at the same time?

Bugs often made several different substances—"all kinds of garbage," as one of the Lederle chemists has described it—and one of the problems of production was to remove the unwanted materials in the process of purifying the antibiotic that was being produced.

But the question was loaded. For if *Streptomyces aureofaciens*—the tawny bugs that made Aureomycin—also produced tetracycline, even in minute quantities, could the drug be described as new? Would it not mean that unknowingly Americans had been swallowing it, along with the antibiotics that had been prescribed, for four years? If this were the case—novelty being one of the bases of the patent laws—then it could be argued that it was unpatentable.

Edelblute went back to his research experts for guidance and, the next month—according to the Federal Trade Commission —assured the patent examiner that this was not the case—an act for which Cyanamid was strongly criticized later on. For under certain circumstances, the answer to Lidoff's question was that the bugs did produce both drugs—even though the amount of tetracycline was very small indeed and its presence was largely academic.

Meanwhile, as Lederle's army of detail men called on doctors throughout the nation, Cyanamid's sales of the new drug soared. By the end of 1954 they were through the million-dollars-a-week mark and were still rising. By contrast, demand for Aureomycin was lagging way behind.

Against Cyanamid's brilliant performance with the new drug, McKeen's decision to use the sales force of its Roerig subsidiary to promote tetracycline was not proving very successful. After only nine months, he switched the new product to his main sales force, which was pushing Terramycin and the other Pfizer lines. However, there was still conflict in the management thinking between fear of inhibiting Terramycin, its "seventy million dollar baby," and its reluctance to be outsold on tetracycline.

McKeen tried to bridge these two aims, which were probably incompatible, by mounting a furious new sales drive. In September, when the new selling arrangements were effected, Thomas J. Wynn, Pfizer Laboratories' general manager, issued a memorandum with instructions that it was to be read to the detail men. Emphasizing that the "Number one pushed product" was Terramycin, which was to take precedence "over every other product in the Pfizer labs line including Tetracyn," he issued the battle orders:

> Competition is going to be tough. . . . We have invested thousands of man hours of sweat and energy and millions of dollars in the broad spectrum business . . . and have no intention of losing one percentage point of our proper share of the market. . . .
>
> We have the finest and most complete antibiotic line of products in the industry. . . . With Terramycin you have the conviction that it is the best, proven with billions of doses and millions of patients all over the world in five years' experience. For those physicians who want the newest, you now have Tetracyn [tetracycline], another Pfizer discovery and development. . . .
>
> For the continuing success of our Company we'll have to work like we never have before! It's going to mean early in

the morning until late at night. . . . Your men must get into every hospital and live in them. You and your men will have to get close to the purchasing agents of institutions and governments. Fasten down tightly friendships and cooperation of the medical students, interns and residents. . . . I am confident, too, that you will personally accept the challenge of our lives . . . the challenge of becoming the world's leading antibiotic house. . . . Best personal regards. It's great to be alive!

All the irony of the new type of industry that had emerged in the age of the wonder drugs was starkly revealed in that official memorandum. No directive to salesmen in any other industry that was unconnected with ethical issues of human health could have been harder-selling in character. But that hard drive —which was a reflection of the Pfizer boss—was also producing results in the laboratory.

The Pfizer salesmen did as they were asked. They mounted a sustained campaign on hospitals and other bulk purchasers. The company's regional sales managers were given great freedom of action—in particular with the amount of the drug they could supply free in order to win a contract. McKeen believed that hospitals were vital for his public relations. "If they got their drug into a teaching hospital," he explained in court about his salesmen, "top doctors, with great influence throughout the country, would be using it."

In the sales office at Pearl River, the cries for permission to give away more free goods were soon heard. The Chicago office reported desperately that Pfizer was giving the Michael Reese Hospital its entire tetracycline requirement free of charge.

Cyanamid went along with the trend, as it always did whenever faced with Pfizer's techniques, but Henry Wendt kept it down to controlled limits. Regional managers were told that they could offer free goods up to 20 percent of the value of an order as an incentive to get the business.

Meanwhile, as the salesmen were slugging it out in the field across America, the situation in the executive suite was growing more complex. Back in early October, 1953—before Mc-Keen paid his important visit to Rockefeller Plaza—Malcolm had been approached by the head of another drug firm: John P. Remensnyder, president of the Heyden Chemical Corporation.

Heyden was a medium-size company that made both chemicals and drugs. But the main lines of the pharmaceutical division were penicillin and streptomycin, neither of which was a healthy area in which to operate any longer. The Heyden board had decided to pull out of the antibiotics business and to devote its total resources to chemicals.

The reason for the Heyden president's call on Malcolm was —according to testimony—to discover if Cyanamid would be interested in buying his drug division.

"Why should we want to do that, Mr. Remensnyder?" asked Malcolm.

The Heyden president's reply was significant: His research scientists had developed a bug that made tetracycline directly. Heyden had applied for patents in both the product and the process.

In court later, Malcolm said that he discounted Remensnyder's claims. He did not believe that he could possibly have discovered tetracycline before Cyanamid or even Pfizer. He was, therefore, no real threat. However, Heyden had a good plant, and Cyanamid bought it for $12,000,000.

In the package were the rights to Heyden's new process—and the microbiologist who discovered it—and, for all Malcolm's protestations, Cyanamid was not slow to press the *process* patent application—for the method of making the drug with a bug by direct fermentation instead of using Aureomycin.[4]

Malcolm received another caller that month with a purpose that, if not exactly the same, was fairly close. His visitor was Frederic Schwartz, president of Bristol Laboratories.

The role in the tetracycline battle of this balding man with thick eyebrows was fascinating. If Bristol's drug division had been in trouble in 1950, it had been doing well by comparison with the gloomy prospect that faced it in 1953. The brief boost that the Korean War had given to the penicillin business was over. Once more, surplus production had sent prices spiraling down to uneconomic levels. That year Bristol's ethical drug business was to lose close to a million dollars.

Schwartz, however, had a card to play. His microbiologists in Syracuse, New York, had, like Heyden's scientists, developed a bug that made tetracycline directly. They, too, had applied for patents. Would Malcolm be interested in a cross-licensing arrangement, depending on which company was successful at the Patent Office?

He was, in fact, proposing the same deal that John McKeen was to put forward a few weeks later. But from Malcolm's point of view, although Bristol-Myers was a very substantial company, its drug division was a very different quality of antagonist from Pfizer, which was a major producer in the antibiotics business.

Malcolm, as he testified later, was blunt with his visitor. "Mr. Schwartz," he said, "I don't believe you've got a bug that doesn't infringe our Aureomycin patent. If you have, it'll be unique in our experience. But there's a simple way of settling the matter. Send us over a sample of your fermentation broth and let us examine it for the presence of Aureomycin."

But this was going too fast for the Bristol president. "In that case," Malcolm said, "I don't think we're interested in discussing a cross-licensing agreement with you."

Frederic Schwartz returned to his office determined to go ahead with his plans to break into the tetracycline business despite the implication by Malcolm that if he did, Cyanamid would sue him. The future existence of the drug division depended on the team of research scientists at Syracuse. If it was to survive, it was now vital that they should work up the yields of their new bugs so that they could set up economic production of tetracycline.

In his plans to compete with Cyanamid, Schwartz seemed bound to lose. Because the main business of the drug division was in bulk penicillin, it maintained only a handful of salesmen. These would be pitted against Malcolm's army of 800, who, with a whole range of big national trade names behind them, were trained in talking to doctors and drugstore managers about antibiotics.

But when Schwartz heard the rumors that Cyanamid and Pfizer had agreed to cross-license each other and realized he would be facing the combined opposition of the two corporations that dominated the market, the news was daunting. Since his position was so weak, he must have considered withdrawing from the fight and, like Heyden, devoting the Bristol-Myers resources in other directions. However, this persistent man still hoped he could negotiate a deal and avoid a direct confrontation in which he would be so heavily outnumbered.

In February, 1954—four months after his unsuccessful meeting with Malcolm—Schwartz saw his chance, though it was pretty slim. In January a party of security analysts had paid a formal visit to the Pfizer plant in Brooklyn. Among the company's executives who addressed them was John McKeen. The Pfizer president—with his eye presumably on the stock market —was dogmatic about the tetracycline patents. His company expected to get them; it was not going to license anyone else, and it would sue any firm that infringed its rights—a statement that was subsequently reported in the *Drug Trade News*, where Schwartz read it.

He immediately called McKeen, who confirmed that the report was true. Pfizer would sue.

"We'd like very much to sit down and talk this thing over with you," said Schwartz.

But the Bristol president was wasting his time. "The article was meant as a factual statement, not as a threat," asserted Mc-Keen. "When we're in a position to legally do so, we'll slap a suit on you. That is our indicated position."

Warily, however, McKeen instructed vice-president John Powers—today president of the company—to maintain contact with Schwartz. He had already been in a patent conflict with Bristol over a special type of penicillin—procaine penicillin—and he did not underrate the rival company's chief executive.

Despite the rebuff by both Cyanamid and Pfizer—which between them maintained 1,600 detail men in the field—Frederic Schwartz went ahead steadily with his plan to fight, naming the project Operation Sphinx. The two big tetracycline makers were not his only competitors. In a memo suggesting that the Bristol sales team should be increased to 91 men—pathetic by comparison with the opposition—his sales director pointed out that the makers of other antibiotics maintained a combined sales force of 2,400. He was referring to Parke, Davis, Abbott and Ely Lilly, all of which were promoting broad-spectrum antibiotics that competed with the tetracyclines.

In May, Bristol went into production. Its little group of detail men began to call on doctors to extol the merits of their directly fermented tetracycline, which was named Polycyclin.

Schwartz was not relying entirely on his puny sales effort. He had plans to supply bulk tetracyline to other companies which maintained adequate distribution machines. During one of his meetings with John Powers, the Pfizer executive challenged him with negotiating with the well-known Squibb drug company, sneering—according to Schwartz in court—that the firm was "the biggest price-cutter in the business."

Powers' information about Bristol's negotiations was accurate. Schwartz had already made a deal with Squibb and was soon to complete negotiations with Upjohn.

"I'm rather unhappy about this," said Powers, according to testimony. "We're going to have a fight."

"I hope the fight won't be dirty," said Schwartz.

"It won't be dirty—but it'll be a tough one."

Powers had just returned to New York from Washington, where he had learned the latest position regarding the patent proceedings. At the end of that meeting—according to testimony by Schwartz—he had called his people together to consider tactics. "The Patent Office route is too slow," he told them. "We have to find a new way to stop Bristol."

If Schwartz was perturbed by what can only have been a warning, it did not prevent him from going ahead with his plan. As soon as he started supplying his two big bulk customers, Cyanamid moved back into the fray for a brief period and sued Bristol for infringing its Aureomycin patent—only to settle out of court four months later by licensing the company formally in return for a royalty on its sales.

Meanwhile, Bristol was fighting fiercely on the patent front, but Schwartz was losing ground. It was fast becoming clear that if he had ever had much chance of gaining the tetracycline patent, his prospects were fading. So he changed his tactics—as applicants in his position very often did—and directed his efforts at breaking up the neat agreement between Cynamid and Pfizer. It was now apparent that he wanted tetracycline, as a product, to be declared unpatentable. For then, even though he would have no control over any other makers, there would be nothing that McKeen could do to stop him from producing the drug.

With their new strategy, the Bristol lawyers were thinking on the same lines as the patent examiner. For H. J. Lidoff was still unhappy about the possible existence of tetracycline in aureomycin. Eventually, in November, 1954, Lidoff made his decision: The drug, he declared, was unpatentable.

Schwartz was delighted by the news. But just to make sure that the examiner did not change his mind, he had his chemists analyze a sample of Aureomycin. They reported that it contained between 2 and 4 percent tetracycline. Schwartz asked one of them to file an affidavit to this effect at the Patent Office.

But McKeen was a fighter. And Lidoff's decision did not deter him. He sent his attorneys back into the attack.

In a meeting with the examiner, they argued that his whole theory—that the bugs that made Aureomycin also made a little tetracycline—was wrong. The minutes of that meeting are couched in careful legalese, but what, in effect, Lidoff said was: "If you can prove this in an actual Aureomycin fermentation by analyzing it with modern methods, then I will reconsider my decision."

Werner H. Hutz, Pfizer's patent attorney, took up the challenge. Back at the plant, two chemists were instructed to run an Aureomycin fermentation and to try to recover tetracycline from the broth by three different methods. In affidavits, they reported that they were unable to recover "products clearly identifiable as Tetracycline."

Later Pfizer was accused by the Federal Trade Commission of misleading the examiner in these tests—not by stating facts that were basically incorrect, but by running the fermentation in a way that it knew would produce a poor antibiotic potency.

However, at the time the new evidence impressed Lidoff, and in January, 1955—to the astonishment of Frederic Schwartz —he issued the tetracycline product patent to Pfizer, which promptly instituted a suit for infringement against Bristol and its two big customers: Squibb and Upjohn.

The three companies countersued, claiming that the patent was invalid because it had allegedly been obtained through misrepresentation at the Patent Office.

For Bristol's drug division, the stakes were enormous. If it could carve itself even a small corner in the tetracycline market, this would place it firmly in a highly profitable position. Failure would almost certainly put it out of business. If Schwartz needed any proof of this, he had only to look at his sales figures. For during 1955, Bristol's total gross was only $14,000,000, of which Squibb and Upjohn bought tetracycline worth more than $11,000,000. Sales under Bristol's own trade names were less than $1,000,000.

If Bristol lost the fight with Pfizer, its drug business would be left with a gross of less than $2,000,000.

Schwartz was determined not to lose. During the pretrial depositions, which preceded the hearing in court of the case with Pfizer, his attorneys—with Bristol chemists in court to guide them—pounded McKeen's scientists with questions about the tests they had conducted as evidence for the Patent Office. The proceedings filled more than 2,000 pages.

However, as the summer came and went, Schwartz began to grow nervous. The case was not shaping up as firmly as he had hoped. His attorneys were beginning to talk more and more about its weak points. Most important of all, his two big customers were showing signs of restlessness. Donald S. Gilmore, president of Upjohn, called on Schwartz and told him frankly: "We're a bit distressed by the lack of progress in the lawsuits. We've got to face the fact that we're liable for thirty million dollars."

Gilmore even met McKeen to explore the possibility of negotiating a separate license with Pfizer but broke off negotiations when Bristol agreed to indemnify him against his damages and court costs.

But the cards were stacking up once more against Frederic Schwartz. In a desperate move, he called McKeen again and asked him for a license. This time McKeen was not quite so adamant, but the ideas of the two men on terms were wide apart, and as a ploy, it failed.

Then, in December, Bristol's negotiating position changed dramatically. Suddenly, Schwartz was able to exercise powerful pressure on Pfizer.

Three months earlier, in September, Schwartz had been in his office one morning when he had taken a call from the district attorney's office: "My name's Birt, Mr. Schwartz," said the caller. "I'd be much obliged if you could drop down and see me."

"What's it about?" asked the Bristol president.

"I'd rather not say on the telephone, but I'll be happy to tell you all I can down here."

Accompanied by Bristol's general counsel, Schwartz drove down to the assistant DA's office. For a company in the throes of a very tough lawsuit, Birt's first question was alarming: "Did you know that your telephone wires had been tapped?"

Schwartz assured him that he did not.

The assistant DA told him that the operation had been conducted by a private detective named Broady. He wanted to make sure that Schwartz had not given permission for the tapping to take place. This question was not as surprising as it might seem at first because many companies, if they suspect employees, have their own lines bugged by investigators.

Schwartz insisted with growing anger that it had certainly not been carried out with his permission.

"Are you prepared to testify to that effect?"

Schwartz was more than happy to agree, but what was vital for him to know was: Who was employing Broady?

"That's something," replied Birt, "that at this time I'm not permitted to tell you. But you'll find out in court."

Schwartz was fairly certain—as he testified later—that Pfizer was responsible for Broady's operation. It fitted into the pattern, too. In March he had seen a news story about a private investigator who was arrested for tapping Squibb's telephone lines. Pfizer, he guessed, was making completely sure that it was fully informed about the plans of the firms it was suing.

In December, 1955, the Broady case was tried in court—and the whole unsavory story came out: how Robert Porter, Pfizer's general counsel, had paid Broady $60,000 for investigating Bristol and Squibb; how the detective's assistant would listen for hours on the tapped wires for the word "tetracycline" or anything about a patent fight; and how Broady would meet Porter in the evenings at the entrance to the Holland Tunnel —which links Manhattan and New Jersey—to report any information he had obtained.

Pfizer denied that it had ever hired the investigator to tap Bristol's wires. He was, it said, instructed to conduct an internal check within Pfizer concerning suspected leaks of one of their secret processes. Whatever the truth, the Pfizer version sounded pretty lame. "We had," said McKeen in court later, "some very bad publicity."

It was so bad that it gave a very angry Frederic Schwartz his opportunity. He ordered his attorneys to send a marked copy of the Broady trial transcript to the Pfizer lawyers with a warning that his company was going to use it as evidence in the patent suit. Bristol would introduce it as proof that Pfizer came into court with "unclean hands."

As a maneuver it was effective. Three days later the Pfizer attorneys called the Bristol lawyers to suggest they talk over the issues that divided them. In a private meeting, McKeen faced the wrathful Schwartz, who apparently felt that even in the jungle that the drug industry had become, Pfizer had gone too far. "I used," said Schwartz in court, "some pretty forceful language, I am afraid sometimes profane, and I was outraged at what had been done to our company. . . ."

However, their mutual interests were too big for personal resentments to hamper negotiations. They settled. The lawsuits were dropped. In March, 1956, Pfizer licensed Bristol formally to make and sell tetracycline. Squibb and Upjohn—the two big outlets that were vital to Schwartz—were licensed only to sell the drug.

Temporarily, the turmoil surrounding tetracycline—one of the most important drugs that have yet been developed and even today prescribed in enormous volume—eased back to a calm that the government later asserted was far too tranquil.

For the prices charged by the firms tended to be the same—as indeed did those of Aureomycin, Terramycin and Chloromycetin.[5]

Throughout the fight with Bristol, the Pearl River executives had remained aloof. It was not their battle. They would, it appeared, have been a lot happier to have had no links with Pfizer at all. As it was, they were selling more tetracycline than the others put together.

Meanwhile, within the Cyanamid complex, Lederle had acquired considerable status. By comparison with its modest role in the thirties before the big speculation in research, it was now the star performer, far outdistancing the chemical companies in the group. In fact, within four years, in 1959, it was contributing no less than $37,000,000 of Cyanamid's total profit, after taxes, of $52,000,000.

Considering the loss it suffered in 1939 or even the profit of $1,800,000 it made in 1940, this was an achievement that must have appealed to the stockholders—even if it did not appear in so admirable a light to certain politicians who were growing interested in the prices that supported these fabulous results.

In the ever-changing power structure of large corporations, the men who bring in the big money inevitably thrive. In 1955, while McKeen and Schwartz were still punching out their patent suit, Malcolm was promoted. He left Pearl River to become vice-president in charge of the marketing of all Cyanamid's products. He did not have the job long. Two years later he became president of the corporation.

His place as general manager at Pearl River was filled by a lanky, graying, expansive forty-five-year-old named Lyman Duncan.

For Duncan, the job of running the most profitable company in one of America's major corporations was a big opportunity. When Malcolm became president, the fact that Duncan was nursing projects that had been initiated by the group's chief executive gave him an open line to the seat of power. But although he did not know it then, Duncan was due for a rough ride.

In Washington and, in fact, as far away as Italy, the currents that were to shake the industry in general—and Cyanamid in particular—out of its opulent complacency were already gaining momentum.

3

THE beginning of the reaction against the drugmakers, the moment when the idea that miracles did not entitle their creators to unlimited affluence was first conceived, is hard to isolate precisely. Probably, it was the same incident that Richard Harris reported in his book *The Real Voice* as the seed that grew eventually into the Kefauver investigation of the industry.

In February, 1951—a year after Pfizer had launched Terramycin so spectacularly—Walton Hamilton, a Washington attorney, awoke one morning with a strep throat. His doctor prescribed Chloromycetin.

Illness was clearly a rare occasion in Hamilton's life, for when he called at his local drugstore for the pills, he was appalled at the price—$8 for a four-day supply. Angrily, he refused to pay and telephoned his GP to find out if there was not a cheaper alternative.

"They're all the same price," said the doctor.

"Exactly the same?" Hamilton asked.

"To the penny."

"I presume they're all made by the same company, then."

"No," the doctor replied, "they're made by three different companies."

Since he had no choice—other than sweating out his infection—Hamilton bought the Chloromycetin but went home furious. He had, he felt, been overcharged by a rigid system that he could not buck.

In fact, of course, the belief that something is expensive or not is largely a matter of attitude. Even then, in 1951, Hamilton would probably have spent $8 on a meal in a first-class restaurant in Washington without feeling he had been cheated. But he felt outraged at the idea of spending the same amount on curing an illness that would otherwise have given him an unpleasant week and diminished his working capacity.

In purely rational terms—disregarding such issues as excessive profits—clearly the Chloromycetin was far better value for money than a dinner would have been. And it is interesting that an intelligent man's irrational response to what is, after all, an everyday occurrence in the lives of millions of people set off the series of events that ultimately erupted into a major chain reaction of repercussions around the world.

For Hamilton's wife, who used her maiden name of Dr. Irene Till in her profession as an economist, had a part-time job in the Federal Trade Commission—one of the U.S. government's watchdogs over monopoly. Hamilton, formerly a professor of law at Yale, had been employed as a consultant in the Antitrust Division of the Justice Department, so he, too, was accustomed to probing the excesses of big business. To both of them, the common cost of the three antibiotics smelled of intrigue and private agreements—even though equal pricing is a regular feature of many mass consumer products.

The next morning Dr. Till discussed her husband's experience with her boss, Dr. John Blair, who headed the FTC's Division of Economic Reports. Blair agreed that the situation merited investigation and recommended that the commission make a preliminary study. A dedicated trustbuster, Blair was a tall man with slightly stooping shoulders and pale-blue eyes that revealed a keen and often mischievous humor. He was to perform a key role in the government's attack on the drugmakers.

Hamilton's infection occurred at an important stage in the FTC's policy development. At the time, the commission attorneys were conducting a carefully calculated campaign in the courts to broaden the practical effect of the monopoly laws. "Antitrust cases," commented Blair, "are essentially different from other legal areas because evidence of conspiracy is, by its nature, often impossible to get. This kind of agreement is not written down and filed—it's done on the telephone or over lunch.

"For this reason, we wanted to get the courts to accept a far bigger element of presumption than they would in other actions. In some cases, we were even holding back hard facts that would have strengthened the prosecution in order to force the judge to rule on indirect evidence."

By the time Dr. Till discussed with Blair her husband's experience in the drugstore, the FTC had already won two important precedent-making cases—against the cement makers in 1948 and against major groups in the iron and steel industry in 1950—and was just about to go into court to fight several combines in the rigid steel conduit business.

In both the iron and steel and the conduit trials, the judges ruled for the FTC on indirect evidence. The law—created by these precedents—was, therefore, changing in a way that could easily be criticized. If there was enough reason to suppose from appearances that a conspiracy existed, then actual proof was not required.

These changes were to be important to Cyanamid. Months before the research chemists had even discovered tetracycline, the links that were to lead Malcolm, McKeen and Schwartz into the criminal court of New York were already being forged.

At the time, however, it seemed that events were running in their favor. The report on the antibiotics business that the FTC authorized, on Blair's recommendation, did not materialize. After a cursory look at the industry, the investigators suggested that the file should be closed.

It was—but it did not change the suspicions either of John Blair or his assistant, Irene Till.

In 1955—while McKeen and Schwartz were fighting over the tetracycline patent—a more powerful man in Washington had come around to the same view. Senator Warren G. Magnuson, chairman of the Senate Independent Office Appropriations Subcommittee—which holds hearings on the annual budgets of federal agencies—had received complaints on drug prices from some of his older constituents. On a trip to Sweden, he had noticed that some pharmaceuticals cost only 20 percent of their prices in the United States.

When Edward F. Howrey, the FTC chairman, appeared before the subcommittee to explain its request for a budget of $4,300,000, Magnuson suggested that the commission study antibiotic prices and forecast that an investigation might show "mark-ups running to four hundred and five hundred per cent of the cost of production."

Howrey acted on the proposal. The report—written by the FTC's chief economist, Dr. Simon Whitney—took more than two years to produce. In the summer of 1957, Earl Kintner, the FTC general counsel, was asked to review it by John Gwynne, who had by this time taken over from Howrey as chairman.

The report detailed the history of the antibiotics business, explored the intercompany agreements—including those that had resulted from the tetracycline patent fight—and described in detail the factors affecting prices and profits.

Kintner, a well-built, cigar-smoking lawyer with thick black hair, had a clear, uncomplicated view of the role of the FTC in American life. This was to ensure that in this democracy, competition continued to act for the benefit of the public. He was a great advocate of "educating" industry and of urging voluntary cooperation. He had stopped what was known in the FTC as the Tar Derby—competitive advertising by the tobacco manufacturers on a copy pitch that the tar nicotine content of one cigarette brand was better than another—without making any move in court. But he was a fervent antitruster, and when conditions were not suited to behind-the-scenes diplomacy, he believed in tough action. In his view, there was no room for negotiating with the tetracycline firms. They merited attack.

When Kintner read the antibiotics report, he saw it as a whitewashing operation. He believed that it was not nearly strong enough in its criticism of the drugmakers and that it skated too delicately around what he sensed was a conspiracy of the tetracycline firms.

So he rewrote parts of it to make it harder-hitting and sent it back to chairman Gwynne.

When Whitney learned what the general counsel had done, he complained furiously to the chairman. Gwynne summoned the two officers to his office to discuss their differences, and in front of him, the economist and the lawyer fought, as one FTC staffer put it, "like Kilkenny cats." Angrily, quarreling heatedly over every word of certain sections, they hammered out a new version of the controversial pages.

The FTC published the report in June, 1958. Lyman Duncan—who by then had been in charge at Pearl River for three years since Malcolm had moved to the corporation headquarters in New York—read it carefully. To him it seemed a pretty fair document, despite the fact that Kintner had toughened the original version.

But the report did not indicate what was taking place behind the scenes in the triangular white granite FTC building on the corner of Pennsylvania and Constitution avenues. For Kintner sent the file on the tetracycline makers to the FTC Bureau of Anti-Monopoly and urged it to consider the case for prosecution. The bureau staff studied the papers and recommended action to the commission.

On July 28, 1958, the FTC announced formal charges against the five companies selling the drug, alleging that they had rigged the market. Hearings, to be conducted by an FTC examiner, would start in January.

Although the FTC is a federal government agency with the authority to order certain actions by big corporations, it has only civil power. If criminal prosecution becomes necessary, this is initiated by the Antitrust Division of the Justice Department, which maintains a liaison officer in the commission building.

Back in 1955, during the early stages of Pfizer's suit against Bristol, the Justice Department had, in fact, shown a sudden interest in the tetracycline patent. It had subpoenaed some of the documents in the case, then appeared to let the matter drop. Now, with the FTC's new interest, the department began to explore the situation once again.

Meanwhile, Senator Estes Kefauver—famous for his highly publicized probe into organized crime—had taken over as chairman of the Senate Subcommittee on Antitrust and Monopoly. He had raided the FTC for staff, inviting John Blair to become his chief economist and one of the commission's senior attorneys, Paul Rand Dixon, to be his top counsel.

Later Blair had asked Dr. Irene Till to be his assistant on the subcommittee staff. During the first two years after Kefauver took over, it investigated three industries—steel, automobiles and bread. But neither Blair nor his assistant had lost his zeal to investigate the prices of drugs. They were put off only by the complexities of the industry.

By then other hearings on Capitol Hill—while not exactly probing the industry—had, at least, provided John Blair with some firmer grounds for advising Estes Kefauver that drugs were an area his subcommittee should consider for investigation.

In February, 1958, Congressman John A. Blatnik, chairman of the Legal and Monetary Affairs Subcommittee of the House Committee on Government Operations, had held hearings concerning the advertising of tranquilizers. Although most of the witnesses praised the industry, there were some criticisms. Dr. J. Murray Steele, professor of medicine at New York University, attacked the drugmakers for "the distorted literature which some of the drug houses are distributing to the medical profession" and stated that some of it contained little or no mention of side effects.

Dr. Ian Stevenson, chairman of the Department of Neurology and Psychiatry at the University of Virginia, supported Steele but campaigned also on another front: the marketing of drugs after clinical testing that was far too limited.

These were straws in the wind of change that was blowing in America's most influential city. They were noted by a burly, ruddy, gray-haired admiral named William Knickerbocker, who, as head of the Military Medical Supply Agency, was spending more than $41,000,000 a year on drugs for the U.S. armed forces. Knickerbocker did not believe he was getting a fair deal from the drugmakers and, in particular, from the tetracycline producers. Too often, after inviting tenders for his big contracts for the drug, he found himself considering bids that were identical. What irritated him even more was the inflexibility he met in the companies' negotiators. If he increased the size of the contract, he usually found that the price of the pills per bottle remained the same. When he complained, he was met by an adamant attitude that he deeply resented.

Temporarily, in view of the patent situation, there was little the admiral could do but pay up. He needed tetracycline in great volume. But growing within him was an angry determination to break what appeared to him to be an artificial price barrier. In a few months' time he was to make a dramatic move that would bring yet another government agency into conflict with the drugmakers.

One afternoon long before then, however, John Blair was idly scanning the FTC's quarterly report—which contained a current analysis of American industry—when he noticed the profit figures listed for drugs. In previous reports, these had been accumulated with chemicals—presumably because many companies operated in both areas. In this issue of the report they were isolated for the first time, and they revealed the spectacular performance of the pharmaceutical firms. Profits, after taxes, were as high as 18.9 percent of invested capital—higher than any other industries included in the report and twice the average earnings.

Blair telephoned Irene Till and asked her to come over to his office. "My God," he said, "just look at those profits."

At the time, Dr. Till was preparing material for the subcommittee's investigation of the bread industry. On Blair's orders she dropped what she was doing and—six years after her husband's appalled reaction at the price of Chloromycetin—started a detailed exploration of the U.S. drug business.

Meanwhile, on the first Sunday in August, when the New York *Times* front paged the story of the FTC's charges against the tetracycline companies, a New York attorney named Walter Mansfield was weekending on Martha's Vineyard—a popular island retreat off the coast of Massachusetts. His host was Ralstone R. Irvine, his senior partner in the big Wall Street law firm Donovan, Leisure, Newton & Irvine and a director of the American Cyanamid Company.

The two men spent the morning casting for striped bass. By the time they strolled back to the Irvines' house, the *Times* had been delivered. When they walked onto the veranda, Truda, Mansfield's blond Czech wife, remarked: "I think you'll be interested in something on the front page."

Together, the attorneys read the news of the market-rigging charges against their big client, conscious of the serious implications.

A few minutes later, as they lounged with drinks in basket chairs, Irvine asked, "What do you know about antibiotics, Walter?"

"About as much as anyone else," answered Mansfield. "I've taken them a few times."

"I ask," Irvine went on, "because I think this is a case you ought to handle."

For Mansfield, as he sat watching the Atlantic surf, this conversation was the first episode in an intriguing assignment that was to reach far beyond the boundaries of the U.S. antitrust laws to encompass the prosecution of an international conspiracy in an entirely different area: industrial espionage.

The big profits in the successful wonder drugs had bred a market for expert process knowledge—and for the vital pedigree bugs that had been bred up to make the antibiotics. For a really good organism with associated know-how could double a company's production overnight.

It was inevitable that with fortunes there for the making, some men would think in terms of shortcuts. Why invest in a highly speculative research program with no guarantee of success when the bugs and the know-how necessary to handle them could be bought? As a technique, this would be far cheaper, and success—in theory, at any rate—would be certain.

In America the patent laws were more than adequate to prevent piracy of this kind, but in many other countries they were by no means so protective. In Italy they did not exist at all, for pharmaceuticals had been specifically excluded from them by Mussolini in 1939. For practical purposes, any Italian company could make and sell in Italy a product patented elsewhere with little fear of legal action.

What seems fantastic, in retrospect, is the fact that the dangers to the drug companies in this situation were not foreseen. For bugs used in production were available to a large number of employees. They could even be isolated by an experienced microbiologist from a teaspoonful of the fermentation broth. It was not strange that when one of the Pearl River production workers was faced with charges of handing Cyanamid's million-dollar organisms to a friend who was a member of a spy ring, he was astonished: "Gee," he said, "this was trash. It was something I had to sweep off the floor several times a week."

This combination of high profits, easy access to these valuable bugs, and patent-free conditions in Italy created an ideal opportunity for exploitation—a situation that, ironically, was about to be boosted by the direct action of the U.S. government.

Inevitably, both in America and in Italy, men were moving into this lucrative vacuum in search of the big money that was inherent in it. Managements of companies, situated in other countries that recognized patents, transferred their operations to Italy. Entrepreneurs, planning to establish drug firms, thought immediately in terms of Milan.

The demand for bugs, for information, for expertise that followed this development attracted a motley group of American and Italian contact men—most of them with names like the cast of a Verdi opera—who set out to bridge the gap between the buoyant market in Italy and the valuable merchandise in America that it needed.

However, there was one aspect of their operation that was

vital: They had to have sources, in key areas inside drug plants, with access to the bugs and know-how—men such as a discontented PhD at Pearl River who had grandiose plans to improve the condition of his life.

His scheme was simple enough. Under normal circumstances, it would almost certainly have achieved at least a modest success. But he chose to put it into operation at a time when political tensions were building up within the drug industry. As a result, he found himself at the center of a pitched battle between Cyanamid and a whole range of powerful adversaries.

4

ABOUT eight fifteen on a cold, misty morning in November, 1958, Bill Fulton, assistant security chief of the Lederle plant at Pearl River, drove his old Plymouth along Middletown Road, which skirted the company's land. As usual, one of his gray-uniformed security guards was standing in the center of the road, opposite the main entrance, controlling the lines of cars that were streaming into the plant.

And as usual, he waved to his boss as Fulton checked the Plymouth, swung the wheel over, and drove into the entrance roadway, which, cutting through the broad parkland with its elegant oaks and firs, provided the setting for the ugly complex of red-brick buildings that constituted the plant. Fronting and flanking them were two vast parking lots—thousands of automobiles, neatly ranged like a protective army of disciplined beetles.

Fulton drove on to the wire fence that encircled the plant
—part of the protection system against pilfering of drugs from
the warehouse—and stopped the car while another security
guard hauled open the big gate.

Then he moved the Plymouth slowly past the Hundred
Group block that housed the process research laboratories and
the tableting plant and on through the network of buildings he
knew intimately—between the large red brick administration
block and the long, low gray quality control building, past the
steroid research section and the cafeteria and the printshop,
where clattering machines produced the Lederle labels for the
packs and bottles, and the technical reference library, and on
by the back of the vast experimental therapeutic complex,
where, with the help of some of the 100,000 animals maintained
at Pearl River, the chemists and biologists tested out new products.

At the end of the road, by the whitewashed photo laboratory,
he turned left and moved down the hill toward the eighteenth-
century farmhouse, trimmed in white and blue, that—except
for the ground floor, which was still furnished for the benefit
of visitors as it was in 1798—housed the security offices.

Once, apart from the stables and the cattle sheds, the old
house had been the only building for miles. That was before
the construction gangs had moved in to build on the farm meadows one of America's most modern drug plants. But even now,
situated as it was apart from the main blocks, it still retained a
kind of old-world dignity.

Fulton parked the Plymouth and stepped out into the roadway, conscious of the faint acrid smell that indicated there was
a fermentation run in progress on the other side of the plant.
He opened the blue front door of the farmhouse and climbed
the creaking stairs to the first floor. Terry Kraemer, the quiet
dark girl he shared as a secretary with Frank Allen, Lederle's
security chief and Fulton's boss, was at her desk in the small
room at the head of the stairs.

That day—like the morning in 1951 when Walton Hamilton, the Washington lawyer, awoke with a strep throat—was to see the beginning of a chain of incidents that were to mushroom into an importance that would straddle the Atlantic and cause big repercussions in Washington. What happened is still fully recorded in the greatest detail in Bill Fulton's files.

Terry Kraemer had a message for him. Dr. Scholz, she said, had called to arrange an appointment in the old farmhouse at nine thirty. Dr. Phelps would be with him.

Fulton was intrigued. Dr. Phelps, as head of the chemical production section, controlled the work programs of many of the 1,000 scientists at Pearl River. Ted Scholz, in charge of the process improvement department, was responsible to Phelps for a big group of chemists and microbiologists whose function at Lederle was to improve production methods and solve chemical problems that occurred in manufacture.

In the normal way, if they had wanted to see one of the security officers, they would have asked him over to their offices. The fact that they sought the meeting in the old farmhouse suggested that something important had occurred that they did not choose to talk about in the research buildings.

Fulton walked on into his office and sat down at his desk. He was a tall, bulky man of thirty-five, with light ginger hair and wide blue eyes.

It was just over a year since he had left the FBI, but at Pearl River, he had plenty of reminders of it. On his wall was a signed photograph of J. Edgar Hoover. Also, both Frank Allen and Jack Stewart—the management executive to whom Allen reported—were ex-bureau men.

He took the old sheriff's star, mounted on copper, that he used as a paperweight from the pile of papers on his desk and began to fill in time until nine thirty.

"We may, of course, be on quite the wrong track," said Ted Scholz after Terry Kraemer had shown the two research executives into Frank Allen's room. "We certainly haven't got much to back our suspicions, but we thought it was something you ought to know about."

Scholz had a group leader in his department named Dr. Sidney Fox.[7] Two weeks before, one of his other chemists had come to him with disturbing information. Fox had asked him if he would be interested in doing some work in the evenings for a small firm in East Paterson, New Jersey, called Biorganic Laboratories.

"I don't suppose we'd have regarded it as all that serious in the normal way," Scholz explained. "The employment contracts forbid it, of course, but you'll never completely eliminate moonlighting, and it's probably better to ignore it so long as it's on a small scale. But Fox has been causing us some concern in other ways."

During the past few months Fox seemed to have been working with large quantities of triamcinalone, a new steroid hormone that Lederle had introduced to doctors at the beginning of the year. Sold under the trade name of Aristocort, it had a revolutionary advantage over other hydrocortisones used in the treatment of arthritis: Unlike them, it did not stimulate patients to the point of insomnia.

It seemed strange to Scholz that Fox should need so much triam because the experiments would normally involve working with quite small quantities of crystals. Apart from this, though, the chemist had been displaying all the signs of a very disgruntled man. He picked quarrels easily, was often feuding with one of the other chemists, and complained repeatedly about his pay to Bob Winterbottom, his supervisor.

Scholz met Dr. Phelps regularly every Tuesday morning to review progress in the department, and at this meeting, he told his boss what his informant had revealed about Fox's apparent link with Biorganic Laboratories.

Phelps suggested that they keep Fox under close observation within the department in the hope of discovering something more tangible than they yet knew to back their concern. The chemist who had first alerted them was instructed to inform Scholz of any suspicious incidents that might take place in the laboratory.

"Of course," Scholz told the security men, "the idea of spying is not pleasant—especially when a PhD is involved—and we wouldn't normally consider it, but Fox is working in a highly secret area. He has access to information and to organisms that are extremely valuable."

For two weeks, Dr. Scholz had kept watch on Fox, but it had revealed little.

"On several evenings, after the staff had left," Ted Scholz told them and confirmed later in a written memorandum, "I visited his lab. I searched his desk drawers and examined the trash in his wastebasket." The only thing he found that was slightly strange was the fermentation procedure, written in Fox's handwriting, for A.8, the code number for Declomycin, a new antibiotic planned for launch next year.

Fox had nothing to do with A.8. On the other hand, his interest in Lederle's newest antibiotic could have been entirely professional. As Scholz conceded, it was "unusual but not impossible in a diligent person."

A few days later Scholz's informant reported that while he had been running an A.8 fermentation in the electrically vibrated shaker flasks in his lab, Fox had questioned him closely about the organism's behavior. Later, he noted, the chemist had obtained a mash sample from the pilot plant.

Fox was not a microbiologist, but he knew enough to stand a good chance of isolating a bug colony by plating out the mash in a petri dish.

"The point is," said Scholz, "that the test tube was stored in the chill room for a few days. Now it's disappeared."

Also—according to Scholz's information—Fox had been leaving the plant for long lunch hours and going home early in the evening. Often he carried a bulging briefcase, and on one occasion, there was something in his pocket that had the round, flat shape of a petri dish.

"Of course," conceded Scholz, "these are just suspicions. We've got nothing conclusive. We just don't like the smell of it."

The lack of any hard evidence clearly made immediate action impossible. So Frank Allen asked Scholz to continue his vigil over the chemist within the research block. At the same time, the security department would set up a random external surveillance. If Scholz could tip them off sometimes when the chemist was leaving the plant, they would tail him.

The situation that the two research executives suspected could be very serious. The ruling philosophy behind the patent laws was that the process descriptions should be written with enough detail to enable anyone "skilled in the art" to make the product.

If this could not be done without a special kind of organism —as was the case with the production of antibiotics and certain steroids such as triamcinalone—then samples of the bug must also be made publicly available by being deposited in one of the national culture collections maintained by the U.S. Department of Agriculture.

In short, any firm that wanted to make a patented organic drug could obtain a description of the process and an appropriate organism in return for a small fee. In the case of some drugs this was enough for a potential competitor in some other part of the world, where the patent laws were less effective, to go into business.

But drugs, such as antibiotics, that depended on a living organism presented a very different proposition. The Patent Office was concerned with facts about the product—not with the economics of making it. The whole process of production of triamcinalone or any of the tetracyclines was a highly skilled operation involving a great deal of know-how that was not written in the patent as part of the basic description. As it was, even with all the experts that Lederle retained at Pearl River, fermentations often had to be stopped when something went wrong—when, for example, it was discovered that the yield of antibiotic had suddenly dropped. On these occasions, a sample of the mash would be rushed over to the process improvement lab, where the chemists—sometimes Fox himself—would work desperately to find out what was going wrong.

And each time the cause of the trouble and the technical information that resulted were recorded in process documents that added to the constantly expanding store of know-how—to which Sidney Fox, of course, had access.

A similar situation existed with the bugs. No company put its high-yielding pedigree organisms in the public culture collections. It deposited organisms that met the specification claimed in the patent—namely, that they could make this particular substance—but they did not certify that they could do so profitably.

Technically, a skilled microbiologist could in time breed up the organisms in the public collections so that ultimately he had possession of high-yielding strains, but this process could take years, and even then, it might fail.

Fox, in short, had access to top-yielding pedigree organisms —which could boost immediately the profits of a competitor that was not so well equipped with this microscopic livestock— together with all the detailed production secrets relevant to the particular bugs. It was not surprising that his bosses were anxious even if—since industrial espionage was not then as well known a risk as it is today—they had not figured out exactly what they thought he was doing. For no American company could make the drugs in which he appeared to be interested without a license from Lederle under its patent.

At any rate, the situation, even if it was a bit obscure, seemed to merit full investigation.

As soon as the two research doctors had left the old farm-house, Fulton—on Frank Allen's orders—set up the first lines of the investigation.

He sent his secretary, Terry Kraemer, over to the personnel department for Fox's file, then called Wally Hoffer, an executive in the purchasing department that bought the chemicals and raw materials used in the plant. Fulton inquired if Hoffer had ever heard of Biorganic Laboratories.

A few minutes later Hoffer phoned back. Biorganic, he reported, had been in business only a short while. It supplied Lederle in a small way with one or two chemicals. As routine procedure, Hoffer had taken out a status inquiry on the firm in May. The report had suggested nothing adverse.

Fox's personnel file gave Fulton little in the way of leads, but it was a base on which to start building a dossier. He would have liked to have talked to the people in the research block who knew Fox well so that he could develop a profile that could guide him in deciding the best way of investigating the chemist. What kind of man was he truly? How would he be likely to react to certain situations? But this he could not do. He had to follow one of the inviolate rules that had been drummed into him in the FBI. It was essential that as few people as possible should know about their suspicions—until they were ready to act. And that looked at present as if it would be quite a long while.

Fulton had another long interview with Ted Scholz, who had talked casually to Fox's associates. Gradually, he was able to build a picture, sketchy though it was, of the man he was tracking.

Sidney Fox, then aged thirty-seven, was short and stocky with round shoulders. He was bald, though the brown hair on the sides of his head grew thickly, and like many chemists, he wore thick-lensed glasses.

He was the son of Russian Jewish immigrants who had settled in Philadelphia. His father, who worked in a clothing plant as a machine operative, was a quiet, meek man while his mother was voluble and dominant.

Fox worked his way through Temple—a university in Philadelphia—then, when he was twenty-nine, took his PhD in organic chemistry at Purdue. He married a slim dark girl, who, like his mother, had a strong personality. Joyce had been brought up in an affluent home. Her father was a successful New York attorney and played an important role in local Orthodox Jewish circles.

According to the people who knew them well—so Ted Scholz reported—Jo, as Fox called his wife, was very conscious of their different backgrounds. Fox's salary of $10,000 seemed inadequate by contrast with the wealth of his father-in-law.

This background, Scholz suggested, could be one reason that contributed to Fox's feeling that he was underpaid. "Sid," Bob Winterbottom, his supervisor, would say to him when he voiced his constant complaint about his salary, "you should never have been a chemist." Sometimes they used to joke about the potential for industrial espionage. "All you need," Bob cracked, "is a ship outside the twelve-mile limit, a good process engineer and a microbiologist."

Fox had joined Lederle four years before. He had been given several salary raises, but his personnel file—which contained replies to status inquiries at various stores, as well as from the finance company that had granted the mortgage on his house —showed that he lived extensively on credit.

There was a significant note in the file from the personnel manager, who, on approving his appointment as a research chemist, warned that "Dr. Fox may be a problem insofar as finances are concerned as he seems to be a man who lives above his means and he may cause Dr. Phelps salary problems."

During the next few days Fulton opened files on Biorganic Laboratories and the company's two officers, who, he learned from the report that Wally Hoffer sent over from the purchasing department, were named Nathan Sharff and Seymour

Salb, but none of his facts about them were suspicious.[7] They had not been in business long, but financially they seemed sound.

The information did not take them very far. In fact, it was obviously possible that there was nothing behind Ted Scholz's suspicions. However, as Frank Allen remarked to Fulton, "It's a screwy way for Fox to behave if he's not up to something."

Early on the morning that Ted Scholz and his boss first alerted the plant security men to the possibility that there might be an industrial spy in the research block, Lyman Duncan, Lederle's general manager, strode up the steps of the administration building. The scene in the spacious marble-floored reception area was the same that awaited him as he arrived at work every day.

The receptionist was sitting at her desk behind a battery of telephones waiting for the stream of salesmen, hoping to do business with Lederle executives, who would keep her busy for most of the day. One of the guides, in a well-cut blue uniform, was fixing the placard of welcome that faced visitors scheduled to tour the plant as soon as they stepped through the swing doors. Suitably personalized for public relations purposes, it listed their names—members of medical schools, housewives' guilds, doctors, drugstore operatives and Lederle detail men who had been successful in sales competitions. Some of them would be arriving at 10 A.M. in the big black Cadillac limousine that drove to Pearl River every morning from the Cyanamid head office in New York City.

As he hurried into the building, Duncan greeted the two girls, turned right under the four big paintings of Cyanamid presidents—including Weed Malcolm, the current occupant of the office—acknowledged the "Morning, Mr. Duncan" of the security guard, and took the elevator to the fourth floor.

As always, Caroline Reutter, his slim fair-haired secretary, was at her desk in the small room adjoining his big office, thickly carpeted in green.

As he walked through her room, she gave him the previous day's sales figures and followed him into his office. He laid the sheet of figures on his desk and examined them while he took off his heavy overcoat, which she placed on a hanger in the cupboard. Duncan's reaction to the daily sales reports was a kind of private ritual between them. When they were good, he would say, "Well, there seem to be a lot of sick people about." When they were down, he would comment, "I don't know how we're going to pay our salaries, Caroline."

Duncan was tall and lanky with the jerky, rather ungainly movements that often characterize men of that build. His gray hair was usually slightly ruffled. He was a courteous man who laughed a great deal and spoke with a Midwestern accent. At forty-eight, he was responsible for Cyanamid's total Lederle operation at Pearl River with its annual drug production of more than $100,000,000, its research investment, which had now risen to $14,000,000, and its force of 800 detail men.

His progress through the Cyanamid hierarchy had followed a firm line of development. He had just moved from job to job, each one bigger and more important than the last. There was, in fact, nothing in his background to suggest that he was destined to become a top executive in a giant corporation. He was the son of a small-time farmer in Flat Rock, Illinois, who—like almost everyone else in the district—had been virtually bankrupted in the Great Depression, although no one had ever considered it worthwhile to administer the *coup de grâce*.

Duncan had been educated only in the winter months. The rest of the year he had been needed on the farm. But even during his months at school, his father had never allowed him to do homework on the principle that if he concentrated properly in the classroom, there was no need.

Duncan claimed that this had done a great deal for his concentration, but in fact, he disliked the written word. He loathed reading or writing letters, which he would dismiss to Caroline Reutter as "that stupid paper work that doesn't make the company any money." It was one of her constant problems that often two or three days would go by without his even looking at his correspondence. "Anything there is in the mail I can learn by talking to people," he would tell her.

He disliked conferences, too, and when he could, he had his executives chair the inevitable stream of meetings that feature modern business life. He liked talking to people individually, and that was how he controlled the plant. That was why, when Jack Stewart strolled into his office that morning and asked, "Got a moment, Lyman?" Duncan welcomed him in warmly.

Stewart—head of industrial and community relations—was wiry, with a manner that was relaxed and casual. He told Duncan that the security office was a bit suspicious of a PhD over in the process improvement section. "He's got some kind of contact with a little outfit in East Paterson called Biorganic Laboratories," Stewart explained. "We haven't got much to go on yet, but we're keeping him under surveillance."

"A PhD?" Even today Duncan can remember vividly his feeling of shocked surprise when he heard Stewart's news. For in Lederle—which had been transformed into Cyanamid's most successful company purely because of its research brains—the PhD's enjoyed a special kind of star status.

Apparently, Stewart said, Fox had been showing a great deal of interest in Declomycin. He would report again when they had discovered anything more definite.

It was to be a long time before anyone at Pearl River knew anything that, by the wildest stretch of the imagination, could be described as definite. Dr. Scholz's internal surveillance came to an end very soon. One evening, shortly after the meeting in the old farmhouse, he noticed on one of his evening visits to Fox's lab that the drawers of the desk were sealed with light sticky tape. If he opened any of them, it would be obvious to the chemist when he came in the next morning. Then, looking up at the glass partition that divided Fox's desk from the rest of the laboratory, he saw that a picture had been fingered in the dust on the dirty pane.

It was a rough sketch of Big Brother—Fox's way of indicating that he knew he was being watched.

Fox's interest in A.8—Declomycin, Lederle's newest antibiotic, which was still under test—was the most serious factor in the situation that had emerged.

The bug that made it had first appeared in a petri dish in a microbiology lab one afternoon back in 1954. Ursula Hirsch, a dark-haired German girl, was examining the few mutant microorganisms that remained after the havoc caused by exposure to ultraviolet rays. Suddenly, she called to her boss, "Hey, Dr. Growich, come over and look at this!"

The colony she was examining was quite different from the usual pattern of glossy, wormlike *aureofaciens* organisms. This one had a ring of fluorescent coloring she had never seen before.

John Growich agreed that it was different all right. But their enthusiasm was dampened when they sent it over to the assay section for testing. For its yield of antibiotic was very poor. Yet it was an interesting bug because the substance it made, though small in volume, had characteristics that none of them recognized.

Clearly, however, it needed a great deal of study. The research division was then straining under a very big work load. Tetracycline had been in production for only a few months. Other new drugs were at advanced stages of development—a diuretic for treating epilepsy; vitamin B complex for the senile; several different products for the anemias; triamcinalone for arthritis; and Artane, a real breakthrough drug, the first to be effective against Parkinson's disease.

Growich was ordered to store the new bug until work on it could be scheduled. So he lyophilized it in a vacuum-sealed glass tube in which it would stay alive and potent for years. Twelve months later a team of chemists headed by two PhD's —Dr. Jerry McCormick and Dr. Newell Sjolander—began working on the Declo bug to explore its potential as a commercial proposition: building up its yield; improving the purity of the drug it produced in fermentation; solving the complex chemical problems; discovering what conditions suited it best—all the same operations that the research teams had laboriously carried out with *Streptomyces aureofaciens*. McCormick handled the fermentation end. Sjolander, who was a microbiologist, bred the bugs.

A few weeks after the Declo program had been set up McCormick walked into the microbiology lab to see his partner on the project. In his hand he carried a long paper sheet spotted with moisture. Sjolander knew that he had been running a paper chromotography test of the ingredients of the fermentation mash of the new bug.

"Find anything interesting?" he asked.

"You could say that," answered McCormick. "See what you think of this."

The two men moved to the ultraviolet compartment in the lab and examined the sheet of paper. Sjolander saw immediately why McCormick had come over. In addition to the other familiar markings on the paper, the ultraviolet rays revealed two yellow fluorescent spots, which meant only one thing. "My God, it is," he said. "It's a new antibiotic."

Although low yields were a problem, the product stood up well to the early tests. They sent it to the animals in the experimental therapeutic building for the long series of trials before it was tried out on human beings. What qualities did it have? How lethal was it against disease bacteria? Was it toxic? Did it cause damage within the body, as well as destroy harmful organisms?

By the fall of 1958 McCormick and Sjolander were in the later testing stages. They still had some way to go before Lederle could go into full-scale production of the drug. It needed a lot more testing in clinical trials on human beings. And the inevitable manufacturing snags would have to be smoothed out in the pilot plant.

But they were far enough along the road to know that they were working with a very good product—better than tetracycline for the same reason that Terramycin had been superior to Aureomycin. It was less toxic. It was absorbed in the body more slowly. It stayed in the bloodstream longer, retaining its potency as an antibiotic. This meant smaller doses with fewer side effects.

If Fox had stolen some of the Declo bugs and accumulated the process data—which, voluminous though it was, he could very easily have acquired—he could have put someone in business. But this, at the time, was pure theory in the minds of Ted Scholz and Bill Fulton as they groped to establish the chemist's motivation. For whom could he put into business? Not Biorganic Laboratories. That, at least, was certain. For that was a two-man business, and Declomycin production would need a substantial plant with a staff of highly qualified experts. Was it possible that Biorganic was a kind of agency for the marketing of bugs and know-how?

In any case, Bill Fulton had found no evidence to support Fox's alleged links with Nathan Sharff and Seymour Salb, who ran the Biorganic firm. Often after Ted Scholz had called the old farmhouse to tell them that Fox had just left the lab, Fulton had tailed the chemist in his old green Oldsmobile as he drove out of the parking lot. But on every occasion he had just driven home to Anthony Court in Spring Valley.

Then in May, 1959, Fox bought a new car—another Oldsmobile, this time in powder blue. This was not remarkable, but as Bill knew from his inquiries, the chemist did not buy it on credit. He paid cash—the full price of $2,064—and this did cause the security man to ponder. For just where had a $10,000-a-year PhD got this kind of money?

A few weeks after Fox had taken delivery of his new car, Ted Scholz made one of his routine calls to the security office to tip them off that Fox was just leaving the lab. It was 4:15 P.M.—a quarter of an hour before the plant hooter howled the official work-stop hour for everyone except those working shifts on the production lines. This time Fulton was tempted to let the chemist go on his own, unwatched, since he had followed him so often on innocent journeys. But he resisted the inclination. Wearily, he picked up his hat and clattered down the farm-house stairs to his car.

It was just as well he did, for on this occasion his highly detailed surveillance report would not be as negative as those he had written before.

The Oldsmobile was already moving up the driveway toward Middletown Road as Bill skirted the blocks of cars in the parking lot.

But instead of swinging left toward Spring Valley—as he had done on every other occasion that Fulton had followed him —the chemist turned right and drove swiftly toward Pearl River Township. Fulton stayed well behind him—leaving a good 150 yards between the two cars to be as inconspicuous as possible. Fox was driving at 65 miles an hour. He swung out to pass a Chevrolet station wagon. The Chevy was moving quite fast, and Fulton stayed purposely behind it so that it would screen him in Fox's mirror.

In the narrow main street of Pearl River, Fox swung the Oldsmobile right at a light and drove in the direction of the Garden State Parkway.

By the time he had gone through the toll barrier, Fulton was feeling cautiously optimistic. For the two cars were heading for East Paterson—the New Jersey town where Biorganic Laboratories was located. At last, maybe, he was going to get information that was not just hearsay. But he had problems. Now that Fox was on the parkway, he was moving at more than 85 mph. Fulton's Plymouth was no match for Fox's new Olds 88. He had his foot down to the floorboard, but the distance between the two cars was growing.

Fortunately for the security man, they were not going far. Fox was almost out of his sight when he checked his speed to drive off the parkway at Exit 158 onto the County Expressway. It was now virtually certain he was traveling to Biorganic Laboratories. When the chemist left the expressway at East Paterson, Fulton braked and deliberately let the Oldsmobile go out of vision.

Biorganic Laboratories was on Chamberlain Avenue—a dull, characterless side street of nondescript buildings—almost opposite Van Riper Avenue. Fulton parked the Plymouth well up Van Riper and switched off the engine. From his surveillance point he could just see Fox's blue Oldsmobile, standing in front of a house farther along the road from the yellow-brick Biorganic building.

For a few minutes, the chemist sat in his convertible reading some papers. Then he got out, walked around to the back of the car, opened the trunk, took out a thick red folder, and went through the Biorganic entrance.

Parked in the roadway outside were a pink Cadillac and a black Oldsmobile convertible. Fulton waited for two hours.

Just before seven, Fox emerged from the building, accompanied by a tall angular man, with gray hair, whom Fulton had never seen before. They talked for a few minutes; then the stranger got into the pink Cadillac and drove east toward the county expressway. Deciding it would be more productive to exploit his new lead than to tail Fox further, Fulton followed the Cadillac.

It took him to Mountain Avenue, Monsey, New York, and he was pretty certain—since the name of the owner of the red-brick house was in his files—that the driver was Seymour Salb.

The next morning, after Frank Allen had reported to him, Jack Stewart walked along the passage on the fourth floor of the administration building to Duncan's office to report the new information, sparse and inconclusive though it was.

"At least," commented Stewart, "we've got direct evidence that they're in touch."

At this stage, with the evidence skimpy and the motivation uncertain, Duncan regarded the investigation as a routine inquiry.

In September, however, after he had taken his annual vacation, Sidney Fox resigned. If he had been handing over the company's property to the two proprietors of Biorganic Laboratories, Lederle now had very little chance of proving it.

By this time, however, events that were to have a deep effect on the destiny of the chemist were materializing in Washington.

5

IN Washington on September 25—a few days after Fox resigned from his job at Pearl River—Senator Estes Kefauver summoned the press to the Old Senate Building on Capitol Hill and announced that the Senate Subcommittee on Antitrust and Monopoly would investigate the drug industry. The hearings, he said, would start in December, and among the four drugs to be probed would be the biggest sellers of all: the antibiotics.

This meant that the Cyanamid executives—who ran one of the largest antibiotics operations in the world—would have to appear before the Senators to face questions that, with so many ex-FTC people on the subcommittee staff, were certain to be hostile.

The probable areas of attack could, to some extent, be assessed. Following the market-rigging charges of the previous fall, an FTC examiner had been conducting hearings in New York since January—a long, tedious process of legal technicalities that was to consume most of two years and fill 11,000 pages with testimony. Walter Mansfield, who was in charge of Cyanamid's legal interests in the case, and the attorneys for the other companies were not too worried for their clients because they just did not believe the FTC could establish a case.

In fact, however, neither Weed Malcolm nor Lyman Duncan had any conception of what lay ahead of them in the Senate hearings. In retrospect, the calm with which the drugmakers as a whole received the news of the investigation is testimony to the complacency that had grown around them like a cocoon. Kefauver's announcement was, of course, no surprise to them. Apart from the rumors sparked by the inquiries of his staff, the subcommittee had sent out subpoenas in March to nineteen major firms demanding details of intercompany agreements—especially those concerning patents. Even so, there was no sense of alarm, no anticipation of the effect that would be created by the hearings—or of the worldwide repercussions that would follow them.

Naturally, the drug executives talked to the men in other industries who had appeared before the subcommittee. "They told us," recalls Paul Stessel, Lederle's public relations manager, "that there was only one thing to do: just bow our heads and take the punishment."

But there was one big difference between this investigation and those that had preceded it: The others had stimulated little interest in the press. The revelations that Kefauver was about to produce about the drugmakers were to make big headlines and contain accusations that amounted to little short of a national scandal—which was the reason why the critical groups that had been growing in Washington tended to rally to Kefauver's standard.

Most of the material that Kefauver was about to display accusingly before the men who, regarding themselves benignly as custodians of the nation's health, provided America with its medicines, had been ferreted out by the subcommittee research staff—in particular by Dr. Irene Till, whose husband's strep throat could be said to have started it all.

Several times the various trials they were pursuing led them back to a small company named Premo Laboratories, sited in the flat, ugly industrial hinterland of Hackensack, New Jersey.

Premo was to become closely involved in Cyanamid's fight with the government, but by 1958 it had not yet plunged into the controversial and aggressively protected area of antibiotics. However, it *was* selling prednisone—a synthetic adaptation, made from Mexican yam plants, of the natural hormone cortisone and one of the big postwar wonder drugs.

However, what interested the subcommittee investigators about Premo and its prednisone operation was that it provided them with dramatic material to expose the big drugmakers as profiteers.

For Premo did not manufacture in the normal sense of the word. It bought its drugs in the form of bulk powder, made it up into tablets or capsules, and then sold it.

As a result, the mathematics of its operation was simple to illustrate, for there were no financial complications—as there were in the case of the big firms with their research operations and sales teams and complicated manufacturing cost structures —to cloud the issue. The price at which it bought the bulk powder and sold the finished product revealed a clear profit that was easily assessed. More important, Premo—like some other small firms—was undercutting the big competition by substantial margins.

The Schering Corporation, for example, in common with four other big firms, was selling the drug at $170 a bottle while Premo's price was only $31. The difference was that Schering and its major competitors were marketing their products under their own brand names. Premo, on the other hand, was selling the drug under its generic name—just simply as prednisone.

If a doctor did not specify a brand on his prescription—merely naming the drug required—then the drugstore could prescribe the Premo product. But in practice, doctors normally preferred to instruct the pharmacist to provide the heavily promoted names they knew.

The crucial issue, as Dr. John Blair saw it, was: Did the advantage of a brand name require a price that was five times higher than that of the same drug sold without one? And this thinking was to color much of the interrogation during the hearings.

Meanwhile, Kefauver staff men called on Admiral Knickerbocker at the Military Medical Supply Agency to explore his possibilities as a witness before the subcommittee. He did not need much persuasion because he had become just as antagonistic toward the drugmakers as John Blair. And the targets of his anger were the tetracycline firms who had proved uncooperative in his attempts to cut the Defense Department's drug bill of more than $40,000,000 annually.

The main reason for Knickerbocker's frustration was the fact that the bids for his big contracts were so often the same—sometimes even to a cent. On occasions there would be one low bid, while all the others, as the admiral testified later, "came in at higher but identical prices." In other words, he concluded, they were carving up the business between them.[8]

Throughout the long battle between the government and the tetracycline producers, a good deal of evidence has been produced that certainly suggested a degree of market sharing.[9] If this was the case, then the method was astonishingly naïve and transparent for men who displayed a considerable sophistication in their other operations.

At any rate, Knickerbocker was not merely concerned about the similarity of the bids. He was incensed by the fact that the common price level was rising and he was impotent to do anything about it—at least, he was until he eventually decided to adopt drastic measures.

In May, 1957, for example, he bought tetracycline hydrochloride tablets at a price of $11 for each bottle of 100. Nine months later he was forced to pay $17.24—more than 50 percent more for an order of 93,476 bottles. His next procurement was the same to the cent, and the one after that at $17.15 was so near the previous figure that it made little difference.

Angrily, he sent a blistering memo to the Navy Department about the powerful common front he seemed to be facing.

It was then that Commander Arnold Weiss, Knickerbocker's tall, affable procurement director, remarked casually, "We could, of course, buy abroad at half the price."

At first, the admiral was horrified. It conflicted diametrically with the government's Buy American policy. Worse, the holocaust that this would cause in Washington when the industry's public relations machine struck back made it seem impractical. He shook his head. But the thought remained.

It was an old and well-worn fact that companies could often sell abroad at prices considerably below those charged in the domestic market, where they had to recover their manufacturing costs. It was for this reason that most nations had antidumping laws against this kind of import.

Italy was an obvious source that Weiss had in mind primarily because, owing to its lack of drug patents, U.S. firms could do little to curb competitors there.[10] In other countries, they could pressure licensees. Also, Italian manufacturing costs were low. By American standards, labor was cheap and research expenditures were small—artificially small, in some cases, as was proved later, because espionage provided a low-cost alternative method of obtaining information and organisms.

For the time being, Knickerbocker took no action following his procurement director's drastic proposal to break the tetracycline price barrier. Then, for a short period, he thought he was at last getting the cooperation from the drug firms that he had been demanding. Pfizer cut its next tetracycline bid to $14.36. But the admiral's belief that this was a new policy was to prove mistaken. When the following procurement was announced, Pfizer's price was back at $17.15—only cents off those of the other tetracycline firms.

The possibility of buying abroad that Arnold Weiss had suggested became more appealing. Knickerbocker made a few inquiries in the higher echelons of the Navy Department to whom he reported. Would overseas purchase be a contravention of the Buy American act? Would it be allowed under the U.S. Code, which contained a section permitting the government to infringe on U.S. patents under certain circumstances? Then he invited the Pfizer executives to a meeting in the old red-brick building on Third Avenue in Brooklyn that housed the MMSA offices.

Tom Cooney, a wiry, hard-hitting executive in charge of Pfizer's sales to the government, attended the meeting together with a vice-president and the company's top medical executive. Today Knickerbocker recalls the occasion in vivid detail and did, in fact, testify about it before the Kefauver Subcommittee.

At first, the admiral took a fairly easy attitude. "Gentlemen," he said, "we think your price is just too darned high. If you could supply us before for fourteen dollars, we just can't see why you have to bid so much now. However, I'm going to help you reconsider it. I'll double the procurement."

Tom Cooney had been over this area with the admiral many times before. It was an argument that never got anywhere. They had conflicting points of view. Suddenly, he grew irritated. He pounded Knickerbocker's desk with his fist. "Admiral," he said, "the price of tetracycline will stay where it is until Pfizer decides to do something about it."

Knickerbocker glared at Cooney through the lenses of his tortoiseshell glasses.

"Well, Mr. Cooney," he said, "we're not going to wait until then. We're going to do something about it now."

"What can you do," asked Cooney, "in view of our patent position?"

"We can introduce a bit of competition." Knickerbocker paused, knowing the effect his words would have. "We can go abroad."

Cooney looked at him with astonishment. For he knew the admiral could not believe that Pfizer would allow the government to bring the drug into the country without taking action. The company could put an embargo on it. It could sue for triple damages.

For the first time during that meeting, the admiral smiled. "We've done our homework, Mr. Cooney—we suggest you do yours."

Commander Arnold Weiss already had a contact with an Italian drug company—Joseph Anselmi, the New York agent of Farmochimica Cutolo-Calosi, a firm that did not actually make tetracycline. Like Premo, it bought bulk powder from other companies and then tableted the product. Weiss asked Anselmi to make a few discreet inquiries.

In the meanwhile, Knickerbocker and his production director went on a barnstorming campaign to Washington to obtain approval to buy abroad. Grimly, they trailed from office to office asking the various officials whose permission they needed to endorse their plan.

One of these was Henry Welch, head of the Antibiotics Division of the Food and Drug Administration. The FDA would have to approve the drugs that the MMSA bought.

As Knickerbocker walked into Welch's office, the first thing he saw was a large signed color photograph of the man who had so far thwarted his efforts to get the price of tetracycline down —Pfizer's John McKeen. "You guys are really asking for it," said Welch. "You'll never get away with it—but, as the representative of another government agency, I'll help you in every possible way."

At last, the Assistant Secretary for the Navy gave his authority, which meant that Knickerbocker could proceed. In December the MMSA announced that it had accepted a bid for the supply of tetracycline hydrochloride tablets from Farmochimica Cutolo-Calosi. The price was $469,440 compared with $964,-641, which the MMSA would have had to pay if it had accepted the lowest U.S. bid. Jubilantly, Knickerbocker claimed that he had saved the American taxpayer nearly half a million dollars.

The news brought a fast and angry response from the drug industry, which was only too conscious that although Knickerbocker was striking initially against the tetracycline makers, he did not have to limit his purchases to this drug alone. The Defense Department, they asserted accusingly, was distorting an act of Congress, passed in 1910 to deal with conditions of emergency. The contract was a direct attack on the American patent system, which had inspired many important drug discoveries. The savings claimed were nothing as great as they seemed when such hidden costs as royalties and taxes lost on reduced company revenue were taken into account.

Ironically, Farmochimica Cutolo-Calosi, Knickerbocker's first Italian contractor, proposed to make the tablets from bulk powder supplied by Farmitalia—a company licensed by Cyanamid to use Lederle organisms and know-how to make the drug.

Meanwhile, the announcement of Knickerbocker's tetracycline deal with the Italian firm sparked off a keen response in an office in Hackensack. Theodore Blackman, president of Premo Laboratories, saw in the situation a potential for big business. If Farmochimica Cutolo-Calosi could buy bulk powder from Farmitalia, make it up into capsules, and supply it in one vast delivery under contract to the U.S. Defense Department, why should he not do the same from New Jersey?

He placed a call to Knickerbocker's office in Washington to explore this possibility and, in particular, to discover what Premo's position would be if Pfizer sued. The answer was encouraging: The government would indemnify him against a patent suit.

Blackman flew to Italy to investigate possible supply sources, so that he could bid for the next MMSA tetracycline contract.

Later two of his suppliers were to feature prominently in Cyanamid's head-on clash with the government.

For the time being, however—angry though both must have been—Malcolm in Rockefeller Plaza and McKeen in the Pfizer head office in Brooklyn were powerless to take any action at all. Meanwhile, came the trauma of the Kefauver investigation.

Only four days after Admiral Knickerbocker signed the tetracycline contract with Farmochimica Cutolo-Calosi, Senator Kefauver called to order the Subcommittee on Antitrust and Monopoly in the large marble-pillared Senate Caucus Room in the Old Senate Building near the Capitol. Although it had not yet dawned on the drugmakers, this occasion had been directly spawned by the decisions of their directors years before to speculate in research. The pendulum had swung. All the excesses that the Kefauver staff objected to—high prices, exaggerated claims in advertising, minimizing of side effects, marketing after insufficient testing (although this could be controlled by the FDA)—stemmed from the element of fierce competition that had entered the industry's thinking from the moment the drugmakers became gamblers.

There was, however, nothing to suggest the character that the occasion was soon to assume when the Senators—accompanied by the subcommittee counsel and, of course, John Blair—took their places on the rostrum on December 7, 1959. The press benches were crowded. It was the first day of a new investigation. Television arc lights glared down from the ceiling.

Like executives in other companies who might also have to testify later, Lyman Duncan flew down from Pearl River to attend the first few days of the hearings. He took a seat at the back of the hall with Bill Kavanaugh, Cyanamid's man in Washington.

Kefauver gave an impression that was misleading. Bespectacled and untidy, his appearance suggested that he would be more at home in a community in Tennessee—which had sent him to Washington as a Senator—than in the powerhouse of the Capitol. Also, he tended to mumble, often to the point of being inaudible, and this, too, contributed to the general rather woolly, hillbilly aura that surrounded him. But in truth, the Senator was a highly skilled tactical politician and as shrewd an operator as could be found in Congress at the time.

Kefauver, speaking with his quiet Southern drawl, outlined what the subcommittee was there to do and welcomed the first witnesses—Francis Brown, the president of the Schering Corporation, and two of his executives, who sat at a small table facing the six-Senator committee and their advisers on the rostrum.

Cortical steroids were the first big group of drugs to be investigated, and the Schering executives had been selected for investigation because the company was one of the biggest producers of prednisone and its sister product, prednisolone.

Prednisone occupied a position in the steroid hormone market that was similar to the role of tetracycline in the antibiotic sector. Scientists had long known that cortisone was an effective palliative of rheumatoid arthritis—even though it produced unpleasant side effects—as well as a treatment for other diseases. But there had been no way of making it economically on a mass-production scale until a method had been discovered of producing it from the Mexican yam. This revolutionized the treatment of arthritis and produced an enormous demand for the drug.

There had been a battle for the patent, involving two of the same contestants as the tetracycline fight, Pfizer and Upjohn. Nevertheless, despite the competition, the drug had played a role in the fortunes of Schering that was similar to the dramatic effect of Aureomycin on Lederle's situation in 1950. The company's profits bounded. From Schering's point of view, the timing of this success was, to say the least, unfortunate. For although Francis Brown did not anticipate the ordeal that lay ahead of him as he took his place at the witness table, it had lain the company out on a slab for the Kefauver hatchets.

By their nature, Senate investigations are often biased. "The most notable committee investigations are seldom in point of fact 'investigations,'" Douglass Cater, the then Washington correspondent of the *Reporter*, has commented. "They are planned deliberately to move from a preconceived idea to a predetermined conclusion."

Even Kefauver did not claim that his hearings were fair. "If you hope to accomplish anything in an area as controversial as the Monopoly and Anti-trust field," he said, according to Richard Harris in *The Real Voice*, "you've got to have an issue, and then you've got to stir up the people about it. Otherwise you don't have a chance of getting a piece of progressive legislation through Congress."

However, the Senate Subcommittee on Antitrust and Monopoly started off with all the superficial appearance of impartiality.

Kefauver encouraged Brown to read a long and defensive statement about Schering's contribution to the fight against disease. At one point, speaking of the cures effected with his steroids, Brown said, "Men walking who were crippled, and working who were incapacitated, at a cost of between 30 and 60 cents a day, seems to me to be pretty reasonable."

Then, as Brown finished and sat down, the mood changed drastically. Paul Rand Dixon, Kefauver's dark, muscular counsel for the majority party—who had been schooled in the FTC—opened the questioning for the subcommittee. At an exhibition point there was a large stand that, until now, had been covered. Dixon asked for the first chart to be revealed. It showed a cost breakdown of prednisolone, the price of which Brown had described in his statement as being "pretty reasonable."

"Mr. Brown," asked Dixon after a few introductory questions, "I put this question to you: If you can make a pill for 1.6

cents, do you still consider it pretty reasonable to charge 17.9 cents to the druggist?"

Brown—a scholarly figure with an aquiline nose—was completely unprepared for this question. Floundering, he said that the figures ignored overhead, development and selling costs, and especially research. Swiftly, John Blair interposed the fact that Schering's research expenditure of nearly $8,000,000 annually was only 8.5 percent of sales.

Idly, with his eye on the press benches, Kefauver asked Blair if research were included in the cost, what that would make the percentage profit markup.

"Mr. Chairman," answered Blair, "it is 1,118 percent."

Immediately, the television cameras started whirring. The reporters on the press benches began scribbling, the headlines forming vividly in their minds—despite the fact that Peter Chumbris, counsel for the minority party, emphasized that this figure was completely misleading. Schering's profits overall, after taxes, were 16.6 percent of sales. This was high, but it was not absurd.

This opening sortie by Dixon established the pattern for the grilling that continued for two days. Question after question—put either by Kefauver or by Dixon—caught Brown off-balance, often because they probed areas in great detail in which he, as president of a large corporation, had not been fully briefed. At one point he said rather desperately, "Mr. Chairman, I would like to ask if we can have an opportunity to study these charts and compilations which have been shown to me by surprise today."

Bluntly, Kefauver dismissed the request. "These charts on profits are well known to everybody," he said. "They were prepared by the Federal Trade Commission. They were published in *Fortune* magazine. You have been in business for a long, long time and I don't like to hear you say that this is a great shock to you. . . ."

At the back of the hall, Lyman Duncan muttered to Kavanaugh, "This is fantastic. This isn't an investigation—it's a crucifixion."

Kefauver and his team had ideal material to exploit in Schering's situation at that time. Owing mainly to its new steroids, profits of the company had more than doubled in three years.

Brown insisted that when his chemists made these discoveries, Schering was small and inadequately capitalized. Promptly Kefauver attacked him on the ground that its profits were 47 percent of the value of the company in that one year alone. "Don't you think that would have been a good year to reduce some of these prices?" he asked.

In his answer, Brown revealed the fear that lies in the heart of all the drugmakers. "That was a year of crisis," he said. "We learned that a competitor was supposed to have a compound that was about six times as active as our compound. We tested it and we found this wasn't true in man. It was true in animals. . . . If this product had proven to have this ratio of activity to our own in man, we would have been out of business overnight insofar as this product is concerned."

Kefauver tried to nail down Brown's constant justification of research by comparing drugs with other industries. "The petroleum refining industry probably has a larger research expenditure than you do," the Senator insisted. "So does the tire industry. These industries have large research programs, just as drugs do. We are glad you spend a great deal on research. But just as a matter of public policy, Mr. Brown, isn't 22 per cent after taxes a pretty high profit? . . . When the product you are dealing with has to be sold to a captive market, there is nothing people can do about it. They have to buy these drugs."

With growing desperation, Brown—sweating visibly, complaining that the glare of the arc lights prevented him from seeing the charts—fought back against his inquisitors who presented their fact-packed evidence so clearly. He talked of the immense cost of tests for quality that marked every stage of the production process. He explained the high expense of maintaining a coast-to-coast distribution network. He spoke of the after-sales service to doctors. He even pleaded that competition existed, not only between products, but also between companies selling the drugs they were questioning him about. There were the four big competitors—selling admittedly at the same price as he was—and also the small firms whose low prices Kefauver and Dixon had quoted to him.

Repeatedly, he insisted that these small companies did no long-term research, had minimal overheads and minute distribution costs. He argued that it was misleading to analyze the profit on a single drug because the successes had to pay for the failures and for those lines on which profit was either very low or nonexistent.

Brown was not just speaking for Schering. He was arguing for the whole industry. He was mouthing the same words that many other chief executives were going to speak from that small table during the months to come—the only difference being that by then they would be prepared, while Brown was an innocent, digging the ground away from beneath his own feet.

Kefauver was preparing to trap him, and he quietly blocked Brown's only exit. "You say," drawled the Senator, "that you have to make a big profit on prednisolone in order to make up your losses on some others. Now just where is the big bargain that you have on some other drugs?"

Brown floundered. He had already explained that prices depended more on competition than on production costs. "What I said, Senator," he answered, "was that we work on the basis of overall averages. We do not work . . . on the basis of cost of raw materials." Earlier, for comparison, he had held up his watch, asserting that it was absurd to strike a profit purely on the cost of the steel in it.

Now Dixon moved in with a body blow that put his previous punches into the category of pure sparring. "Mr. Brown, you sell a generic product under the trade name Progynon. . . .

In 1958, you purchased it from Roussel—Roussel is a French drug firm—at $3.50 a gram."

Schering, said Dixon, sold Progynon to drugstores at a price of $8.40 for a bottle of sixty tablets while the bulk cost they paid for it worked out at only 11.7 cents. "Now the mark-up from 11.7 cents to $8.40," he declared, "is 7,079 per cent!"

Immediately, there was a stir on the press benches.

Desperately, Brown tried once more to argue that the figure was a distortion of the situation. Since it had already been shown that Schering's profit was 16.6 percent, this kind of gigantic markup was "aimed at headlines."

It was all over but the shouting. The Washington *Evening Star* headlined the story of the first day's hearings: SENATORS find 1,118% DRUG MARK-UP. The next morning the New York *Times* covered the afternoon session under the words in bold type: SENATE PANEL CITES MARK-UPS ON DRUGS RANGING UP TO 7,079%.

Duncan, conscious that in a few months he would be sitting with Weed Malcolm at the little table where Francis Brown had been castigated, returned to New York. To his president he suggested: "We've got to prepare for this with great care. We need to treat it like a public relations campaign. We've got to have all the answers to those loaded questions."

The Kefauver investigation, with the headlines it provided to the nation's newspapers, placed the drugmakers in the stocks. For a decade, they had been public heroes. They had been the miracle workers. Overnight, their image had been transformed. Now they were gross profiteers. They were exploiters of the poor.

The patent system—which is more protective in the United States than it is in most countries—was violently criticized. It sometimes provided cover, its opponents charged, for drugs that were not truly new or different at all—merely combinations of existing products. The whole notion that it had inspired a large number of new drug discoveries was, they implied, a lot of nonsense. Most of the major drug discoveries had been made in other countries. The idea that strong patent laws inspired invention was pure public relations.

As evidence of the inadequacy of the patent laws, John Blair submitted two lists of major drug discoveries: Forty-eight, he said, had been originated by U.S. companies, but 110 had been developed abroad—a contention that infuriated the drugmakers. For on the foreign list—so they claimed—29 of the discoveries dated back to the nineteenth century and before. Two, in fact, were developed in the 1500's. More than half were originated before 1939. By contrast, more than 35 of the 48 drugs in the American list were discovered after that date—when the big spending on research by drug companies truly started—compared with 14 from Germany, 7 from Switzerland and 5 from France. Of the drugs on Blair's list no other country came up with as many as four new products during this period.

Perhaps the most serious of all the criticisms was the suggestion that the drugmakers were using the word "research" as a smokescreen. The industry claimed to spend $190,000,000 a year in its laboratories, but how much of this was devoted to finding cures to disease? Suddenly, drug research—which, until then, had been regarded as fairly self-explanatory—acquired new propensities in keeping with the new image of the pharmaceutical firms that had been created by the investigation. To what degree were research budgets inflated artificially?

Although some expert witnesses from outside the industry praised the contribution to the fight against disease made by the drugmakers, it was the critics that tended to catch the headlines. Mike Gorman, executive director of the National Committee Against Mental Illness in Washington, D.C., crystallized the views of the skeptics. "How much of this is honest-to-goodness research," he demanded during his testimony, "and how much of it is in support of drug evaluations designed to prove that Pill A (the pink one) is infinitely superior to Pill B (the blue one)?

"During the past several years, scores of articles have appeared in medical publications questioning the validity of some of these so-called drug evaluations. . . . How much of this figure [the research total of $190,000,000] is for research on whether people like blue or pink pills? How much of it is for research on what shape pill appeals to the American esophagus?"

Seymour Blackman, executive secretary of Premo Laboratories, was far more dogmatic. "The vast majority of the research done by the pharmaceutical manufacturers," he stated bluntly, "is applied research, motivated by self-preservation and the profit angle."

Others attacked the drugmakers for using their research departments to exploit the Patent Office. Dr. Frederick H. Meyers, associate professor of pharmacology at the University of California Medical School, asserted that much of the work done by American drug firms was "mostly to modify the original drug just enough to get a patentable derivative."

The whole system of distributing drugs under trade names was attacked. Would it not be better to force doctors to write generic names—such as tetracycline instead of Achromycin— in their prescriptions? This would almost certainly have the effect of reducing prices and would also remove much of the incentive from high-pressure promotion. The drugmakers' implicit argument that because they had spent millions of dollars promoting a brand they clearly had a vested interest in its quality was not rated highly. The critics of the industry have always taken the view—challenged by the drugmakers as logistically impractical—that quality was something that could be controlled by law.

Inevitably, implications that the FDA and the Patent Office

were not strong enough threaded the hearings. In all, the impression imparted by the hearings painted the drugmakers as very evil men.

Maybe some of them were. Certainly, the speculation in research had bred some big excesses that, in the case of some companies, were outrageous. However, it had also produced a range of drugs, such as Cyanamid's Aureomycin, that only a few years back had been regarded as miraculous. But in the atmosphere of hostile suspicion that had been created by the hearings, these discoveries were forgotten or regarded skeptically as exploitation of America's sick—as, in the sense that large profits were made from them, they were. All the same, the fact remained that they were still curing disease and saving lives—even if this aspect was temporarily obscured by the volley of abuse that was hurled at the drug firms.

The paradoxes within the industry—the fact that the doctor who controlled the purchase did not pay for it, that the profit motive was linked to human health—clearly justified a cool, hard look at the whole system that was operating within America and, for that matter, in other countries. It was probably time for the pendulum of the drugmakers' fortunes—which had reached for so long in a direction that was favorable to them—to start swinging back.

Without question, Kefauver stopped it dead and gave it a gigantic push in the opposite direction. And one of the methods he set out to exploit from the start was public opinion.

"Kefauver, who had what one observer called 'a genius for publicity creation,'" wrote Richard Harris, who was a clear admirer of the Senator, "made it a point to bring out his biggest guns half an hour or so before the reporters had to leave to file their stories—ordinarily, 11:30 A.M. for the afternoon papers and 4:30 P.M. for morning papers."

This was when the truly damaging evidence was staged. The drugmakers found themselves answering allegations at times when the reporters were away phoning through their stories.

On one occasion, John McKeen—who was not the kind of man to accept this kind of strategy without a fight—leaped to his feet from the public benches and shouted, "Stop those men!" The reporters were heading for the exits after a particularly damning criticism of Pfizer that McKeen claimed was misleading. He wanted the newsmen to stay to hear the rebuttal. But even McKeen was no true match for the Senator from Tennessee, supported as he was by the powers given him under the U.S. Constitution.

On the morning that Senator Kefauver opened the drug hearings in Washington, another meeting started in New York. The fact that the two events coincided was evidence, if any was needed, of the reluctance or inability of the drugmakers to realize until then the threat that they were facing. Despite the documents and contracts that had been subpoenaed by the subcommittee from some of its major members, the Pharmaceutical Manufacturers' Association (PMA) saw no reason to postpone the big conference it held in December every year.

In fact, it *had* dawned on a few of the drugmakers that times might be on the point of changing, that the attention of a Senate subcommittee and the limited press criticism that had then been published could, in the long term, be damaging. Back in April the PMA had decided that its staff of one man and five girls was too small to protect the industry's interests. It planned to follow the lead of other more progressive manufacturing associations and establish an organization that could promote its public image. It hired a new director—Austin Smith, formerly editor of the prestigious *Journal of the American Medical Association*—a full-time public relations officer, and Hill and Knowlton, a PR firm well known for its experience at handling the problems of whole industries. Also—and perhaps most important of all—the PMA employed outside counsel to represent its interests in Congressional lobbies.

This refurbishing of the trade association, however, was not conducted with much dynamism. It was a leisurely development that had only begun to shake down by the time the Kefauver hearings opened in December.

By lunchtime of that first day, however, drug executives attending the PMA conference in New York learned from phone calls from shocked colleagues that they were facing the biggest crisis in their history. Although some of them had anticipated the need for protection—Austin Smith had even approached Kefauver with the unsuccessful request that he should be permitted to testify first—none had expected an assault of the size and intensity that was taking place on Capitol Hill.

For the first time, the drugmakers attending the PMA conference realized that they were going to have to fight hard if they were to preserve a remnant of the reputation which they had enjoyed before. But the methods open to them were limited. Unlike most manufacturers in other fields, they had no direct contact with the public. They depended entirely on doctors. They spent vast sums on the promotion of their products, but this was all directed within the medical profession. By tradition, they did not advertise in the daily newspapers or magazines. They bought no time on television.

On the other hand, many of the members of the PMA were large and wealthy firms that had prospered from the profits they had made through the 1950's when research had paid off so spectacularly. They employed top advertising agencies and PR firms to conduct their own company campaigns. Apart from the PMA's own advisers, the talent that was available to the industry to mount a defense was, therefore, very great. By the time the newspapers, carrying the story of Schering's markups, were on the streets of Manhattan, the drugmakers were already discussing the ways they might adopt to fight this new and very serious danger.

If the PMA's first moves to change its character to conform with the new age had been unhurried, the association was now fired with a new and angry purpose. It would not be long before it was accused by critics of maintaining the most efficient lobbying organization in America.

By June, 1960, the flurry at Pearl River caused by the strange behavior of Dr. Sidney Fox, particularly his keen interest in the Declomycin bugs, had almost been forgotten—until the sunny morning when Jack Stewart walked into Duncan's office and plopped a trade journal on his desk. "I thought maybe this might interest you," said Stewart dryly.

The journal was *Chemical & Engineering News*—one of the trade magazines read by the drug industry—and it was folded back to display a page in the classified advertisement section. One ad had been outlined in ink.

As Duncan began to read it, he was appalled. For it was an invitation to industrial espionage.

Headed PROCESSES WANTED, there was no subtle veiling of what the advertiser wanted: "Foreign manufacturer, seeks information or consulting services for production of antibiotics, vitamins, steroids and pharmaceutical chemicals. . . . Products will be sold only in foreign countries where patents do not apply. All replies held in strictest confidence. Unusually attractive compensation. Write to representative presently in the U.S.A., Dr. Angelo Mancuso, 15 Bergen Boulevard, Fairview, N.J."

"And who in hell is Dr. Mancuso?" asked Duncan.

"I don't know yet," said Stewart, "but Bill Fulton's finding out."

Fulton did not, in fact, discover who Dr. Mancuso was for some while, but with the help of a friend who was still in the FBI, it did not take him long to find out who lived at 15 Bergen Boulevard, Fairview. It was the home of a man named George London, who provided a direct link to Dr. Sidney Fox. For London was the brother-in-law of Nathan Sharff, one of the two partners who ran Biorganic Laboratories—the little firm in East Paterson to which Fulton had tailed the Lederle chemist.

This was the first time Fulton had been able to link Fox, Biorganic Laboratories and the Italian drug industry.[11] For there was little doubt that although there were other places where patents were ineffective, the most likely country to be involved was Italy. Apart from this rather vague connection, the information did not move his investigation much further forward, but it supplied a small piece in the mosaic of evidence that, in due course, was to become extremely important. Meanwhile, Duncan grasped the opportunity to use the advertisement in the political arena. In September the time came for the Cyanamid executives to face Kefauver and his subcommittee.

With Malcolm and three other executives, Duncan took his place at the rectangular table in the blue-white glare of the television lights.

On their right were the press benches and, among the rows of faces, Duncan noticed Barbara Yuncker of the New York *Post*. A few days before, he had met her at a party. "Why do you only print Kefauver?" he asked her. "Why don't we ever get a look-in?"

"I'm in the news business," she answered. "You give me some news—I'll print it."

"Maybe I can do that," said Duncan. "I hope you'll be ready for it."

Behind the Cyanamid executives sat Walter Mansfield and the other lawyers. Nine months had now gone by since the hearings had started, and Duncan had made certain that the time had not been wasted.

Cyanamid's attorneys had made a careful study of Kefauver's methods. They had analyzed the interrogation of witnesses and isolated the favorite areas of Dixon and John Blair, the economist.

By this time several men who ran small drug firms had testified, as well as the chief executives of the industry giants. Always the background question was: How can these small companies make drugs so cheaply when the big companies charge so much? Repeatedly, the large firms gave what they claimed to be an adequate answer: the small companies did not carry large ranges of products—such as Cyanamid's 800 regular lines —some of which were unprofitable; they did no research, provided no service to doctors and hospitals following the introduction of new drugs, and operated on far smaller overheads.

In the prevailing climate of opinion, however, this argument was regarded as specious and exaggerated.

As head of the drug division, Duncan would have to face much of the questioning on detail. Early in the preparation, Walter Mansfield asked him: "Lyman, have you ever been cross-examined?"

Duncan admitted that he never had.

"Then we must put you through a bit," said Mansfield.

Systematically, Mansfield and two of his partners grilled the Cyanamid executives in the boardroom of the corporation's head office in Rockefeller Plaza—a process known as horse-shedding from the days when attorneys prepared their witnesses in the stables behind the courthouses. Taking it in turns, as Kefauver and Dixon did in the hearings, the lawyers fired questions on prices, profits, research, promotion, detail men and—because this was clearly going to be an important target area—the license arrangements Cyanamid had with the other tetracycline companies.

By the time they attended the hearing in response to the subpoenas, the Cyanamid executives felt like students on their first day of examinations.

Malcolm read a long statement of Cyanamid's role in the drug industry—the opening privilege that Kefauver normally granted his witnesses before Dixon was offered the field. It was dull but pointed, aimed at the record. By contrast with its breakthrough with Aureomycin, he said, the company had spent $137,000,000 on research projects that had yielded no return. Examples: $7,000,000 on a chemotherapeutic cure for cancer, $12,500,000 on a live virus vaccine for the treatment of polio.

He defended his prices. In ten years the cost of milk, footwear and gasoline had risen by 20 percent. Lederle's antibiotics had dropped by two-thirds in the same period.

After lunch, Dixon moved in to interrogate with the help of economist John Blair's charts, which drug company directors had now learned to fear. He asked why the prices of the five tetracycline firms had, until August, remained static since 1955, while those of streptomycin and penicillin—which were not controlled to the same extent by patent—had dropped steeply. He wanted to know, too, why they were all the same.

"Ride down any road," said Duncan, "and check the prices of gasoline . . . you'll find they're the same. . . ."

It was, in fact, in the area of profits that Dixon was most revealing. For the profits of Cyanamid's drug division in 1959 had been more than 17 percent of sales income—three times the average of industry in general. Duncan countered that it was difficult to control profits. A research program took ten years to mount.

Suddenly, when questioned on competition, Duncan attacked the government for buying in Italy. "We've got a nest of pirates there operating in a sanctuary which this lack of a patent law actually provides. . . . Just to show you how brazen they have become, I have a copy here of the *Chemical & Engineering News*. . . ."

As he flourished the magazine, he glanced at Barbara Yuncker on the press benches. She smiled at him and started to write in her notebook. Dramatically, Duncan read out the advertisement of Dr. Mancuso.

"This is an open invitation to our employees to attempt to steal our cultures on which we have expended sometimes three and four million dollars. . . . What is even worse . . . what the Italians are really doing is dumping in this country . . . in general the quoted price in Italy is almost exactly the same price as ours . . . So now we find our own Medical Procurement Agency . . . are not only condoning this practice, they are encouraging and helping to finance it. . . ."

That evening Duncan got the headlines in the evening papers. Barbara Yuncker's story was printed in the *Post*.

A few days later, following Admiral Knickerbocker's evidence before the subcommittee, Donald I. Rogers, financial editor of the New York *Herald Tribune*, moved to Duncan's support. "Senator Kefauver, the self-appointed guardian of the public interest, nearly fell off his dais," he wrote, "extending to the MMSA the heartfelt thanks of a grateful nation. . . . The point is that in the realm of higher authority a subcommittee of the U.S. Senate has the nerve to invite applause from the American people as the armed services of the nation import at discount rates goods that were plundered from their own domestic industry and with the U.S. Government acting as a fence in the thievery."

On the information that either Duncan or Rogers possessed at that time, this was going a bit far. Certainly there was nothing to suggest at any time that Farmochimica Cutolo-Calosi was involved in any way with espionage. But the accusation was, in fact, well founded so far as some other Italian firms were concerned—even though their identities were still unknown.

Duncan's dramatic gesture had introduced into the political arena a new element, and as the pace of the conflict increased, the reflected role of espionage was to grow very large indeed.

Meanwhile, Kefauver appeared to have sensed the danger. The next day, when Dr. Philip Bowman of Bristol Laboratories testified about the Italians' "copy-cat approach," the Senator cut in: "Dr. Bowman, I made a mistake yesterday in not inter-rupting a witness who was referring to the same subject that you are. I am going to warn you now that this committee is not going to be used as a forum to disparage the people or the scientists of a friendly allied nation."

By that time the testimony of the Cyanamid executives was over. Kefauver had congratulated them on their advertising—false claims in promotion being a common criticism of drug firms—but attacked them on their high prices.

The investigation had now been in progress for nine months. The worldwide effects, which spread from the steady stream of publicity of the hearings, were greater than that of the bill that President Kennedy eventually signed. Government and state attitudes hardened. In overseas countries, where politi-cal thinking was often well to the left of American attitudes, the results were tangible. Pressure for legislation designed to weaken the effect of patents grew stronger. Some foreign gov-ernments—which did not already have laws forcing holders of patents to license any applicants—considered introducing them. In Britain, one of the world's biggest markets for drugs outside the United States, the Conservatives took similar action to the Defense Department's. Exploiting a law designed for wartime emergencies, the Ministry of Health began to buy from Italy for UK hospitals.

This was truly dangerous because the British National Health Service paid for more than 95 percent of all ethical drugs consumed by the public. If the ministry developed its theory—limited then to hospital purchases—and bought from Italy all tetracyclines sold in drugstores, the damage would be colossal.

Returning to New York from Washington, Duncan consid-ered Cyanamid's position after its testimony. Generally, he fig-ured, the company had emerged from the ordeal pretty well. Later he wished that its appearance before the subcommittee had been deferred. For he was suddenly to receive a stream of alarming information that—even if some research by drug firms was ineffective—proved without question that the work in Cyanamid's laboratories was regarded in certain quarters as having great value.

6

THE big speculation by the drugmakers in research—even if some of it was, as the Kefauver critics insisted, directed at such nonscientific areas as marketing—produced a range of very diverse repercussions. Of these, the most dramatic, the most inevitable and, potentially, the most damaging was industrial espionage.

In fact, several U.S. drug firms were victims of espionage, although, by the beginning of 1961, few of them had yet realized it. Even the suspicions within Cyanamid of Dr. Fox had grown cool since no one knew exactly what had happened, if, indeed, anything had happened.

That January, 1961, however, the situation changed drastically. The possibility that the company was being savaged by espionage moved from the category of surmise to unquestionable fact. Strangely, the source of new and vital information was a man who barely knew Sidney Fox.

Austin Phillips, a quiet, bespectacled lawyer in his late forties, was a senior patent attorney in Cyanamid's headquarters in New York. One cold morning early in January, he was called by Caesar Bottone, an Italian-born physician who had decided that business was more lucrative than medicine.

"Mr. Phillips," said Bottone, "I seem to be in trouble with your company. Maybe I could come and talk to you about it."

Phillips knew his caller quite well. He had first met him in this same office on the fifteenth floor of the Rockefeller Plaza building three years before in 1958.

The attorney had been glancing through the published list of successful bids for the big orders put out for bids by Admiral Knickerbocker's Military and Medical Supply Agency. Among them was a contract for the supply of sulfadiazine, one of Lederle's old sulfa drugs that was still used sometimes in preference to antibiotics because it was particularly effective in the treatment of meningitis and pneumonia. The winning bid had been made by a Dallas firm called International Pharmaceuticals, which Phillips had never heard of.

No one else he checked with had ever heard of it either. It was not even listed in the trade directories. Eventually, he discovered the address through the MMSA and wrote to the company—which was directed by Caesar Bottone—drawing attention to Cyanamid's patent in sulfadiazine.

A few days later, following a phone call, Bottone and his attorney called to see him. Apologies during the meeting were profuse. "Caesar didn't realize what he was doing," explained the lawyer. "Until recently he was just a student at a hospital in Dallas. He didn't have the kind of money to pay for patent attorneys. Then he got this idea for a little business."

In retrospect, bidding for a government contract did strike Phillips as a little adventurous for a young student starting a little business. However, at the time, the thirty-year-old Caesar—good-looking, fresh-faced, smiling—seemed such a pleasant young man that it was not hard to accept that this was, in fact, what had happened. Also, since the two men emphasized that Bottone would be happy to pay a royalty, the meeting ended on a very friendly basis. Cyanamid would license International Pharmaceuticals to sell the drugs to the MMSA under this contract.

Phillips' views about the affable Bottone changed when no royalties were paid under the agreement. A phone call to his lawyer revealed that he had left the country.

It was not long, however, before he was back in Phillips' life. Essentially, though, Bottone's lawyer had told the truth. His client had had a little idea for a business that—with the emerging political background of antagonism to the big pharmaceutical firms—was very sound.

But the offense that Phillips had to investigate in the fall of 1960 was more serious.[12] The lawyer discovered that a drugstore in New Jersey had been offered imported sulfadiazine at cut prices in Lederle drums on which the company's identification had been concealed by labels bearing the name of a dealer. This not only was an infringement of the Cyanamid patents, but was also a violation of the food and drug laws.

On checking the supplier of the drug, Phillips found that it was a firm registered in Canada—Kasal Trading Company. From Montreal, investigators reported that Kasal was owned by Bottone and Elio Salvetti, a handsome Roman who was his partner at the time.

Bottone operated from an office in Fort Lee, New Jersey, just across the Hudson from Manhattan. So Phillips instructed the Cyanamid lawyers to file suit against the two men—an action that precipitated Bottone's phone call that January morning in 1961. As the attorney fixed a date for a meeting, he guessed that he would be treated to the same performance as before—a display of charming apology.

Phillips got what he expected. Bottone's explanation was

complex, but he admitted he had done wrong. As usual, however, he would like to make amends. What did Mr. Phillips suggest?

The attorney dealt with the situation in the normal way. Bottone agreed to sign a consent decree, admitting the infringement.

The doctor then did something that was extremely strange.[13] Even today—after his alleged role in the industrial espionage conspiracy has been explored in court—his motivation has never been adequately explained. He leaned back in his chair expansively and remarked that he had some information that Phillips should know. Was he aware that Lederle organisms and processes were being sold in Italy?

Phillips knew nothing of the suspicions of Sidney Fox or of Bill Fulton's investigations, but he was fully alert to the dangers presented by the patent situation in Italy. He encouraged Bottone to continue. The story Bottone told—according to Phillips' testimony—was alarming for a corporation already engaged in a battle with a government. For if it was correct, it meant that a very successful raid had already been made on the product of Lederle's multimillion-dollar research investment—and was still continuing.

Bottone named three men who, he said, were the nucleus of a ring selling Lederle organisms and secrets: Sidney Fox, Irving Rosenblatt and John Casei.[14] They had—so he said—offered bugs and know-how to Italian firms to make Declomycin. Bottone named big companies in Italy. Among them were three in particular: Le Petit in Milan, Pierrel in Capua and Leo in Rome.

There was, Bottone continued, a pilot plant in Suffern, N.Y., operating under the name of Kim Laboratories. Fox was in Rome at present working for Leo under the alias of Dr. Joseph Martin. He had also been in touch with a new outfit in Milan that had only been in business for a short while—a company called Ankermann.

Austin Phillips could write shorthand—a fact that was very useful when he was challenged later in court on the accuracy of his notes—and he carefully recorded all that Bottone told him. It was a revelation that could be of the utmost importance to Cyanamid. Not least was the significance that it might put on Admiral Knickerbocker's bulk purchases in Italy. For it was obviously possible that some of the firms supplying tetracycline under his contracts were making the drugs with organisms stolen from Pearl River.

If Bottone was telling the truth, Lederle was clearly facing a serious commercial threat that could damage it badly—especially in overseas markets where patent litigation would have to be mounted in many different countries, some of which had very loose or ineffective patent laws. But the situation did carry a significant plus. It could help put teeth into Lyman Duncan's charge during his Kefauver testimony that the government was promoting industrial espionage—an accusation that, though widely reported, was backed by little in the way of hard evidence.

As soon as Bottone left him, Phillips called Lyman Duncan at Pearl River and told him the story.

Phillips, as a lawyer, was trained to treat hearsay evidence with great caution. But he was positive that Bottone, for all his suspect business methods, had told him the truth. The only aspect that bothered him was why he had made the revelation. "Maybe he was just grateful we didn't force him to pay damages in the sulfa suit," he said.

For Duncan, fully briefed as he was on the background to the Sidney Fox affair, it was illuminating. He put down the phone and strode along the passage to the room of Bob Parker who—since Duncan had been promoted to Cyanamid vice-president in charge of medical affairs—had now taken over as general manager.

Parker was on the phone as Duncan entered the room, but

as soon as he saw his chief, he finished his conversation quickly. "Lyman," he said, "there isn't any doubt any longer."

Parker had information that had nothing to do with the Bottone tip-off. "That was Gerald Furman of George Uhe on the phone," he said. "They're New York brokers."

Furman had called on behalf of one of his clients—a Roman drug company named Leo which had asked him to make inquiries about a firm in Suffern, Kim Laboratories, and two men associated with it: Joseph Martin and Sidney Fox. "I know Furman slightly," explained Parker. "He called me because he'd heard that Fox once worked here."

For the first time since Ted Scholz had first voiced his suspicions to the security men back in 1958, Fulton had some leads that could possibly tie Dr. Fox into an espionage network. He went to work immediately, contacted a status inquiry agency in New York, and asked for confidential reports on the Italian companies Bottone had mentioned to Phillips.

Then he drove over to New City, the capital of Rockland County in which Spring Valley was situated, to check the company registrations for Kim Laboratories—the pilot plant that Bottone had described as being linked to Sidney Fox.

When he got back, Fulton reported to his boss on his progress. He had discovered that Kim had been registered in March, 1958, under a PO box address in the name of Joyce Boxer.

This, as he explained, linked it very closely to Fox. "His wife's called Joyce. Her maiden name was Boxer. Obviously, Sid didn't want to register the company in his own name in case we did some checking."

In any event, it did not take long to prove that Fox ran Kim Laboratories. The inquiry from Rome that had come through to Bob Parker, the Lederle general manager, had referred to it as a Suffern company. Suffern was only six miles from the plant at Pearl River, and Fulton found the Kim premises without much trouble—a small drab shop overlooking the railroad tracks near the station. Kim's business, so Fulton learned after a few phone calls, was in chemicals, although the little firm had a strange and unrelated sideline that, in view of the news from Italy, was significant: It sold photocopy machines and even offered a microfilm service. All the same, it was not a bad cover.

A few days later, the status reports that Fulton had called for on the Italian companies arrived in the old farmhouse. They did not supply him with a great deal more information, but they gave him two more names that, if Caesar Bottone had been telling Austin Phillips the truth, could be important—Helmuth Wawretchek,[19] president of Ankermann Italiana, and Count Niccolo Visconti di Madrone, who was head of the Pierrel Company.

By then the name Pierrel had thrown the Lederle executives into a state of shock. For the most alarming news that they had yet received had just arrived in the plant. It came in the form of an advertisement in *Il Tempo Medico,* a promotional magazine distributed by the company that Count Visconti directed: Pierrel was to launch a new tetracycline under the trade name Demetetra. But the reason for the traumatic effect of the advertisement was that Demetetra was chemically identical to Cyanamid's new top-selling product, Declomycin.[18]

Lederle had launched Declomycin in the fall of 1959—only a few weeks before the Kefauver hearings had opened—in the same way that they had introduced tetracycline to the U.S. medical profession. Like its battle-scarred sister product, Declo had been the subject of papers read before the annual Antibiotics Symposium at the Mayflower Hotel in Washington—only a bus ride from Capitol Hill, where so much attention was now concentrated on the drug industry.

Since 1954, when microbiologist Ursula Hirsch had first peered through her microscope at the new bug with its fluorescent ring, Lederle had spent $2,500,000 on development.

Duncan had been happy with his company's investment.

From the start, the drug had done well. Within only a few months, sales in the United States had topped the $10,000,000 mark. Now it was to face stiff competition—in overseas markets and, possibly through Admiral Knickerbocker, at home.

Duncan was working at his desk when Jack Stewart reported to him on Pierrel's new drug. Suddenly, all the attacks that had been made during the Kefauver investigation welled up in him in a violent sense of injustice. The marketing of tetra or triam by an Italian competitor, would have been bad enough, but Declo was his new bright patented star. Summoning Frank Allen and Bill Fulton to join them in his office—a scene that Fulton still recalls vividly—he demanded action.

"Lyman," said Stewart, "I'd certainly like to see some action. We'd all like some action. But we've got to face it: At the moment, we haven't got a ghost of a case. All we've got is one hell of a lot of rumor and hearsay."

Was that not enough, demanded Duncan, to hand over to the FBI?

Stewart was doubtful. They still had no hard evidence. And even if they had, what was the crime?

To prove that Fox had stolen know-how seemed almost impossible. The line between a chemist's experience—which he was entitled to sell—and confidential information belonging to Cyanamid was very narrow. Clearly, their only hope of mounting a prosecution against him was to prove he had stolen Lederle's bugs. "At least, they're tangible property," said Stewart, "even if you can't see them without a microscope."

Duncan was not truly interested in the detail—just results. He strode up and down the room angrily.

"The way things were going in Washington at that time," he has explained since, "these people were looking like Robin Hoods. As a big drug firm, we were one of the robber barons. The only difference was that these Robin Hoods were putting the money in their own pockets. There we were, spending fourteen million a year on research, and it was being stolen under our noses for sale in Italy. Worse—for all we knew, it was still going on."

The possibility that the ring was still operating at Pearl River was the most worrisome aspect of all. Bottone, in his tip-off to Phillips, had mentioned a source that was still active in the research block. When Ted Scholz had been watching Fox in the fall of 1958, he had noticed his contacts with a chemist named Siegfried Muller.[16] Fulton had, in fact, run a detailed investigation on him, but it had revealed nothing to suggest that he was implicated in any way. Now, however, in view of Bottone's tip, Muller came under suspicion once more—and he was not to be cleared until much later. In the hope of finding more leads, Bill ordered a detective agency to keep him under surveillance.

Two days later his suspicions increased sharply. Siegfried Muller resigned. Detectives reported that he had negotiated with an Englewood, New Jersey, auto dealer to buy a Volkswagen for delivery in Munich.

The news precipitated a violent reaction of activity. Jack Stewart took over day-to-day control of the investigation and gave orders that he was to be informed of every detail. Ted Scholz went to work in the research block to find out what he could among Muller's colleagues.

But he was not very successful. There was nothing in Muller's contacts to support the suspicions of the security staff.

When the chemist finally left International Airport on February 19, he left behind him a sense of frustrated anticlimax. By that time investigators had reported that his destination was not Munich, but Milan—a city that, with its patent-free environment, was a far more alarming destination. But when Fulton analyzed the results of the concentrated investigations, he was forced to conclude that they had produced nothing of practical value. Muller's most suspicious action was to put a note in the suggestion box urging that Cyanamid's executives might gain advantage from a course of mescaline—a hallucinogenic drug that increases the perceptions.

On the same day that Muller announced he was leaving Lederle, John Cancelarich, a process engineer in the production plant, also tendered his resignation. In the atmosphere of alarmed suspicion that colored Pearl River at that time, this placed him under immediate suspicion. But this eased when he told the personnel department he was joining a small New York company that was not even in the drug industry. However, John Cancelarich, in due course, was to prove very important indeed to Cyanamid.

At that time in February, 1961, Lyman Duncan held a position of power in Cyanamid that was exceptional for a vice-president. This was due to his special relationship with Weed Malcolm. Apart from the fact that Malcolm had run Pearl River before Duncan, the Cyanamid president had a PhD in bacteriology, and drugs held a deep fascination for him.

As a result, he was always pleased to see Duncan when he dropped into his office in Rockefeller Plaza. He understood his problems. He knew his executives. He liked to keep in touch with the research programs that had been born under his control.

It was because of this close link with his president that Duncan rarely had any trouble with the committees in which the true power in large industrial combines is normally concentrated.

"Weed," said Lyman, after reporting on the January developments, "I propose to go after these people as hard as I can. I hope you'll back me."

Malcolm called in George Martin, Cyanamid's general counsel, to talk over the long-term issues. That conversation among the three men—almost casual in character—was, in effect, the decision that led to the expenditure of nearly a million dollars to get the evidence that was to jail the conspirators. At the time Duncan did not realize what was involved. As he saw the situation, it was merely a question of supplying the FBI with evidence that seemed to be streaming into Pearl River from several different sources. In practice, however, it was not quite as simple as that.

Muller's resignation—even though this was proved later to have no significance—strengthened the Lederle case for police action. Frank Allen called Joe Lucca, the resident FBI agent at Suffern, and asked him to come to Pearl River for a meeting with Jack Stewart. There is a freemasonry among men who have been in the bureau. Joe Lucca wanted to help if he could, even though the evidence was still very weak. He agreed to ask permission from the U.S. Attorney's office to open an investigation. For the only time in Lucca's career, the U.S. Attorney asked him to make a report in writing before agreeing. Three weeks later he was ordered officially to open a file.

The investigation, boosted as it was by the sudden rush of information at the beginning of the year, soon lost its momentum—despite the fact that the FBI man in Rome was working to find the answers to Lucca's questions.

As it happened, Bill Fulton—carefully co-opting the help of Cyanamid's companies in Germany and Italy under conditions of close secrecy—made more progress than the FBI. Many of the gaps in the sketchy picture he had been able to draw of the threat facing Cyanamid—and other U.S. drug companies —were filled by a Lederle chemist who spent a few days in Milan during a European vacation.

Once a week Joe Lucca would drive over to Pearl River to lunch and discuss the case with Bill Fulton and Frank Allen. However, on that morning in August when Bill had talked to his research contact, who was just back from Europe, they were able for the first time to piece together the situation that they faced in Italy.

"By then," Fulton has recalled, "we pretty well knew the

whole setup. There were still one or two things we hadn't got around to—some of Fox's customers, for example, and a bit of quarreling among the group—but we were aware of the basic situation. By this time Fox had been shouldered out. He was no longer in the conspiracy. All the same, he had had a good run.

"There was no doubt that he had been in touch with the Leo firm in Rome—the inquiry by their brokers proved that. We assumed he had made a deal with Pierrel [17] since they were selling a product that was chemically the same as Declo. Bottone had implied that Le Petit was involved[18]—and it was the second biggest group in Italy. But the company that we were watching the closest of all was Ankermann in Milan." [19]

Ankermann Italiana was the sister company of a German firm with the same name that was based in Friesoythe in Lower Saxony. Helmuth Wawretchek, its founder and managing director, was a short, round man, with thinning brown hair, a buoyant sense of humor and a deep fascination for Don Quixote. His home in West Berlin was filled with statues and pictures of Cervantes' sad hero.

In 1952, West Germany established patent laws which—though not so protective as the U.S. legislation—began to restrict Wawretchek's plans. For he wanted to manufacture two drugs with which he knew he could make an enormous amount of money—tetracycline and vitamin B_{12}.

Vitamin B_{12} was one of the postwar wonder drugs, patented by Merck, that was vital to people suffering from pernicious anemia, which once killed 6,0000 Americans every year. It was also a basic ingredient of most multivitamin tablets and, since it was the growth factor in animal protein, had a big sale as a method of quick-fattening poultry and cattle. But one of its most dramatic features was that it was effective in microscopic doses; this was why, in its basic form, it was extremely expensive. In 1958, with a going rate of $180 a gram, it was far more valuable than gold.

It was because the patent holders could stop him from making these two drugs in Germany that Helmuth Wawretchek —as he has admitted freely—decided to plunge into what was to prove an ill-fated business in Italy, where he would be free from suit. By the fall of 1958, when Fox was under suspicion at Pearl River, the German's plans were far advanced. The contractors were working on the site he had bought in the Milan suburb of Cinisello. The giant fermentors had already been transported across the Alps from his plant in Friesoythe.

By 1961 Ankermann's new plant was in production, but what concerned the security staff at Pearl River was the fact that it had acquired some new stockholders, who were by then well known to them—Nathan Sharff and Seymour Salb, the two partners in Biorganic Laboratories at East Paterson with whom Sidney Fox had been in such regular contact.

Another shareholder was Caesar Bottone, a fact that made his revelations to Austin Phillips seem even more curious than they had appeared before and certainly moved him several points up the list of suspects. Also, Fulton had now learned that Siegfried Muller had joined the company.

By the day that the FBI agent, Joe Lucca, came over to Pearl River for lunch, Fulton knew that Ankermann was already making tetracycline and was trying hard to get into production with Declomycin. "They still had technical problems," he recalls. "But with Siggy Muller in their labs, we were pretty sure they'd soon get over them. By then, too, we knew they'd got another of our men. Their production manager was a young process engineer who had been making both tetra and Declo here at Pearl River. He had resigned on the same day as Muller. His name was John Cancelarich."

Most galling of all the information that had been collated and analyzed in the old farmhouse was the news that Ankermann was preparing to bid for Admiral Knickerbocker's lush Defense Department contracts. This time there was not much doubt in the minds of the security men: The drug that Knickerbocker would be buying, if Ankermann bid successfully, would be made from Lederle organisms.[20]

Lucca sympathized with the two security men, but the fact remained that despite all their efforts, they had no proof. Furthermore, as they well knew, the FBI did not like keeping files open unless progress seemed likely. If they did not come up with some evidence very fast, Lucca hinted, he would be ordered to stop work on the case. The situation, from an investigator's point of view, seemed hopeless.

Meanwhile, the pace was quickening in the conflict between the government and the tetracycline producers. Back in April, 1960, only a few weeks before the Cyanamid executives testified before the Kefauver Subcommittee, a grand jury had been convened in the traditional horseshoe benches on the fourteenth floor of the Federal Courthouse in Foley Square, New York. Harry Sklarsky, an Assistant U.S. Attorney from the Justice Department's Antitrust Division, asked the jurors to indict Cyanamid, Pfizer, Bristol and their presidents. There were a range of charges under the Sherman Act, but they centered on the allegation that the companies had conspired to corner the market in tetracycline, that they had helped Pfizer obtain a patent that was, in fact, invalid and then fixed the prices, not only of tetracycline itself, but also of its sister products, Aureomycin and Terramycin, at "substantially identical" and "unreasonably high" levels.

These charges by the Justice Department covered much of the same ground as those that had been leveled by the Federal Trade Commission two years earlier, but there were vital technical differences. For one thing, while the FTC proceedings were civil, this indictment—if the jurors voted it—would accuse the companies and their chief executives of criminal actions. The possible penalties included jail. Second, while the FTC was concerned with a continuing situation, Harry Sklarsky's charges were based solely on events that had so far taken place.

By the end of August, 1961—when Lyman Duncan was facing the bitter advice of his security staff that there was nothing he could do about the espionage raids on the Lederle plant—the grand jury was still considering Sklarsky's evidence.

The tenure of a grand jury is limited to eighteen months. Only four weeks remained for the jurors to decide whether or not to vote the indictment. If they took no action, all the evidence would have to be resubmitted to a new jury. So there was an incentive for Sklarsky to press them to reach a decision.

In the Wall Street offices of Cyanamid's attorneys, Walter Mansfield had guessed the policy behind the Justice Department's strategy. In the last big antitrust case—involving General Electric, Westinghouse and other makers of heavy electrical equipment—only relatively junior executives had gone to jail. The senior men had stayed free. In this action, vice-presidents had been subpoenaed to appear before the grand jury, but—since testimony in antitrust matters gives automatic immunity against prosecution—it was significant that the three presidents had not been called. This fact, added to other signs from Washington, suggested that Attorney General Robert Kennedy had issued orders: This time get the top brass.

On a hot afternoon in August, Harry Sklarsky telephoned Walter Mansfield's offices. It was a courtesy contact. "I thought you ought to know," he said. "The grand jury has just voted an indictment."

7

AT 10:30 A.M. on September 6, 1961, Weed
Malcolm, accompanied by three attorneys, walked up the steps
of the Federal Courthouse in Foley Square to answer the
charges against him and the corporation over which he presided. For all three men—for McKeen and Schwartz, similarly
attended by their legal retinues, stood before the judge with
the Cyanamid president—it was a traumatic experience that
was shared by their executives. In particular, Lyman Duncan
felt deeply for his president, who had also been his patron and
his friend.

For this reason, Duncan was possibly more angered even
than he might otherwise have been when, a few days after the
indictment, Jack Stewart walked into his office and told him
that—as Joe Lucca had warned the Lederle security men—the
FBI file on the Fox case was about to be closed.

For the first time, in a sudden moment of clarity, Duncan realized that the whole character of their strategy would have to change. At that stage, this was more a question of attitude than of action. He did not know precisely how he would alter the campaign. He just knew that the dynamic would have to move from the old farmhouse into his big office on the fourth floor of the administration block, that he would have to exercise his power as a vice-president of a giant American corporation. That afternoon he held a meeting with Jack Stewart and the two security officers to consider what action was open to them. It was a tense, frustrating occasion, still remembered clearly by three of the four men who were present. The security men produced no new ideas, no fresh leads, no different avenues of approach. They had long done all their thinking. They knew the conspiracy existed, but they could not prove it.

Duncan leaned forward, his elbows on the red morocco covering of his desk, his fingers clasped. "If the FBI, with all their resources, don't figure there's a case," he said, "then what in hell can *we* do? Well, we've got to do something."

He pushed his chair back sharply from his desk, got up, and began to stride about the room.

"I was brought up," he recalls, "on a Middle West farm fifteen miles from the nearest law enforcement officer. We had a big English sheepdog. If it barked at night, my father would climb out the back window with a big full-choke twelve-gauge shotgun and stalk anyone who might be prowling around. We knew we couldn't always rely on the law. If you needed protection, you often had to fix it for yourself.

"That afternoon at Pearl River, I found myself thinking that maybe we were in the same position as we had been at home. Maybe our problems weren't important enough for the law enforcement agencies—but they were certainly important to us."

Both for the industry and for Cyanamid, that summer of 1961 was a period that was marked by deep emotional conflictions. The drugmakers had been staked out and probed—in what they regarded as extremely unfair and prejudiced hearings—in the full public gaze of the nation. Their claims for their research investment had been mocked, and their discoveries had been denigrated. And in Congress, Kefauver was now actively promoting his drug bill that was aimed, among other targets, at the U.S. patent laws. As a result, they were ultrasensitive, wounded, wearing giant chips on their shoulders.

In addition, the tetracycline producers—who had borne a big part of the Kefauver assault—were facing the combined attack of two government agencies and, as they saw it, an unfair mauling by a third: the Defense Department.

To Duncan, who had not been at Pearl River in the days of the fight for the tetracycline patent, the attitude of the government was blatantly unjust and the result of emotional bias.

Meanwhile, the executives of Italian companies were basking in official approbation, acclaimed by government officials as public-spirited men who were helping bring down the prices of vital drugs—men who, as Duncan saw it, were exploiting American brains.

Worst of all, some of them were financing the theft of organisms that his Lederle microbiologists had bred over years. They were buying secret information that his research teams had aquired at great cost.

To Duncan, as he paced the thick green carpet of his big office, the situation in which his company was placed not only was unjust, but was the wrong way around. In effect, his company was being accused of plundering, whereas, in truth, they were being plundered. They stood accused as the villains, while, as he saw it, they were victims.

One event had taken place during the past few days to support his view of Cyanamid's situation at that time. An official document had arrived by first-class mail at the company's attorneys' offices on Wall Street. The examiner, appointed by the Federal Trade Commission to hear the evidence in the charges against the tetracycline companies, had at last announced his decision. After considering 11,000 pages of testimony and hearings since 1959, he declared that there was no case for the companies to answer. They were exonerated.

It was an ironic reflection of the U.S. legal system that despite this result—which was, of course, subject to appeal—a grand jury only days before had taken what was, in effect, an opposite view. Even though the two cases were technically different, they both stemmed from the same alleged conspiracy to fix prices starting from the fight for the tetracycline patent and the cross-licensing deals that followed it. Much of the basic evidence was common to both actions.

It was, therefore, particularly tormenting for Lyman Duncan to witness the big impact made by the indictment, which accused Cyanamid, by comparison with the small amount of attention given to the ruling of the FTC examiner, which in effect cleared the company of very similar charges. Under these circumstances, Duncan's frustration at the lack of progress in the espionage investigation—which, even though it was not concerned with the same issues, would at least provide some firepower to direct at his hostile, persecuting government—was greatly aggravated.

He was quite clear in his mind about what he wanted even if the precise method of obtaining the objective was in doubt. He wanted the Italian drug firms—or those, at least, who had traded with the espionage ring—exposed as thieves. He wanted to stop his government from buying dumped drugs from tainted overseas sources. He wanted to prove that research—at any rate the research conducted at Pearl River—had a big value with a substantial price tag in the market. He wanted Cyanamid's companies throughout the world to be able to exploit these facts in the patent litigation—which was always in progress—and in their negotiations with overseas governments. Most important of all, perhaps—raw and smarting as his emotions were at that time—he was motivated by a deep need for justice.

For the achievement of these purposes, one event was necessary: the condemnation of the espionage conspirators after a full public trial in the criminal courts mounted by the U.S. Department of Justice.

At that moment in August, with the FBI closing its investigation because it could find no evidence, Duncan's chances of success in his aim were remote in the extreme. He could not figure out how to begin to go about it.

"Suddenly," Bill Fulton recalls, "he stopped walking about the room. 'I've got an idea,' he said. 'There's just one man who might be able to break this conspiracy, if he'd agree to take it on—Walter Mansfield.' "

Walter Mansfield was the trial attorney who had been conducting the Cyanamid case before the Federal Trade Commission. But this was not, as it might appear, an overdramatization of a simple decision by a corporation vice-president that, since they were in trouble, maybe they should consult their lawyers.

The average attorney working for a big law firm would not have been a great deal of help. He would just have advised Duncan to drop the whole thing. In fact, it was not Mansfield's role as a legal man at all that was dictating Duncan's new thinking as much as his background.

At fifty, Mansfield was a man of presence, with thick white hair, a tanned rectangular face and bushy brows over blue eyes that held a suspicion of a smile even when he was not smiling. Relaxed and courteous, he looked what he was: a successful lawyer with an Ivy League education. In fact, his father, also an affluent attorney, had been a mayor of Boston.

Mansfield, however, was a lot tougher than he seemed. In World War II, he had served in the OSS, working as a guerrilla fighter in the mountains of Yugoslavia. Later he had operated in China, organizing the mercenary warlords to attack Japanese supply lines. As a trial attorney, he had handled many clashes between big clients and powerful opponents.

If some people are born losers, Mansfield was a born winner. He was marked by a determination that had in it a quality of ruthlessness. More important, perhaps, he was aggressively tenacious. And just at that particular time, tenacity was just what Duncan needed.

Despite his possession of this quality, however, the attorney did not display it immediately when, after driving to Pearl River the next day in answer to Duncan's summons, he listened to Bill Fulton's outline of their evidence. In fact, he reacted at first in the same way as any other lawyer would have done. "Lyman," he said, "you haven't got a prayer. There's not even a glimmer of a case."

Duncan brought his fist down hard on the desk top. "I *know* we haven't got a case, Walter. That's just why we've asked you to come out here. Now let's start thinking how we can develop a case."

Quietly, the attorney outlined the legal position, emphasizing the weakness of their case and their complete lack of evidence. Their only hope—and it was a remote one at that—was to find the weakest link in the conspiracy and break it. That might possibly give them enough leverage to put pressure on other links. If they could break them, too, then at least they would have some witnesses.

The obvious place to start, he suggested, was Italy. Fox had obviously been in touch with several companies there. There could well be others that were unhappy about their negotiations with him. They might be willing to talk or even testify. "How about your overseas sales side?" he asked. "Haven't they got some contacts there?"

Two days later Bob Bogan, executive director of Cyanamid International—the company that controlled the corporation's foreign operations—came out to Pearl River for a meeting with Duncan, Mansfield and the security staff.

Bogan had already planned to go to Italy in early October. When Duncan explained his problem, he agreed to do what he could.

Bill Fulton laid out on the table three photographs: of Sidney Fox and of the two experts from Pearl River who were now working for Ankermann in Milan—John Cancelarich, the engineer, and Siegfried Muller,[16] the chemist.

"These are the men we think are involved," said Mansfield. "We want any evidence you can get that they sold our production bugs—or our process information."

When Mansfield returned to his office, he told Gail Mitchell, his twenty-one-year-old secretary, to open a new file. "Call it Cyanamid-Tallyho," he said.

She grinned at the symbolism centered on the name of Fox, then walked along the corridor to her room and marked the first of many files that, in time, would bear the title.

The noise of traffic outside in the Sulla Tibertinn rose in waves—an ever-changing background of auto sounds, overlaid with the clatter of scooters, that was curiously Continental in character. It was two weeks later, and Bob Bogan was talking with Dr. Giovanni Auletta in his big office in the Leo plant in the suburbs of Rome.

Auletta was a handsome man with black hair, precisely tailored clothes and a figure that was beginning to thicken. Though still only in his twenties, he was a millionaire, owned a yacht and a richly furnished penthouse apartment that overlooked the Tiber in the exclusive Lungotovere Flaminia.

His uncle—who had been a prominent figure during the Mussolini regime—had owned *Il Giornale d'Italia,* a leading Roman daily, had a major holding in the Banca Nazionale della Agricoltura, and controlled the drug firm Societa Leo-Industrie Chimice Farmaceutiche, known usually as Leo. When the old man died, Giovanni and his mother, the Countess d'Armenise, had inherited much of his fortune, including Leo.

Leo had been founded in 1949 to make penicillin under license from a Danish drug firm but had since expanded into broad-spectrum antibiotics with Aureomycin, as well as the sale of a number of other drugs. It was not a big firm, but it had a very modern, well-designed plant.

Bogan knew Auletta quite well. He had often met his uncle when he was alive and had first come in contact with "Nino," as he knew the young executive, when he was a teen-ager. Leo was a customer of Cyanamid's Italian company, from which it bought drugs in bulk powder for tableting and sale under its own brand name.

For this reason, when Bogan called Auletta after checking into the Excelsior Hotel on the Via Veneto, the Italian responded warmly and sent his Mercedes to collect him.

The two men chatted cordially for a while, their conversation ranging over general topics. Then Bogan confided that he wanted to discuss a subject of a somewhat delicate nature. Opening his briefcase, he drew out the three pictures he had been given at Pearl River and handed them across the large desk. "Nino," he said, "do you know any of these men?"

The first photograph that Auletta studied was of Siegfried Muller. He shook his head. Then, as he examined the others, a broad smile slowly creased his face.

Without saying anything, he unlocked a drawer of his desk, took out a check, and passed it to Bogan. Drawn on the Chemical Bank New York Trust Company, it was for $50,000 and made payable to the Countess d'Armenise, Auletta's mother. It was signed by Elio Salvetti.

"Have you ever met Mr. Salvetti?" asked Auletta.

Bogan had barely heard of Salvetti, let alone met him. His name was one of several that Bill Fulton had mentioned to him in his briefing at Pearl River—mainly because he had at one time been Caesar Bottone's partner. Also, he was of interest to the Lederle security staff because he held a small block of stock in Ankermann Italiana, the Milan firm that was partly owned by Nathan Sharff and Seymour Salb.

However, had Bogan ever come in personal contact with him, Salvetti would almost certainly have made a lasting impression. A strikingly good-looking Roman with curly ginger hair, he had a remarkable personality that made a big impact on most of the people who met him.

Certainly, Salvetti got along very well with quite a number of tough and hardheaded businessmen, possibly because he was immensely enjoyable as a companion. An accomplished pianist, a skillful conjurer, a brilliant raconteur, he displayed a certain brash style—drove a Ferrari, loved parties and high living. He was married to a beautiful German girl and lived in an elegant villa near Milan with classical statuary in the garden and a panoramic view of Lago Maggiore.

It was in October, 1960—only six weeks after Lyman Duncan, in the Kefauver hearings, had publicly accused the Defense Department of encouraging industrial espionage—that Elio Salvetti had called on Dr. Giovanni Auletta at the Leo plant.[21] The purpose of his visit was to offer Auletta a deal.

Salvetti—so Auletta told Bogan—explained that he was the owner of high-yielding organisms to make tetracycline, Aureomycin, and Declomycin, as well as vitamin B_{12}. He was prepared to sell these to Leo—and to provide the technical assistance needed to use them in production—for $150,000.

Realizing that the Leo president was clearly wondering about the source of these bugs, Salvetti volunteered the information that he had acquired them from an American research group.

The offer had big attractions for the young Auletta. At the time he had many problems, most of them caused by the resignation after a bitter quarrel of the executive who had run Leo while his uncle was alive. As a result, the company was under pressure from internal and external strains. There was little doubt that Auletta needed help. Also, he wanted badly to join the other Italian firms that were supplying drugs to Admiral Knickerbocker in Washington—a source of business that would ease many of the company's difficulties.

The following Sunday, Auletta met Salvetti again and offered him $70,000 for the bugs and process help to make only two of the drugs he had mentioned—Aureomycin and tetracycline. The deal was conditional on successful production.

A month later Salvetti returned to the Leo plant. With him were two men whom he introduced as Dr. Joseph Martin and Mr. John Jane—the technicians, he explained, who would guide Leo through its initial production problems with the new bugs which they had with them in four screw-topped test tubes—slants, as the chemists called them.

Auletta began to probe Martin's experience. The chemist said he had worked for Squibb, a big U.S. drug firm and, until a year before, Lederle Laboratories. Since then he had devoted all his energies to a research organization of which he was part owner—Kim Laboratories of New York, where the organisms they now had with them had been developed.

Martin produced a Kim Laboratories visiting card on which was printed the name Dr. Sidney Martin Fox, which he then admitted rather hesitantly was his own name. For reasons of his own, he explained, he did not want it to be known he was in Italy and would like to be called Joseph Martin.

Meanwhile, Mr. Jane—whom Auletta identified in Bogan's pictures as John Cancelarich, the Lederle process engineer—had said very little. Martin—or rather Fox—had done most of the talking, with interpolations from Elio Salvetti. Jane, Fox said, was one of his assistants in Kim Laboratories. And Auletta's technicians confirmed later that he had seemed knowledgeable of production methods.

It was a pretty suspicious setup, and clearly Auletta was anxious about it. For when his visitors left the office, he put a call through to New York to Gerald Furman of the George Uhe Company, his U.S. representatives, and asked him to investigate Kim Laboratories and the strange chemist who called himself Dr. Martin but was, in fact, Dr. Fox.

All the same, his disquiet did not prevent him from settling a deal with Salvetti and Fox—who agreed to return to Italy the following month to start work with the new bugs—or from handing Salvetti a check for 22,500,000 lire, approximately $35,000

Certainly, from Auletta's point of view, his initial concern was in no way palliated by his first experiences with this new research group controlled apparently by the ingratiating Elio Salvetti. For examination of the tetracycline bugs revealed that they were contaminated, and the Italian had to cable Fox for some more.

Then Auletta heard from Gerald Furman, who had driven out to Suffern to inspect Kim Laboratories. He reported that the research laboratory consisted of a small shop in a poor section of the town with a window on which was pasted a card bearing the name of Sidney Martin Fox. A local policeman had told him that there seemed to be no regular activity at the place except for an occasional visit by one individual.

Toward the end of December, Fox arrived in Rome with his family to take up his role as "consultant." In his luggage was another glass slant containing a tetracycline organism.

Fox was a chemist—not a production man. He was fully able to work with test tubes and flasks, but he knew little about complex machinery or large-scale manufacture. It was not strange, therefore, that Leo was not very successful in its attempt to make tetracycline economically—despite its valuable new bugs.

The situation deteriorated rapidly. The fermentations were dogged by contamination—which is often a problem even in the hands of experts—and Fox's experience was not adequate to help them prevent it. Eventually, Auletta fired him and looked around for other consultants to extricate him from his difficulties.

Salvetti tried to preserve the deal by calling on the Leo president with Mr. John Jane—alias John Cancelarich—the engineer who had been present at the early meeting. But by then Auletta had had enough of the group. He told Salvetti he was no longer interested. Salvetti insisted and, to prove his good faith, wrote out the $50,000 check that Auletta later showed to Bogan—but admitted that right then he did not have the funds to meet this in his bank account. It was a gesture to prove his integrity.

By this time, Auletta told Bogan, he had guessed the true source of the bugs, and when Gerald Furman wrote to him from New York that he had received a visit from the FBI investigating industrial espionage at Lederle, he went to the police, who referred him to the American Embassy. There, he saw the legal attaché—who, like most legal attachés in large U.S. embassies, was an FBI man—and told him the whole story.

"I wish," Auletta said to Bob Bogan, "that I had never seen any of them. They've caused me a great deal of trouble."

Cyanamid, big and powerful and spanning the world, was in a strong position to help Leo. Now that the Italian company was supplying the Defense Department, through Premo Laboratories of Hackensack, New Jersey, with tetracycline—made, according to Auletta, from sources other than Fox's bugs—its situation was not so dire as it had been when Salvetti first arrived with his proposition, but it was still fragile.

The young tycoon had some incentive—in the form of Cyanamid's goodwill—to cooperate, and he agreed to draft a letter setting down in writing the account that he had given Bogan of his dealings with Salvetti and Fox.

When Walter Mansfield heard of Bogan's success, he was delighted. The development was far greater than he had expected at this early stage. Auletta, as a direct customer of Fox, would be an invaluable witness. In addition, he had agreed to hand over supporting evidence—notes in Fox's handwriting and some of the bugs that the chemist had sold to Leo.

It was a big breakthrough. Immediately, Mansfield asked one of his partners to fly to Rome to obtain an affidavit from Auletta.

The elation, however, was premature. By the time the lawyer reached Rome, Auletta had consulted his attorneys, who viewed the negotiations with great suspicion—mainly because he was opening himself up to possible criminal action. He had bought stolen goods. The fact that he had not known they were stolen might be hard to prove.

Eventually Auletta decided not to swear out an affidavit. Later, however, he did hand over the other evidence—the bugs and Fox's notes—which had a limited value.

In New York, Walter Mansfield was planning a campaign like a general commanding an army—most of the activity being aimed at obtaining information that would enable him to apply pressure on the members of the spy ring. He ordered Bill Fulton, who had been placed at his disposal, to find out all he could about the assets owned in America by the suspected conspirators—for these could possibly be seized in civil litigation. He persuaded Bob Bogan to go on up to Germany to get him more information about Ankermann's Helmuth Wawretchek and his other company at Friesoythe. He demanded from Ted Scholz a detailed analysis of the secret areas in the process data that Fox had sold to Leo.

From Mansfield's office on the sixteenth floor of 2 Wall Street, he could see the traffic on the Hudson. It was here that he held his planning conferences with Bill Fulton and his legal assistants that later, when the pace was stepped up, became a daily routine.

At this stage, Mansfield's aim was to get enough solid facts to mount suit. "I want to get Sid Fox on the stand," he told his team, "so that I can ask him some questions. Then, maybe, we can give the FBI something to get their teeth into. But, first, I've got to know a lot more than I know right now."

During the next few weeks, the information came into 2 Wall Street from many different sources. By December Mansfield knew what property was owned in America by his suspects. His file on Helmuth Wawretchek began to grow.

Lyman Duncan maintained close contact with Mansfield during those early weeks, but he did not interfere. He had complete faith in the attorney. He never questioned any proposal. He had, in effect, given him a blank check. They rarely even met, but Mansfield would often telephone him in the evening at his home in Hastings-on-Hudson, New York, to report on progress and to talk over campaign plans.

Walter liked to think aloud, to bounce his ideas. Often Duncan would try to interpose a suggestion, but Mansfield would just continue talking, developing his line of thinking. To Ruth, Duncan's English wife, the conversation seemed to consist of her husband saying repeatedly: "But, Walter . . ." and breaking off until at last he grew irritated and insisted: "Walter, may I please be heard?"

After a while, whenever Mansfield called and she answered the phone, she would summon her husband with the words: " 'But Walter' is on the line again."

One evening, shortly before Christmas, "But Walter" called with a definite proposal. "I think we've got all we're going to get, Lyman," he said. "I figure we should go ahead and sue."

In early January, Mansfield swung his team into a new planning stage—the run-in to filing suits, Cyanamid's first open legal move against the ring that, if it were successful, would almost certainly stimulate criminal action by the Justice Department.

At a morning session in his office, he outlined his attack design. He was in his shirt sleeves. Smoke spiraled upward from a cigarette between two fingers of his right hand.

Sidney Fox—alone, angry, evidently deserted by his former colleagues—was clearly the first target. If he could be persuaded to talk, they stood a good chance of making some real progress.

Mansfield's plan was to sue Nathan Sharff in the federal court and to subpoena Fox as a witness. This would give him his first big opportunity to question Fox in the pretrial depositions—and under the court rules, by calling him as a witness, he would have far greater freedom in his interrogation than he would if the chemist were the subject of the suit.

The attorney considered it vital to serve writs on the two men almost simultaneously; otherwise, the warning might enable one of them to disappear. Also, he wanted to sue on his home ground of New York, but he could only do this if the summons were served on Sharff—who lived and worked in neighboring New Jersey—while he was in the confines of New York State. This meant they would have to know the moment he crossed the state line.

The strategy the attorney laid down was both elaborate and dramatic. Private investigators were to install radio telephones in two cars with linkups to both his office on Wall Street and the old farmhouse at Pearl River. Both Fox and Sharff were to be placed under permanent surveillance during the hours that the court sat.

As soon as Sharff moved across the state line into New York, the investigator tailing him was to warn Mansfield's assistant, Jack Stichter, by radio so that he could immediately initiate the technicalities in the court for writs to be issued.

The plan needed finely detailed preparation—especially since, for legal reasons, Sharff had to be served before Fox. Jack Stichter supervised test runs of the cars. Together with the others in the team, he worked to perfect the campaign orders. Gradually, they found the errors and covered the weak points in the plan.

"What's on the menu today?" remarked Mansfield one morning when they took the draft plans to him for approval. After that, it was known as the Menu.

The Menu laid down precise instructions about radio contact. No one was to be mentioned on the air by name, owing to the remote possibility that Fox and Sharff might pick it up on their own radios. Fox was to be known as Subject A, Sharff as Subject B. Bill Fulton was Touchdown. The Wall Street office was to be referred to as the Lawyer.

At 7:15 A.M. on a late January morning, investigators' cars moved into their specified positions outside the homes of their two subjects in Teaneck and Spring Valley. It was a big and highly expensive operation that was marked by anticlimax. For although the surveillance of the two men continued for three weeks, it did not produce much in the way of progress. Sharff never crossed the border into New York.

Reluctantly, because it meant replanning all the legal technicalities to conform with New Jersey law, Mansfield switched the center of his operations to the federal court in Newark. D-day, in fact, was Tuesday, February 27, 1962.

It was still dark as—according to the investigation reports— the two surveillance cars moved into their usual stations near the homes of Fox and Sharff in Spring Valley and Teaneck.

Subject A—as the detective reported over the radio to John Kelly, his boss, in Newark, New Jersey—was at home. The family was rising. But in Teaneck there were no signs of activity in the house of Subject B. Furthermore, his car was not there.

If Sharff were, in fact, away, it could spoil the whole intricate operation. For in the offices of the Newark attorneys— whom Mansfield was using for guidance on New Jersey procedures—his partner, Granville Whittlesey, would soon be waiting for the news that both men were available for writ serving. He would then file Cyanamid's complaint in the court. Two more investigators would then rush the writs to the colleagues who were watching their target subjects.

At Spring Valley, Fox left home and drove to work to the Kim Laboratories office in Suffern—tailed by Kelly's investigator, who reported the fact by radio to Newark. The other detective in Teaneck was ordered to East Paterson to check if Sharff had gone to work early. The fact that his white Ford Galaxie was parked outside the Biorganic building confirmed that this was what had happened.

Kelly phoned the information to Granville Whittlesey, and the legal formalities went into operation. Within minutes the two detectives, who had been waiting in Newark for the writs, were driving fast to their two destinations—East Paterson and Suffern.

At two thirty that afternoon, Jack Stewart strolled into Duncan's room at Pearl River. "The suits are filed, Lyman," he reported. "Fox's pretrial examination is scheduled for nine days' time. At last, it seems, we're rolling."

The suit in Newark against Nat Sharff demanded $5,000,000 in damages for conspiracy in attempting to obtain confidential information on Cyanamid's research and development, as well as microorganisms. John Cancelarich and Siegfried Muller were named as co-conspirators in addition to Sidney Fox.

The investigation was no longer secret. The Bergen *Record*, a local daily, ran the story on Thursday—two days after the suits were filed. On Friday, Sharff's attorneys issued a statement to the press:

> The story which appeared in The Record on Thursday, March 1, 1962, was obviously inspired by the American Cyanamid Company and its attorneys for the same reason that the suit seems to have been brought about: namely for the publicity value rather than any factual basis. . . . The charges . . . are not stated to be based on any knowl-

edge of facts, but only on "information and belief." . . .
This law suit was started so that it could be tried in the
daily newspapers to the prejudice of Mr. Sharff. . . .

There was some truth in this accusation, but in fact, the publicity had not been inspired. It had been picked up by routine
checks at the court by the *Record* reporters. Cyanamid's public
relations divisions had been ordered, on Mansfield's instructions, to do nothing.

On Wednesday—the day before the *Record* ran the story—
Dr. Bob Parker, as general manager, addressed the supervisors
of all departments at Pearl River. It was a dark, drab day, and
rain was falling heavily. They came, dressed in hats and rain-
coats, to listen to him, in the half-finished building that today
houses the engineering department and the guest relations
block.

"Yesterday," Parker told them, "the company filed suit in the
United States district court in Newark, New Jersey, charging
the theft of millions of dollars' worth of technical know-how
and valuable strains of microorganisms by an international ring
that includes former, and possibly present, employees of Lederle Laboratories."

The general manager gave full details of Cyanamid's charges
and the men who were named in the suit. "We have real concern," he went on, "that there may still be disloyal employees
in the laboratories here at Pearl River. It is of the utmost importance that we find out if this is true and so I am asking for
your loyalty and cooperation in trying to determine the facts.
. . . If any of you have any information that might lead to the
detection or apprehension of others involved, please do come
forward. . . ."

The effect on the plant was shattering. They all had read
about industrial espionage in other companies, but the news
that an operation had been conducted successfully by their own

colleagues—and might still be continuing—made a deep impression on them.

The first reaction of the crowd of supervisors was anger. The crime seemed immense. "We left that meeting saying, 'Why, the sons of bitches,' " recalled one of the research doctors, "but later, when the immediate shock was over, people got kind of sympathetic whenever they were cheesed off with the management. They'd say: 'Maybe those guys had something.' "

The next day, Bill Fulton and Joe Lucca, the FBI agent in charge of the case, began interviewing Pearl River staff in the old farmhouse. Now that there was no need for secrecy, they could attack the problem openly.

Fulton already had a list of people who he knew were friendly with Fox, Cancelarich and Muller. Among the men who were interviewed that day was a third-generation Italian named Joe Gerace, who had been a close friend of John Cancelarich's.

Gerace told his interviewers frankly about his friendship with John Cancelarich, but there was one piece of information that he kept to himself. One evening a few months earlier Gerace had been phoned at home by a man named Leonard Fine.

He knew Fine, who was also a friend of Cancelarich's. In fact, the three of them had vaguely discussed going into business together. On this occasion, however, Fine had called with a request from Cancelarich in Milan. He wanted a sample of the tetracycline mash in current production at Pearl River. Would Gerace do him a favor and get one?

Gerace's job as an assistant in the analytical control lab in the research block often took him into the pilot plant where tetracycline fermentations were often run in the big green vats for experimental purposes. The mash was only too available to him. It was lying around the floor, slopped from the round metal carts in which it was drawn off from the fermentor for testing. The notion that it might have any value was ludicrous. To Gerace, the request from Fine was merely a question of his friend John having problems with his new job. If anyone had suggested to him that he was taking part in an industrial espionage conspiracy, he would have been astonished.

A few days later he called Fine and suggested that he come over to his home and collect the sample.

He did not give the matter another thought until the day Dr. Parker addressed the supervisors and broke the story of the espionage conspiracy. Gerace did not attend the meeting because he was not a supervisor, but he heard about it very soon. A friend rushed into his lab, yelling, "Have you heard about John, for Christ's sake? He's been peddling bugs to the Italians. He's part of an espionage ring."

Gerace recalls today the shock he felt when he heard the news—and the awful feeling of nervous unease that followed it. The sensation was still with him when he was summoned over to the old farmhouse for a talk with Lucca, the FBI agent, and Bill Fulton. He answered the questions he was asked, but he did not volunteer any information about the mash sample—which must have been hard for him, for he was a friendly, talkative man.

That night, when he went back to his home in Haverstraw, New York, Gerace was troubled.

At last, on urging from his wife, he called Bill Fulton on the telephone. In the old farmhouse that night he told the Lederle security man and Joe Lucca of the FBI about the mash sample.

The confession that he swore a few days later gave them the most important advance they had yet achieved. Mansfield had always forecast that the key to their strategy would be pressure, and on the information he had, he suspected that Cancelarich —although he did not have the technical importance of Fox— could be the most vulnerable link in the inner chain of conspirators.

Mansfield's planning for the confrontation of Cancelarich was as detailed and thorough as his campaign to file suit against

Sharff, the first practical result of which was now imminent: the questioning of Sidney Fox. But it did not quite work out as the attorney had expected.

At 10 A.M. on March 26—Sidney Fox faced Walter Mansfield across a table in the Newark Federal Courthouse. This was his pretrial examination as a witness in Cyanamid's suit against Nathan Sharff.

The chemist looked confident. He appeared convinced that Cyanamid could not substantiate its charges. Also, as Mansfield conceded later, he was a man who could stand up exceptionally well to aggressive interrogation.

Fox answered the first four questions briefly—his age, his address, his profession and his educational background. Then he gave an answer that surprised Mansfield. The lawyer asked him: "Will you state what your professional background, since you left school, has been?"

"On the advice of my attorneys," Fox replied, "I decline to answer the question . . . on the ground that it might incriminate me at this time."

He was taking the Fifth Amendment—the constitutional right of a U.S. citizen not to incriminate himself out of his own mouth, but extremely rare in a civil case.

With the record in mind, Mansfield persisted with his questions even though it was obvious what the answers were going to be. Was he connected with Kim Laboratories? Did he know Nathan Sharff? Was he acquainted with John Cancelarich or an Italian drug company named Ankermann Italiana? Each time Fox refused to answer.

Mansfield demanded that a judge should rule. The chemist, he said, was not entitled to the Fifth Amendment on all questions.

The judge ordered Fox to answer sixty-two of them. When Fox still refused, Mansfield asked that he should be declared in contempt of court. On April 4 the judge ordered Fox to prison.

He did not go, however. At least, not then. It took Cyanamid's attorney more than a year of legal skirmishing to get the chemist behind bars.

Meanwhile, the events on Capitol Hill in Washington had acquired a new dynamic.

8

"THESE drug fellows pay for a lobby that makes the steel boys look like popcorn vendors," Paul Rand Dixon, counsel for the majority party on Kefauver's subcommittee, has commented. "In the end, they mounted against Estes the most intense attack that I've seen in a quarter of a century in Washington."

What Dixon described as an attack was, of course, a counterattack, an aggressive defense in a conflict that Kefauver, carrying out his duties as a Senator of the United States, had initiated. If the industry's attempt to protect its flanks was spirited, it was because the stakes were enormous.

By 1962—when Cyanamid had begun to play its ironic double role of both accused (by the Justice Department) and accuser (of the Italians and the Defense Department)— the drugmakers had absorbed the body blows that had sent them reeling in that December, 1959, when Kefauver opened his hearings.

If any part of the old character remained from the days when the industry was constituted of gentlemanly family firms, the Senator had stamped it out forever. For more than a decade, the drugmakers, now bossing giant corporations, had been competing fiercely to garner what they could in the research bonanza. At all levels—ranging from high-pressure marketing to skillful in-fighting at the Patent Office—they had developed into hardened combatants.

Now that they were faced by a common enemy who, for all his coonskin-cap exterior, was one of the most experienced tactical politicians in Congress, it did not take them too long to rally their mauled morale and deploy some of the forces they had been directing at one another in a combined operation to fight off the attack from outside—or, at least, to hone down some of its more serious effects.

But if the drugmakers were taken by surprise by Kefauver, the Senator had anticipated pretty exactly what would happen after the first foray when the industry executives got up and brushed themselves off. He had specialized in the antitrust field. His senior staff, whom he had drawn from the FTC, had spent most of their careers attempting to control the excesses of big business. He had fully calculated the considerable firepower that the pharmaceutical men could bring to bear once they got their range right.

Almost certainly, this experience provided the motivation behind the dramatic headline-grabbing tactics he had employed in the hearings. It is doubtful if Estes Kefauver truly questioned the benefits brought to the human condition by the age of the wonder drugs, even though the hearings gave the impression at times that he regarded the whole story as a con trick. What he objected to was the high charges and the overselling techniques that, in his view, had been included in the package.

To his mind, the profits of the drugmakers were far too lush to be justified by their investment in research. As he saw it, they were exploiting the patent system to build comfortable monopolies—linked by mutual back scratching—and spending millions of dollars on promotion campaigns aimed at doctors that, in some cases, were not only highly dubious, but, by omission of facts about side effects, downright fraudulent. The result of these practices, he concluded, was that the sick American —often old and poor—was paying prices for his drugs that were far too high.

The only way that Kefauver could break this system was by successfully promoting a bill through Congress that would change the law. To achieve this, he would have to surmount some formidable obstacles. For the fact is that the political system of the United States—in common with that of most democracies—is designed to make new legislation difficult. Even when bills are backed by numerous powerful supporters, they can often be killed or maimed drastically at many different stages in the legislative process—mainly in the committees that have to hammer out agreement on details before there is any possible hope of a favorable vote on the floor of either house. The proof of this is that the President himself, with all his influence, often fails to persuade Congress to accept his legislation.

What prospect, then, did a lone Senator possess of effecting radical changes to a system of which many Americans, in theory anyway, inevitably approved? The United States had been built on successful enterprise by men who were prepared to take risks. The only difference between the industry that Kefauver was gunning for and other spheres of U.S. business was that the drugmakers were operating in the area of human health. They were handling the material that could make the difference between life and death.

It was only by exploiting this vital and emotive fact that Kefauver had any chance at all of successfully steering any kind of effective drug bill through Congress. And the obvious way—

probably the only way—of achieving this was to shock the ordinary American in the street, to rouse public support to an extent that constituents at local level would pressure Senators and Congressmen to support his drug bill.

This was the key to his tactics during the hearings. Those damaging headlines—even if they were often misleading and achieved by admittedly unfair means—would pay off when the in-fighting started on Capitol Hill.

By the time the drugmakers had faced up to what had hit them, they realized the Senator's intentions and deployed their ranks to fight back in both areas—at the grass roots among the electors and in the lobbies of Congress.

Kefauver, however, had won many points in the first session of the hearings before the drugmakers had even got around to putting up their fists. But Hill and Knowlton, the public relations firm employed by the PMA, was an old campaigner for industries under pressure. Press releases were soon arriving on editors' desks answering charges made in testimony by industry critics. A film was made of the hearings, showing what the industry considered to be a true version of what had happened as opposed to the distorted, damaging picture that—according to the drugmakers—the public had seen on their TV screens. A booklet, in which the answers to highly publicized critical evidence were printed, was prepared under the title *The Untold Story of the Drug Hearings.*

Many drug firms took action on their own in the common cause. Some urged their employees to write to their Senators and Representatives pressing them to oppose the legislation and, in those areas where they maintained big plants, roused the communities to the dangers to jobs that Kefauver represented. Others dispatched elaborate mailing shots to doctors warning them that if the Senator were successful, it would be the end of research and a setback for medical progress.

Cyanamid was not slow to add its efforts to the combined operation. Soon after the first hearings opened, Lyman Duncan lunched in the management dining room at Pearl River with Paul Stessel, the Lederle public relations manager, and Harry McNey, who was in charge of sales. "During lunch, we kept worrying about how we could put over our side of the story to the mass of people," recalls Duncan. "It was a tough problem because, as an industry, we weren't geared to approach the public direct. Then one of us—right now I can't remember who—suggested suddenly: 'What about the detail men?' "

Lederle employed a sales force of 800 detail men spread across the country. They were educated men, college graduates, trained and fluent in their subject. Their job was to talk to physicians, but they were fully equipped to talk to anyone else. They worked and lived at the grass-roots level where the headlines that Kefauver had inspired were creating the most damage.

But if the Lederle force represented a considerable body of men, the combined teams of all the major drug firms in America amounted to a formidable army of many thousands. The scope was obvious.

Until then, the detail men had operated under strict orders that their contacts should be limited to doctors and druggists. But the men promoting veterinarian products—and like Lederle, most of the big firms operated in both markets—worked traditionally with a much wider brief. It was common practice for them to address Grange meetings, attended by farmers who wanted to learn about the new drugs and feeding additives produced by the pharmaceutical companies.

Paul Stessel was not slow to exploit what seemed to be a big opportunity. He prepared notes for the guidance of detail men who wanted to address nonmedical audiences and suggested to the PR section of the PMA that other companies did the same. A PMA speakers' bureau was set up to provide lecturers. A special kit was designed with visual aids, such as wall charts, that was lent to salesmen who wanted to strengthen their speeches with facts in dramatic form.

What results were produced by all this activity is debatable. When a U.S. Senator declares that a whole industry—especially one concerned with sickness—is making excessive profits by charging prices that are far too high, it is a rough chore to persuade the drugstore customer that this is not true—especially when, as many drug executives will concede today, there was substance to the charges.

If, however, the drugmakers failed to repair the damage that Kefauver had produced in the attitudes of the public, they were undeniably successful in the area where in practical terms it mattered most: the lobbies of Congress. At any rate, for the time being, they were.

On April 12, 1961, after he had brought his investigative hearings to an end, Estes Kefauver rose in the Senate and presented his drug bill. Today, when the laws of other countries are considered, it does not seem too revolutionary a document. But at the time, although parts of it even conformed with the published PMA standards of practice, it seemed in total to be a formidable threat.

In essence, it was aimed at removing many of the excesses that had been revealed in the hearings. Quality standards and advertising were to be much more closely controlled by government agencies.

There were many other technical changes to the regulations, but the two most important features of the bill were aimed at the patent laws. Those cozy arrangements under which firms competing for patents could cross-license one another and build a monopoly citadel around a product—as Cyanamid and Pfizer had done in the tetracycline battle—would become illegal under the antitrust acts if Kefauver's bill was accepted by Congress.[22] In addition, a patent would only be exclusive for the first three years of its seventeen-year life. After the initial period, the holder—though entitled to a royalty—would be forced to license other firms that wanted to make the drug.

Although many members of the PMA believed that the time

had come for a new drug bill—even if there was disagreement over what it should contain—they all were determined to lever every ounce of pressure they could produce as a political group into attacking the patent clauses.

For this struck right at the nerve of their whole psychology. They were now seasoned speculators, as toughened to losses as Las Vegas professionals, and they were just as jealous of their rewards when they hit a winning streak. This was what Kefauver was attacking in his clause to limit the protection provided by a patent. And although they would have fought the bill anyway —especially those aspects that were aimed at weakening the trade name system—it was the patent clauses that provided the true inspiration behind the ferocity of the drug lobby.

Like the politicians they seek to influence, lobbyists have a pretty rugged history. Their activities today, however, are a lot less sinister than they once were. In the modern Congress, lobbyists perform a vital function that—along with the deployment of skillful techniques of persuasion—supplies the members of both houses with information and even guidance that they would find it impossible to accumulate independently.

From 1959 on, the PMA maintained a highly active lobby to fight the drug bill under the directions of its special counsel, Lloyd N. Cutler, and its legislative strategist, Edward H. Foley. And there is little doubt that they—or, rather, the Congressmen who supported the opposition—could have killed the bill. Committee after committee had to approve it before it went to the floor of the Senate, and even if it were backed by a majority vote there, the whole process would then have to be repeated before it could be passed by the House of Representatives.

To a political layman it is, in fact, a mystery how any legislation that is opposed ever finds its way onto the statute book.

However, Foley and Cutler did not want to destroy the bill. They and their client were sophisticated enough to know that after all the mud that had been thrown at the industry during the hearings, the public would feel that there ought to be legislation. Also, many of the big firms would have welcomed laws to force all drugmakers—some of whom operated in very primitive conditions—to maintain high standards of hygiene and quality control. The aim of the lobby, therefore, was to get the bill trimmed of the features they did not like—the clauses restricting their advertising were, for example, a very sore point —and, in particular, to draw the teeth, such as the patent proposals, that had a potential for causing real damage.

From the start, they had powerful supporters on the Kefauver Subcommittee itself—Senator Roman Hruska, a conservative from Nebraska and, far more important from a tactical viewpoint, the minority Senate leader, Everett Dirksen. For Dirksen sat on many of the key committees, and he was as accomplished a political strategist as Kefauver.

Dirksen had been on vacation in Tennessee when the hearings opened, and the first he had learned of Kefauver's headline-catching tactics was when he read the reports in his morning newspaper. But in all future hearings he was there on the dais with Kefauver, trying, somewhat unsuccessfully, to curb the chairman's methods, which he attacked as "terribly unobjective and unfair." His support was so vigorous that the *New Republic* charged him with taking on himself "the burden of defending America's medical and pharmaceutical interests for the Republican Party." Later Kefauver, in an angry scene on the floor of the Senate, was to make much the same charge.

Although Dirksen was Kefauver's main political adversary over the drug bill, the PMA lobbyists had plenty of time to fan opposition among the other Senators. After Kefauver introduced the bill, nearly a year went by while the subcommittee held more hearings—this time legislative sessions at which witnesses from the industry, from the medical profession, from pharmacists and other interested groups commented and argued about the specific clauses.

During these months the PMA men were working in the lobbies, emphasizing that if the patent proposals were allowed to become law, much of the incentive to research would be removed—a claim that Kefauver contested—and promoting their own proposals for altering other sections.

Politicians are inevitably nervous of a new law because of its potential for turning into a Pandora's box—and the lobbyists had plenty of scope with the drug bill to exploit this inherent anxiety about possible repercussions that were not immediately evident. This applied particularly to Kefauver's patent proposals. For the patent acts were designed to cover all inventions—not just discoveries of drugs—and amendments to them involved principles that extended far beyond the issues raised by the price of medicines or the way the pharmaceutical firms ran their operations. Could the proposed drug bill be the thin end of a wedge for the attack of patents in other fields? If so, it marked the bill with a very different color.

Until March, 1962, Dirksen could do very little to counter Kefauver's tactics during the hearings except complain. But then the chairman's superior position, by virtue of the political makeup of the subcommittee and his own role on it, came to an end. The minority leader got his opportunity for effective action.

The first tactical clash between the two politicians, which Dirksen very nearly won, occurred when the subcommittee had to vote formally on the various clauses in the bill. It so happened that there were only four members of the subcommittee present—Republicans Dirksen and Hruska and Democrats Kefauver and Edward Long.

With a 50-50 vote, Dirksen could have blocked the subcommittee's formal approval of any clauses he did not like. But at the last moment, Senator John Carroll entered the room to give Kefauver the majority he needed. The subcommittee reported out the bill intact.

But Dirksen still had plenty of scope for maneuver during the weeks to come. The bill had to be approved next by the Judiciary Committee—the parent of Kefauver's subcommittee.

As soon as the session opened, the Republican leader moved that the bill should be referred to the Subcommittee on Patents and Trademarks for consideration of the clauses that fell within its jurisdiction.

Angrily, Kefauver opposed the motion, insisting that Dirksen's proposal was "an obvious attempt to kill the measure." But he was badly outvoted. Among the committee members who opposed him was Senator John McClellan, chairman of the relevant Patents Subcommittee.

The drugmakers were delighted about the way things were going. The *Pink Sheet,* one of the industry's trade journals—which clearly was not aware of the PMA's subtle policy of wanting a bill, but a weak bill—declared that the vote had "killed any chance of Senate approval of the drug bill this year." Prices of drug company stocks rose on Wall Street. Later, columnist Drew Pearson observed somewhat cynically that it had been Dirksen who persuaded McClellan to support his motion. "One of the biggest contributors to the Republican Party," wrote Pearson, "is Spencer Olin of the Olin Mathieson combine, sole owners of Squibb . . . and a generous contributor to Dirksen's election."

Sure enough, the Subcommittee on Patents and Trademarks gave the bill its first serious mauling. The PMA lobbyists had got their message through. The bill went back to the Judiciary Committee with two sections stripped out—including the controversial patent clause with its compulsory license provision and the antitrust paragraphs that had tried to make illegal the negotiating of cross deals during a patent fight.

Soon after the action of the Patents Subcommittee, Kefauver suddenly won what seemed at first to be support from a powerful quarter. President Kennedy—unhappily watching the stubborn resistance in Congress to the Medicare plan, designed to give free hospital treatment to anyone over sixty-five—decided to back the drug bill. He wrote to Senator James O. Eastland, chairman of the Judiciary Committee, that apart from a few alterations that he suggested, the bill "adequately deals with the most pressing problems in the drug field and it is my sincere wish that it be enacted during the current session of the Congress."

Strangely, this intervention was far more helpful to the drug lobby than it was to Kefauver. In June, Ed Foley reported to the PMA board that he had agreed with the Judiciary Committee and the administration a bill that, if not perfect, was at least a piece of legislation that the industry could live with.

The only interested person who had not agreed was the father of the original document—the Senator from Tennessee. In fact, the deal that Foley had negotiated revealed dramatically the power of the drug lobby. For most of the bargaining took place at a secret meeting that was inspired by the President's letter to Senator Eastland. He wanted a bill—and he wanted it this session. And as far as Eastland could see, judging by his admissions later, there was no hope of a quick compromise between Kefauver and his political opponents. So he railroaded him.

The secret meeting was attended by representatives of the administration—from the Department of Health, Education, and Welfare and from its agency, the FDA—and of the Republican interests on Kefauver's own Subcommittee on Antitrusts and Monopoly. Senator Eastland also sent a member of his staff. Kefauver was not even invited to have an observer present. Together with Cutler and Foley, acting for the PMA, they hammered out a bill that they could all agree on—all, of course, except Kefauver and his supporters. For it was a very different document from the bill that Kefauver was promoting.

"The pressure of special-interest representatives in such a meeting," comments Richard Harris in *The Real Voice*, "is, if not unique, rare, for ordinarily everyone prefers a little more discretion when it comes to suggesting where the power lies."

Kefauver learned about the deal only when, in a meeting of the Judiciary Committee, Dirksen handed him the draft of the revised bill. Appalled at what he regarded as flagrant double-dealing, he successfully filibustered the meeting to stop the motion going to the vote. That afternoon, ignoring pressure to stop him that included a telephone call from the White House, he moved onto the offensive on the floor of the Senate.

"Mr. President," he declared, "today a severe blow to the public interest was delivered in the Senate Judiciary Committee. Most of the drug industry and its acolytes have been punching away for some time at S. 1552 [Kefauver's bill] which is designed to make vital prescription drugs available to the people at reasonable prices. Today they swung a haymaker and just about knocked this bill out of the ring. . . . I think the time has come for the spotlight to be turned on so that the people of this country can see who is on which side."

Taunting Dirksen and Hruska, he went on: "The bill as it stands is admittedly agreeable to the Senator from Illinois and the Senator from Nebraska. They have generally, and I think admittedly, taken the position on these issues set forth by the pharmaceutical drug manufacturing industry, so I assume the bill is equally agreeable to the drug manufacturing industry."

Reluctantly, he conceded that parts of the revised bill would make "useful changes," but even these provisions were considerably watered down from those approved by the subcommittee.

His main resentment, however, was reserved for the Department of Health, Education, and Welfare (HEW). "I think the people are entitled to know," he declared as he ended his angry speech, "just how they happened to be there [at the secret meeting] and what the Administration's present position is."

He sat down to a silence that, according to Richard Harris, lasted for a good half minute. If the Senators were speechless, it was because, by political standards, Kefauver had been exceptionally rash. He had denounced one of the leaders of his own party, as well as the administration. By implication, he had criticized the President.

At last, Eastland stood up. "I accept full responsibility for the alleged secret meeting . . ." he said, calmly. "The truth is that the Administration designated certain individuals to handle the drug bill. It was my obligation to do what I think was needed to get a realistic drug program. . . . I admit that I did not call on my friend from Tennessee for consultation because I thought it would be a futile act. I did not think he would make any agreement with respect to anything."

In July the Judiciary Committee formally approved the bill in its new form. But Kefauver's attack had embarrassed the administration. As a result, its support lost some of its earlier enthusiasm, and the future of the bill seemed less certain.

In one sense, this was a victory for the drugmakers, but in another, it was not. For many of them still believed that following the exposure of the investigation, some form of legislation was needed, not merely to deal with some of the excesses, but as a matter of good public relations. "If they get this new bill through," Kefauver commented, referring apparently to the broad range of interests that had ganged up against him, "they can say to the public: 'The industry was investigated thoroughly and Congress did such and such. Now you can have complete faith in drugs again.'"

How long the conflict would have continued, had events taken their normal course, is impossible to calculate. For in that July, 1962, a situation was developing that would soon cap dramatically the allegations made in the subcommittee hearings, a situation that would induce a trauma within the drugmakers deeper than had been caused by any other event in the twenty-five years since the research spree had started.

The full impact came slowly. Back in April, John Blair—chief economist of Kefauver's subcommittee—had read a report in the New York *Times* about a speech given to the American College of Physicians by Dr. Helen B. Taussig, pediatrics professor at Johns Hopkins University. What caught Blair's attention was her reference to the fact that between 3,500 and 5,000 deformed babies—a figure that was later revised upward—had resulted from a sleeping pill taken by their mothers during pregnancy.

Most of the cases had occurred in Germany, where the drug was first sold, but now it was available in other countries. The only reason why it was not already in U.S. drugstores, reported Dr. Taussig, was that the FDA had postponed its decision to approve, pending the supply of more research data.

The drug was thalidomide, but that July it was a name truly familiar only to the more careful readers of the medical journals. The New York *Times* report was not, however, the first reference to it in the lay press. Several weeks earlier, *Time* magazine had run a brief story about the drug and its possible effects. In the PMA offices in the Madison Building off Massachusetts Avenue, Dr. Karl Bambach, assistant director of the association, had clipped it and circulated it to the staff with a memo warning that potentially this could be a great tragedy if the suspicions were proved.

Meanwhile, although Duncan was on the association board, the Cyanamid executives had not been involved with the maneuvering of the PMA lobby in the Capitol, concerned though they were with its results. They had been too occupied with their own conflicts to pay too much attention to the broader struggle between the industry and Kefauver. For by then their campaign against the Defense Department and the Italians had flared into a new stage.

It was in April—just after Sidney Fox had refused adamantly to answer most of Walter Mansfield's questions during the pretrial depositions in the Newark courtroom—that the attorney launched an operation in Italy.

9

THE target of Walter Mansfield's new strategy was John Cancelarich—the likable, easygoing chemical engineer, once employed at Pearl River, who had now joined Ankermann Italiana in Milan as production manager.

From the start of the attorney's campaign to get the evidence to jail the espionage ring, which had raided Cyanamid's plant at Pearl River so successfully, Mansfield had known that his only prospect of achieving his objective lay in pressure. Systematically, he had to break the links in the chain of conspirators until at last he had enough confessions to hand the FBI a case that was so strong that the Justice Department would be forced to take it to trial.

So far, progress had been disappointingly slow. Sidney Fox —even if he had quarreled with his previous colleagues—had shown that he was going to fight Cyanamid fiercely for every inch of ground he conceded. Clearly, Mansfield was going to have to corner him and break him down by sheer weight of legal pressure—a process that, with the appeal procedures open to defendants in American courts, could take a long time.

Leo's Dr. Giovanni Auletta had made some contribution to the case—by handing over notes in Fox's handwriting and the organisms he had bought from him—but the fact that, on the advice of his lawyers, he had now refused to testify made his value almost negligible. Truly, the only significant evidence Mansfield had obtained was the statement by Joe Gerace, after his night confession in the old farmhouse the previous February, that he had innocently supplied Cancelarich with tetracycline production mash—from which, of course, the vital pedigree bugs could easily be isolated by an experienced microbiologist. As evidence, this was pretty meager, but it could at least be used as a lever on the young chemical engineer, who had clearly worked closely with Fox. For according to Auletta, he had taken part in the conspirators' deal with Leo in Rome.

There were other reasons why, as a link in the chain, Cancelarich might be the most vulnerable to pressure. It had been a surprise to everyone who knew him—especially Bill Fulton, who was on the same bowling team at Pearl River—that he had been involved in a criminal conspiracy. Thirty years old, slim and good-looking, he was a pleasant young man, popular in the plant, and he had little of the discontentment that the prickly Sidney Fox had displayed.

He had a pretty young Southern wife named Johnnie Lou and a young baby. Studying the dossier on him that Bill Fulton had prepared, Mansfield suspected that his role in the espionage ring had been out of character. If this was the case, he could well be quite easy to break when he realized that he was faced by a very big, a very powerful and a very angry international corporation.

Also, Fulton's investigation had revealed that, together with his sister, Marie, he was part owner of a house in Dumont, New

Jersey, in which his parents lived. Cyanamid had already named him as co-conspirator in its action against Nathan Sharff. Certainly, it could now muster enough legal ammunition to sue to seize the house—an act that might help to tighten the screws on the young man. If he cooperated, Cyanamid could then graciously abandon the action.

Mansfield gave orders for the technicalities of the suit to be prepared. Then he took a cab to the Federal Courthouse— where a few months before Dr. Malcolm had been indicted— and called on a tall bulky young Assistant U.S. Attorney named Al Gaynor.

The Fox case had been Gaynor's first assignment on joining the staff of the U.S. Attorney for the Southern District, New York—and although technically it was not all that unique, there were complex ramifications. Not the least of these was the fact that the complainant, Cyanamid, was itself under indictment for criminal conspiracy.

Had the circumstances been normal, Gaynor and Mansfield might well have taken to each other. The Cyanamid attorney, as a young lawyer, had had the same job as Gaynor in the same courthouse, and he knew the problems. Both men were excellent trial lawyers, although Mansfield was now one of the most eminent members of the New York bar. Gaynor was bright and ambitious, as Mansfield had been, and would almost certainly have appealed to the older man.

However, the circumstances were not normal, and the relationship between Mansfield and Gaynor—and Robert Morgenthau, Gaynor's boss, the U.S. Attorney—was soon to deteriorate to one of cold, though overtly polite, hostility.

Gaynor has always insisted that neither he nor the other government lawyers concerned with the Fox case have ever deliberately delayed its prosecution. But in time, that was the way it came to look from Mansfield's office on Wall Street, and he suspected that the root cause lay at the headquarters of the Justice Department in Washington. Gaynor, he believed, was acting on orders to hold his hand because of the antitrust case pending against Dr. Malcolm, Cyanamid and the co-defendants.

Al Gaynor's expressed attitude was simply that, as always, they had a lot of cases to try. Mansfield was trying to use the criminal courts to serve a client who was in deep trouble—which was his right. But the young lawyer did not like being pressured. In any event, industrial espionage against a multi-million-dollar corporation did not rank too high in the scale of priorities—especially since any suggestion of partiality in the cause of a big drug company would at that time have attracted prompt and strident criticism from the men in Congress who were fighting the industry.

What is fascinating about the Fox case is that everyone concerned—in both Cyanamid and the government—has always behaved superficially as though it were a perfectly ordinary prosecution, unaffected by outside events. In fact, the case was completely colored by politics from the start.

The truth is almost certainly that the Justice Department was not eager to prosecute, although it eventually did, because of the events that were taking place in Washington. It is also highly doubtful if Cyanamid would have considered the successful prosecution of Dr. Fox to be worth the expenditure of close to a million dollars had it not been for the turbulent political background at the time.

By that March, 1962, however, the conflict between the U.S. Attorney's office and Cyanamid's lawyers had not yet developed. Even Mansfield agreed that Gaynor did not yet have enough evidence to get an indictment, and that was why he was campaigning to obtain some for him.

The purpose of his visit on this occasion was legal etiquette. He had decided to take Joe Gerace to Italy and to use him in an effort to persuade John Cancelarich to talk. Gerace was a potential government witness. Mansfield hoped that this would not interfere with Gaynor's arrangements.

Late on a Saturday morning in early April, the big jet carrying Mansfield, Joe Gerace and Bill Fulton flew low over the broad, flat valley of the Po River and landed at Milan's Malpensa Airport. An hour later, they checked in at the Palace Hotel in the spacious Piazza della Repubblica. Only half a mile away, in the Via Turati, was the head office of Pierrel and its chief executive, Count Visconti. The Ankermann plant was only a twenty-minute drive by cab. They were, in short, in enemy country.

Over lunch, Mansfield laid down the final details of their strategy. Joe Gerace was bait—tangible evidence that Cyanamid had a witness who would accuse Cancelarich, the key aspect of the confrontation of power that Mansfield hoped would swing the engineer onto their side.

The initial contact was to be as friendly as possible. Fulton and Gerace would call informally. Mansfield would handle the tough play once the lines of communication had been set up. Until then, he would stay out of the picture.

That afternoon the two men drove to the Cancelarich apartment in a side street off the main arterial Viale Certosa.

When they arrived, Cancelarich was at work at the Ankermann plant, but his wife, Johnnie Lou, welcomed them warmly and telephoned her husband. If she suspected the reason why Joe Gerace, accompanied by a security officer from Pearl River, had flown some 4,000 miles to Milan, she did not display it.

Cancelarich was in no doubt of the purpose of the visit. All the same, when he arrived home, he greeted them both without reserve and behaved as though he were delighted to see them.

When Johnnie Lou left them, Fulton came quickly to the point. Gerace had revealed everything he knew. Cancelarich himself had been named as a co-conspirator in Cyanamid's suit against Nathan Sharff.

Cancelarich had heard about the case. His sister, Marie, had sent him a clipping from the Bergen *Record*. But he was not committing himself.

"We want to know how closely you're involved," Fulton said at last.

Cancelarich looked blank. "Involved with what?" he asked. As the security man told him more about the information Cyanamid had accumulated, the young chemical engineer shrugged his shoulders. He did not know what Fulton was talking about.

Today Fulton recalls clearly the moment when the crunch came. "Listen, John," he told him, "we know all about Fox's deal with Leo. We know that he used the name of Dr. Martin and"—he paused for a few seconds, eyeing Cancelarich, then added sharply—"we know quite a lot about you, too, Mr. Jane." John Jane was the alias that Cancelarich had used for his contacts with Leo.

Gerace told his old friend bluntly: "John, you've got to know. I shall be there on the stand testifying against you."

Cancelarich continued to play it cool, shadow-boxed with more questions. At last he said that he did not know if he could help, but what exactly did Fulton want him to do?

That evening they all had dinner with Walter Mansfield in a little restaurant near the Cancelarich apartment. Calmly, the attorney pointed out the two alternatives that the young man faced. Either he cooperated with Cyanamid, or he was going to have a fight on his hands. "And if it's the latter," said Mansfield, "I warn you the fight will be vigorous—we'll take it right through to the end."

Cancelarich did not appear to be unduly disturbed, but there was no doubt from his expression that he believed the attorney meant what he said. Nor did he underestimate the power that Cyanamid could bring to bear against him—especially since it maintained a big Italian operation with a plant in Sicily. What concerned him was what would happen if he cooperated and signed a confession. What about the FBI? Could he be jailed?

Mansfield saw that despite the self-assurance the young man was displaying, the front was breaking. Quietly, he outlined his position. Naturally, the FBI was investigating. Almost certainly, the U.S. Attorney would have to ask a grand jury to indict him. There would be a trial, and Mansfield could not tell a judge how to do his job. But he could ask him to be lenient, and since he was acting for the complainant, this would probably affect the issue. If Cancelarich cooperated fully with the prosecution then, no doubt, the U.S. Attorney would do the same.

It was not a very encouraging prospect when compared with Cancelarich's position at the time. Was there any reason why he should leave Italy? Could they extradite?

"Maybe the government couldn't," Mansfield told him. "But make no mistake, John, we'll act against you here. We'll mount suit wherever you go." Then, of course, there was the question of the house in Dumont where his parents lived.

That night, in his room at the Palace, Mansfield wrote a memo to his office: "I analyzed for him what would happen if he fights, pointing out how his house would be attached. . . . He thinks we know more than we do but is impressed by our knowledge about the deals with Leo. . . . He hates Fox. . . . He indicated that he favored talking, but still wanted to talk with Ben Rubinstein, his lawyer. . . ."

The following day, Mansfield reported again to his office: "Cancelarich phoned today, quite nervous and obviously anxious. We played it cool again, indicating that we would not worry because our steamroller was going forward regardless. However, we agreed to pay Rubinstein's fare, provided there was no delay."

Two days later Rubinstein arrived in Milan. Mansfield, anticipating that the attorney would instruct his client to stop talking, called his office in New York and ordered them to serve a writ of attachment on the Cancelarich house in Dumont—a first move toward seizing it. Faced by this sudden teeth-baring display of strength, Rubinstein advised his client to cooperate, and the young engineer, conscious that his only reward would be the vague comfort that the giant Cyanamid would now be his friend instead of an awesome enemy, agreed to talk.

It took him three days to tell the story in the office, near Milan's Duomo Cathedral, of Cyanamid's Italian attorney. In a room thick with cigarette smoke and littered with half-empty cups of coffee, Mansfield and Fulton took turns taking notes. Then, while one continued with the questioning, the other dictated the statement to a secretary.

For the first time, Mansfield heard the overall story of the espionage conspiracy, although much of the detail—especially concerning those events that Cancelarich had not featured in but had learned about from Fox—was supplied later by other sources. It portrayed a strange and sordid picture of amateur criminals, squabbling among themselves for the big money that appeared always to be available for high-yielding bugs and process data.

It seemed to have little relation to the fight against disease, although, ironically, thousands of lives were undoubtedly saved by the drugs made by Italian companies with Fox's bugs. Certainly, it would have horrified Dr. Benjamin Duggar, who had started it all some fifteen years before at Pearl River by developing his tawny organism, *Streptomyces aureofaciens.*

The suite in the Park Sheraton Hotel on Seventh Avenue in New York was functional but coldly formal. As the three men waited, they could hear the sound of a noisy crowd higher up the avenue toward Central Park. For it was early November, 1960, and a Kennedy Presidential rally was in progress at Columbus Circle.

Earlier they had checked into the hotel under conditions that were almost too heavily dramatic even for so clandestine a meeting. Sidney Fox had registered as Dr. Joseph Martin of the Martin Chemical Company in St. Louis and asked his two colleagues—Leonard Fine and John Cancelarich—to assume false identities for the negotiations that were to take place in the suite. Like a lover planning an illicit afternoon, Fox carried a suitcase weighted with old shoes to give the impression that he was staying the night.

This was the first big deal to be discussed by Fox's newly formed espionage ring with an Italian drugmaker. Count Niccolo Visconti di Madrone, managing director of Pierrel, was in town on a business trip. Pierrel, the company he directed, was planning to make dimethylchlortetracycline (Declomycin)—patented in America by Cyanamid but not, of course, in Italy—and the Fox group was ideally placed to help him. So now they waited impatiently on that winter evening to meet the count.

Fox had traveled quite a way since his first exploratory move into industrial espionage that had alerted Dr. Scholz two years earlier in the research block at Pearl River. In fact, he had not planned consciously to become an industrial spy. He was just fed up with Cyanamid, the employers that did not seem to recognize fully his merits as a chemist. Because of this, he was open to suggestions—such as the one that was hinted at by Seymour Salb on a spring evening in 1957.[23]

Fox and Salb, who was Sharff's partner in Biorganic Laboratories in East Paterson, both were on the board of the Rockland County Hebrew Institute in Spring Valley. They had a good deal in common. They were chemists. Their children attended the parochial school controlled by the institute. They often talked together after board meetings.

At the time Fox was working mainly with triamcinalone, Lederle's new drug for the treatment of arthritis, which the company had just introduced to doctors under the name of Aristocort. Fox told Salb about its progress, commenting how well the drug had stood up to clinical testing.

Salb was interested. "We could get a good price for triam," he said, "if we could lay our hands on some."

"I've got plenty in my lab," Fox answered. "I doubt if anyone would miss it."

A few days later—at Salb's invitation—Fox drove over to Biorganic Laboratories' bare yellow-brick building in East Paterson. There, according to Fox's testimony in their trial, the two men agreed to buy triamcinalone from him for resale in Italy.

At first, Fox sold them some of his lab stocks of triam; then he worked out a way of extracting it from the "crude" that was left over after the production process.

Fox set up a business, registering it in his wife's name, and opened a bank account in Haverstraw. Over the next few months, Kim Laboratories—as he called his company—earned $3,500, which was not bad for a chemist earning only a little over $10,000 a year.

Then Sharff introduced him to another potential market—a small firm in New Jersey that wanted the organisms and process data to make triamcinalone. Fox agreed to cooperate.

During the following week, he wrote out the production procedure to make triamcinalone from the Lederle research reports. He walked boldly into the chill room, near his lab in the research block, in search of a triam organism. In the cold windowless compartment—thermostats maintained the temperature at three degrees above freezing—he scanned the long racks of slanting test tubes ranged aggressively like squads of advancing toy soldiers. In each of them, the spores that would grow into bugs when they were rodded into nutrient were a delicate network of silver strands suspended over a dirty gray jelly.

Fox recognized the slants he was seeking from the code numbers on the labels and put one in the pocket of his white coat.

Then he went down to the pilot plant and asked an engineer for a sample of the nutrient they used in production.

In September, 1958, he delivered the results of his work to his new customer, who gave him a check for $2,000—the first payment against an agreed total of $15,000. A few months later, he did another deal with the same firm—this time with a tetracycline bug together with the necessary knowledge. Again, the price was $2,000.[24]

By now, although he had not yet glimpsed the broad horizons, Fox had realized some of the potential of his position as a Lederle chemist. He began to take documents home that might be useful for future deals. He set up a kind of process library, which he kept in boxes in the basement of his home in Anthony Court. He made plans to build up a store of bugs, not only to make triamcinalone, but also to produce the tetracyclines in which the really big money lay.

In retrospect, it is fantastic that with Ted Scholz watching his every move within the research block and Bill Fulton tailing him regularly out of the plant, Fox was able to complete his stock of organisms to make Aureomycin, tetracycline and Declomycin. He kept them in a gold-speckled plastic box in his refrigerator at his home in Anthony Court, Spring Valley.

In September, 1959, Fox resigned from his job in Pearl River and devoted himself full time to promoting Kim Laboratories' "consultancy services." Then, just before Christmas, Sharff offered him $5,000 for an Aureomycin bug and process—which he accepted happily until he found out later that Sharff had sold it to Ankermann Italiana for $45,000.

It was in January, 1960, that Fox discovered for the first time the true potential of the fortunes that lay in the bugs in his refrigerator and the library of process material that he had built up.

Stopping over in Milan, on the way home from a trip to Tel Aviv, he set up a deal with an American chemist named Maurice Rosenblatt, who was consultant to Le Petit, one of the biggest drug groups in Italy.[18] Under this—according to Fox's testimony—he was to be paid $300,000 for bugs and processes to make tetracycline and Declomycin.

In March, Rosenblatt flew to America to collect the merchandise for Le Petit, and a payment of $55,000 was made to Fox, $40,000 of which he deposited in his own account in a Swiss bank and the balance in Rosenblatt's.

While he was in the middle of this operation, Fox's old partners, Nathan Sharff and Seymour Salb, approached him once more. They wanted exactly the same bugs—for tetracycline and Declomycin—that the chemist had agreed to sell to Le Petit. But they did not realize that Fox had now discovered the realistic market rate.

When Sharff offered him $5,000 each for the bugs—the same price that he had paid before—Fox laughed in his face. The price, he told him, was $50,000 each.

It was this clash that led to Lyman Duncan's dramatic gesture in the Kefauver hearings when he flourished the *Chemical & Engineering News,* with its advertisement for processes, and attacked the Defense Department for promoting espionage. For at that particular moment, Nat Sharff was in the final stages of negotiating a $275,000 deal with Ankermann Italiana and Helmuth Wawretchek, whom he had met as the result of an introduction by Caesar Bottone.

He had big plans for Ankermann—his deal carried a royalty on sales—not least of which was to bid for Admiral Knickerbocker's Defense Department contracts. Obviously, Fox could spoil the market by putting too many firms into competition with them. So Sharff initiated a scheme that could have no rational purpose but to curb the chemist. If this was its motivation, it misfired badly. Sharff placed the advertisement for processes in the *Chemical & Engineering News* under the name of Dr. Angelo Mancuso of 15 Bergen Boulevard, Fairfield, New Jersey, which was, in fact, the home of his brother-in-law, George London.[11]

This—according to evidence at Sharff's trial—was bait for Fox. And he rose to it. He asked a friend to answer the advertisement.

As a result, a meeting was set up for him in London—he was, in fact, on his way home from a brief visit to Switzerland—with Dr. Angelo Mancuso, who turned out, in fact, to be Caesar Bottone's erstwhile partner, Elio Salvetti.

Salvetti was doing a favor for Nat Sharff, who appeared to want Fox steered away from the Italian market. But Salvetti—according to Fox's testimony—decided to bring him into far closer contact with the drug firms of Milan and Rome than he had been before. He offered him a deal: He would act as his salesman.

And of one thing there was no doubt. With his good looks, his fluency and his easy charm, Salvetti was a highly skillful operator in this role.

Fox, however, had a problem. By resigning from Lederle, he had cut off his supply of organisms and up-to-date process information. If he were going to supply the services that Salvetti's customers were going to need, he would have to create new lines of communication within Pearl River.

The person he had in mind for the job was John Cancelarich, who was one of the men who controlled the machinery in the actual production of the Lederle drugs. They had come to know each other when Cancelarich was assigned to the pilot plant in the research block long before Fox had resigned.

Now in June, 1960, Cancelarich was working in the main production area and ideally placed to serve Fox's purpose. The mash was available to him all the time, and his duties involved constant reference to current production documents containing the newest technical improvements worked out by Ted Scholz's scientists. And it so happened that, like Fox a year earlier, he was disgruntled with his employers.

Lederle had just introduced a new stock-ownership plan for employees, but this was only open to men on a salary level that was slightly higher than Cancelarich's income. Bitterly, he had complained at what he saw as unfair discrimination.

The two men met in Tiny's Diner—a small aluminum truck stop on the fringe of Spring Valley—and the engineer needed little persuasion. Fox also co-opted Leonard Fine, an analytical chemist who had worked with him in Squibb.

Fox introduced Cancelarich and Fine one evening at his home in Spring Valley. The three men agreed to work together to develop Kim Laboratories.

Kim's aims were broad. In addition to its "consultancy business," it was to supply industrial chemicals and a range of equipment. It did, in fact, obtain franchises to sell laboratory glassware and a line of photocopying machines. Fox planned also to offer a microfilm service, although no one he approached was interested. As a business base, the men rented a small shop, overlooking the railroad tracks at Suffern, about which Dr. Auletta's New York representative was to write so critically only a few months later.

In theory, the setup was extremely good. Cancelarich, still at Pearl River, was a source of bugs and process information. Salvetti, moving between America and Italy, would set up the deals. Lennie Fine was the part-time manager of Kim's legitimate business—for which he even hired a couple of salesmen—which provided an ideal cover. Between them, they could offer the expert services of an organic chemist, an analytical chemist and a progress engineer. The only specialist Kim lacked—and in the view of some people at Pearl River this was fatal—was a microbiologist.

Through the fall, Cancelarich produced the documents they needed. When the photocopying machine that Fox had bought the previous year proved too cumbersome for the volume of work it had to handle, they rented a microfilm camera and reader. Together they copied thousands of papers—most of which Cancelarich would borrow overnight from the production building—containing process or other useful information.

In November—according to testimony—Elio Salvetti set up the meeting with Count Visconti.

Visconti was exceptionally tall. In his early forties, with graying hair and dark, prominent eyes, he looked what he was—an aristocrat of one of Italy's most famous families who had enjoyed great power for centuries. The meeting in New York went well. He was sufficiently impressed with the "Martin" group and the yields they claimed their Declo process could produce that he agreed to pay $50,000 plus royalties, provided the promised production results were achieved—but, in fact, Visconti claimed they never were. In Milan, the deal was formalized by written contract.

Ten days later Fox and Cancelarich—who was taking vacation time due to him—flew to Rome in separate planes. In his attaché case, Fox carried three rolls of microfilm and—with the glass tubes protected in metal cigar containers—the bugs to make Aureomycin, tetracycline and Declomycin.

The day after their arrival, still using false names, they traveled down to Capua to start working at the Pierrel plant with Visconti's technicians. Then they returned to Rome for the meeting with Dr. Giovanni Auletta of Leo that Salvetti had set up.

Fox and Cancelarich flew back to America, confident that they faced an opulent future. The two deals, already negotiated, carried between them a gross price tag of $120,000, depending on production success. Kim appeared to be thriving.

One evening in December, Fox returned to his home, where Cancelarich and Fine were waiting to talk to him. Jubilantly, he threw wads of dollar bills onto the living room table. "This is just the beginning," he said. "There's plenty more where that came from." It amounted to $10,000—the first payment on account under the Leo deal.

The clouds gathered very fast for the espionage ring. Just

before Christmas, Fox flew to Rome with his family to help Dr. Auletta get into production with the new bugs he had sold him. But he failed to produce the results provided by his contract with Leo, and Auletta fired him.

Count Visconti, too, had discovered Fox, as a research chemist, was not a microbiologist or experienced in production and severed the relationship.

Meanwhile, at home Cancelarich and Fine had mutinied, claiming that Fox had reneged on his agreement to give them stock in Kim Laboratories. Unwisely, Fox had left his library of process information and his bugs in their safekeeping. They set up a new group around the leadership of Elio Salvetti.

When he returned home, Fox found that he was out of business—without organisms, without documents, without partners and, of course, without Elio Salvetti as a contact man.

Salvetti and Cancelarich flew to Italy in an attempt to salvage something from the wreck that Fox had left, but Visconti had lost interest. So had Auletta—despite Salvetti's dramatic gesture, described later to Bob Bogan, of writing a check payable to the Italian's mother for $50,000.

However—according to Cancelarich, as he later testified—the two men did negotiate a deal to supply Declomycin processes and bugs to a Milan firm named IBI (Istituto Biochemico Italiano) for $50,000. The president of the company was a well-known Italian politician, Senator Antonio Cremisini.[23]

Like other Italian firms, IBI was bidding for the Defense Department business in Washington. In June, Admiral Knickerbocker granted the company a $115,000 contract for tetracycline.

Meanwhile, Helmuth Wawretchek—with the expensive assistance of Fox's first customers, Nat Sharff and Seymour Salb—was not enjoying much more success than his competitors who had dealt with the ex-Lederle chemist. In the hope of increasing the Americans' incentive in the success of Ankermann, he offered to sell them stock—an opportunity which they were eager to grasp.

By now the two groups, neither of whom would have anything to do with Sidney Fox, had come to realize that they had more to gain by a combined operation than by rivalry—a piece of diplomacy masterfully handled by Caesar Bottone. As a result, Bottone and Salvetti—who took over responsibility for Ankermann's sales—also bought stock in the company. Cancelarich became production manager. Siegfried Muller, the Lederle chemist who had innocently answered Sharff's advertisement in *Chemical & Engineering News,* joined the laboratory staff. And a string of scientists came over from America for short visits to advise on special problems.

Ankermann began to make progress with tetracycline production going well, but the new arrangement did not last long. After a few months Helmuth Wawretchek bought back the stock he had sold but retained John Cancelarich as his production director.

This was the situation when, in April, 1962, Walter Mansfield arrived in Milan. The following Saturday, Cancelarich swore a sixty-one-page affidavit before the U.S. vice-consul in Milan.

The Cancelarich confession provided the Cyanamid campaign with a new dynamic. Back in New York, Mansfield fast exploited his new ammunition. Leonard Fine agreed to follow the lead set by his partner and—after long sessions in Mansfield's office on Wall Street—swore out a lengthy affidavit. He confirmed most of what Cancelarich had said.

Ben Rubinstein, the attorney acting for the two men, took the affidavits to the Justice Department. Mansfield made a separate appointment to see Robert Morgenthau, the U.S. Attorney, and Al Gaynor. "Well, I've got you a case," he said somewhat jauntily. But the two government lawyers were not enthusiastic. They liked to do their own investigations. Even though they were forced to accept it, they did not welcome evidence being thrust on them by a multimillion-dollar corporation with political interests.

There was, however, no doubt that Cyanamid had made a great advance. Of the seven men, who had at times been linked in the conspiracy, three—although Gerace was only an innocent on the fringe—had now confessed to the role they had played. That left Fox, Sharff, Salb and Salvetti—and the most important, because of his key role, was Fox.

At first, despite the fact that the chemist had taken the Fifth Amendment in the pretrial deposition, Mansfield had hoped that Fox could be broken in the same way as his previous partners. He arranged with the Pearl River management for a Lederle chemist, who knew Fox well, to contact his old friend to explore the possibility of a deal.

But Sid Fox was not as awed by the might of the American Cyanamid Company as Cancelarich and Fine had been. He decided to fight—and he won the first round. The federal court of appeals overruled the judge who had ordered him to jail for refusing to answer some of the questions that Mansfield had put to him.

But the advantage was only temporary. In June, Mansfield deployed his new armor and launched the biggest attack that he had yet directed at the chemist. Standing up one morning in a crowded room on the first floor of the State Courthouse, he made a formal motion to a judge that triggered off the first blast of major publicity throughout the world.

Four days earlier, in support of a new action against Fox, Mansfield had filed affidavits by John Cancelarich and Leonard Fine. For the first time, these confessions became public documents. Men who had been involved in the marketing of industrial secrets were openly admitting their crimes and, in effect, accusing major Italian companies of buying stolen merchandise.

It was a good story. In fact, two weeks before, at Pearl River,

Lyman Duncan had held a meeting with the heads of the two public relations divisions concerned with the Fox case—Paul Stessel, PR manager at Pearl River and responsible for domestic publicity, and Ned Candee, PR director of Cyanamid International, who controlled information supplied to foreign newspapers by the corporation's overseas subsidiaries. Since the blanket of secrecy had been removed from the conspiracy by the filing of suits in February, Duncan had held several similar meetings.

Both PR men were anxious to exploit the story. The conflict between the industry and Kefauver was at its height. Throughout America, Cyanamid detail men—in speeches to PTA meetings and social organizations—were trying to correct the appalling impression that the Kefauver hearings had created in the minds of the public. The Defense Department was buying millions of dollars' worth of drugs from Italian firms—or, at least, in the case of Premo Laboratories, from U.S. firms that had imported bulk powder from Italian sources.

At that time in June, Kefauver was throwing his whole weight behind his attempt to fight the drug bill through Congress—against a determined defensive action by the PMA lobby. But even if the lobbyists—and those politicians who shared their views—could keep Kefauver's damaging patent clauses out of the bill, the impression was still there in the public mind: Patents were a means of exploitation, of maintaining high prices and big profits. Their true value had been greatly inflated by the drugmakers.

The affidavits of Cancelarich and Fine provided a dramatic answer. Italian companies had agreed to pay big money for the product of research. Even if Kefauver gave the impression that many of the inventions under patents had no value, the Italians had certainly proved that, so far as Cyanamid's research was concerned, they did not share the same view.

Also, for years now, the PR men had been fighting to defend the Cyanamid image against the bad publicity created by the antitrust charges of the FTC and, finally and most humiliating of all, by the grand jury indictment of the company and its president the previous fall. In the Fox story, their corporation was the injured party—injured, what is more, by foreign interests with the active assistance of their own Defense Department, which was providing so rich a market. From a PR point of view, it was highly exploitable.

But these meetings at Pearl River were always frustrating. Whenever action was contemplated, Walter Mansfield invariably ruled against it. He did not want to answer charges that Cyanamid was trying the case in the press.

This time, however—since the affidavits had been filed— Duncan hoped the answer would be different. He called Mansfield during the meeting. Once more the attorney said no. "Lyman," he insisted, "you're playing with high stakes. The big throws will be in court. Don't weaken my hand."

Duncan sighed and put down the phone. "Sorry," he said to the other two, "you've just got to be patient."

They did not have to be patient for long. Three days after the affidavits were filed, the United Press man in the courthouse covered the story. That night it went out on the agency's overseas service.

The next morning, when Ned Candee walked into his office in the silver birch woods of Wayne, New Jersey—where the corporation's HQ had now moved from the city—London was already on the line. Several newspapers, following up the United Press report, had called Ted McAlister, Cyanamid's PR man in Britain, for further information. What was he expected to tell them?

Mansfield's policy was clearly going to be difficult to support. By that night he had conceded this—but only so far as the foreign situation was concerned. That night Joe Calitri, Candee's PR manager, cabled the Zurich office—which controlled Cyanamid's European subsidiaries—and all other overseas companies in the group with full details of the suit. Lyman Duncan's political thinking was clear in the statement Calitri advised managing directors to issue to the press. "I am naturally shocked to hear," he suggested they say, "that it is possible that antibiotics produced from materials and information stolen from Lederle are being brought into this country. . . . Whoever is purchasing these antibiotics has obviously become the innocent and unwilling accomplice in what appears to be an international pharmaceutical scandal. It is hoped that interested government and industry officials will look into this matter and take whatever action may be deemed necessary. . . ."

In London, Ted McAlister issued the statement, demanding that the Association of the British Pharmaceutical Industry should "examine the implications"—a fact that was duly reported in the New York *Times*.

On the Saturday following the action, the London *Daily Express* splashed the story and was followed the next day by the prestigious *Sunday Times*.

Promptly, Calitri dispatched copies of the British articles to the managing directors of all overseas subsidiaries.

The Italian press was slow to publish the story, but when it did, it printed it prominently. *L'Espresso*—a sensational Roman tabloid—devoted two whole page articles to the conspiracy, highlighting the alleged roles played by Count Visconti, Senator Cremisini and Dr. Giovanni Auletta, since they were well known and wealthy.

They attracted fast and indignant responses from the men and the firms that were named. Cyanamid, asserted some of the Italians accusingly, was conducting the case with ulterior motives. It wanted to switch attention from the antitrust charges that were pending against it in New York. The low prices charged by Italian producers in their overseas markets threatened the alleged conspiracy by Cyanamid and the other tetracycline producers to rig the market.

In Brooklyn, Admiral Knickerbocker learned of the filing

of Cancelarich's affidavit with distrust. Although he suspected its motivation, he realized that if, as was virtually certain, it led eventually to a criminal indictment, it would prove highly embarrassing to the government—which was exactly what Duncan intended. IBI—one of the firms in the affidavit—had been granted a tetracycline contract. Dr. Auletta's Leo supplied bulk powder to the New Jersey drug firm, Premo Laboratories, that had bid successfully three times. And negotiations were at an advanced stage to grant a contract for Terramycin to Count Visconti's Pierrel.

The admiral saw clearly that if Cyanamid succeeded in persuading the Justice Department to mount criminal proceedings against Fox and the others, the government would find itself in an impossible situation. For it would be buying drugs made as a direct result of the crime it was prosecuting.

Knickerbocker was hard-hitting. He had deliberately taken on an industry—and he was proud of it. He figured he had already saved the American taxpayer millions of dollars by his policy of buying abroad. He did not propose to be deflected from his purpose. As he saw it, the whole policy of the tetracycline firms was geared to the cynical exploitation of their patent position. But it was obvious he would have to tread carefully.

It was Count Niccolo Visconti who was causing the admiral's biggest problem because he was alleged to have played a leading role in the conspiracy that Cancelarich and Fine described. Should Knickerbocker proceed with the Terramycin contract with Pierrel, which was now at the final stages of negotiation? He flew to Washington for guidance. The Defense Department had now merged the MMSA into a new organization under its close control called the Defense Supply Agency. When Knickerbocker asked for instructions, the reaction of his superior was: "The Secretary of Defense made that decision personally. Unless there's a damned good reason against it, go ahead and sign."

Despite the concern of the admiral in Brooklyn, Al Gaynor in the Federal Courthouse in Foley Square seemed in no great hurry to ask a grand jury to indict. All the evidence suggested that the department's hackles were up against Cyanamid pressure.

Once a month Walter Mansfield called to discover the status of the case. "Naturally, as complainants," he would say, "we're pretty interested."

"We're working on it," Gaynor would assure him airily. "It's getting due attention."

There was nothing that Mansfield could do to force the hand of the Justice Department. Angrily, he reported to Lyman Duncan that Gaynor did not even show signs of asking a grand jury to indict. By now Mansfield had provided him with more proof than the confessions of Cancelarich and Fine. Independent experts had examined the bugs handed over both by Dr. Auletta of Leo and by Fox's former colleagues. There was, they said, no doubt that these came from Pearl River. Dr. Scholz had pinpointed the secret information in the microfilms that was not included in the patents.

Without question, the case as Mansfield saw it, was strong— certainly strong enough to put to a grand jury. Cancelarich had returned to America. Gaynor had his witnesses. But still the Assistant U.S. Attorney delayed.

Meanwhile, Mansfield pursued his strategy of trying to break, one by one, the remaining links in the chain of conspirators, amassing evidence as he did so that Gaynor could not ignore forever.

During these months of hectic activity in 1962, while Walter Mansfield was pressuring the men who had been connected in various ways with the espionage operation at Pearl River, a time bomb named thalidomide had been ticking away in Washington. Not even the Senators or the lobbyists wrangling over the drug bill were conscious of the megatonnage that was about to be triggered.

In late July it exploded. Once more the drugmakers were shattered by an experience that changed them drastically. This time, however, the tragic effects—revealing as they did the inadequacies and dangers in the production and distribution of medicines—went far deeper.

10

COMING at the time that it did, the thalidomide tragedy appeared on the American political scene as a stark indictment of the drugmakers—a flagrant, awesome, vividly tangible example of the practices for which they had been charged during the Kefauver hearings.

In truth, though, it was not so much an exposure of the industry—although, in its suggestions of inadequate testing, it was certainly that as well—as a revelation of the federal law, of the public control system and even of the practical execution of the powers the authorities already possessed. It had nothing to do with prices or profits, which were Kefauver's main concern. Or if it did, it was linked to them remotely only by the fact that the lack of control was built in to the same concept of free enterprise that characterized the whole industry.

The drugmakers were only just emerging from their gold

rush era, and in retrospect, the laws controlling their activities were—as practiced—almost as limited as those of the Wild West. The powers of the FDA were comparatively small. Before a new drug could be marketed, the promoting company had to submit it to the agency. If refusal was not specifically stated within sixty days, the applicant was allowed to assume it was granted. In the case of a drug, such as thalidomide, that was subsequently found to be dangerous, the FDA had inadequate legal powers to force it out of the drugstores.

This was bad enough, but the regulations concerning the development of a drug *before* it was even submitted to the FDA were extremely lax. The testing of new compounds on animals before they were tried out on people was not legally required. Even then, doctors were under no legal compulsion to inform those patients—or their relatives—of what they were giving them and were subject to no authority. Even though thalidomide was never formally approved for prescription in America, it was administered during clinical trials to an estimated 20,000 human beings in the United States—a massive figure for an unapproved and uncontrolled drug, which underlined dramatically the dangers inherent in the system—or, rather, lack of system. The astonishing fact was not that the thalidomide tragedy should have happened, but that more disasters—there had been a few others—had not occurred.

The system, in short, was antiquated. It was based on the old assumption—as medical professional practice is based—that everybody is a gentleman. The ethics that lay behind it reached back to the days before the research bonanza had transformed the drug industry, to the times when the drugmakers in the main were private family firms untroubled by the movement of their stock on Wall Street.

By and large, the system had worked. Despite the excesses that had emerged over the past twenty-five years, most of the big firms were very jealous of their quality. Their reputations and their future sales depended on it. Doctors preferred to prescribe drugs made by the firms they felt they could trust; this was why the legislators have had so much trouble persuading them to order drugstores to supply their patients with products under their generic names, often made by firms they do not know.

The immense trouble that Cyanamid devoted to the development of Aureomycin—with tests lasting years on a wide range of different animals—was a clear illustration of at least that company's attitude. A spectacular failure would have been disastrous for them because it would have marred the reputation they had built up over decades in the minds of doctors. They did not need a law to make them take trouble or to carry out extensive toxicity tests in animals. It was only good business to do so. But the point was that in the turbulent marketplace that the drug industry had become, they did not *have* to. Other firms, with fewer scruples and perhaps with less to lose, could cut corners—provided they could evade the vigilance, which was not always all it might have been, of the FDA.

Dr. Louis Lasagna of Johns Hopkins University had summarized the position in the Kefauver hearings. "Some drug houses perform extensive animal tests before a drug is first put into man," he said. "Others perform almost none. It is reprehensible for man to be the first experimental animal on which certain kinds of toxicity tests are run, simply because bypassing adequate acute or chronic toxicity tests in laboratory animals saves time and money."

This was clearly a situation that should never have been allowed to exist. Paradoxically, however, even the jealousy of their reputation that was marked in most of the big companies could backlash and transform a motivation that was obviously in the public interest into an attitude that was antisocial.

The withdrawal of a product attracted bad publicity. For this reason, drug executives were often reluctant to accept medical evidence on newly discovered side effects about a product because of the damage that would be caused to the name of the company. Human beings are complex animals, none of whom are exactly the same, and contraindications emerge as a result of any drug from time to time.

Before taking the drastic decision to pull a product out of the drugstores, the boards of drug houses were often tempted to mark time, to wait for more reports, to set up special tests. This reaction—and the dangers inherent in it—was built into the system under which drugs were produced by commercial companies whose success or failure was judged on their profits.

The original makers of thalidomide—though charged in a criminal prosecution for their actions[26]—were probably especially unlucky. The drug, as everyone is now aware, produced a ghastly side effect that only revealed itself in pregnant women —and even then only affected their unborn children. It could have been tested for years in rats or mice or guinea pigs, and this inherent fault could have remained unexposed.

Today research scientists are fully conscious that the drug has the same effect on pregnant rabbits and, especially, on monkeys whose reproduction system is very similar to that of women. It is for this reason that subhuman primates are now employed as study subjects for most products in the obstetric area. But this was not the rule in 1962, when Congress was digesting the various proposals for a drug bill.

Thalidomide first came to the attention of the FDA back in September, 1960, when an application for a product called Kevadon from the old and reputable William S. Merrell Company was handed to Dr. Frances Kelsey, a new medical officer who had just joined the agency. It was her first major assignment. Merrell was planning to market Kevadon—which was a brand name for thalidomide—under license from the German firm Chemie Grünenthal.

Even though thalidomide had by that time been freely available in Germany for two years, Dr. Kelsey was not happy about the drug. So she bought time by repeatedly asking for more research data.

Four months after she received the application, a letter appeared in *The Lancet,* a British medical journal, that increased her sense of apprehension. It suggested that some recent cases of peripheral neuritis—which causes a tingling sensation in the tips of fingers and toes—might have been caused by thalidomide. Dr. Kelsey had worked in medical research, and among the facts that she had learned while studying the effects of quinine in rabbits was that drugs that irritated the nerves of mature animals could cause paralysis and deformity in the fetus. She asked Merrell for its comments on this possibility, but the firm assured her that its studies revealed that it was extremely rare for peripheral neuritis to result from the use of thalidomide.

In April the company was granted official permission to market the drug in Canada, and executives began to press Dr. Kelsey for her clearance for the United States. But by this time physicians in West Germany were growing alarmed by unexplained births of deformed babies. Isolated reports were also coming in from other countries in Europe and as far away as Peru and Australia.

During the summer, in an attempt to solve the mystery, Dr. Widikund Lenz, a pediatrician from Hamburg, conducted a survey among some of the mothers of these deformed infants. Exploring what medicines they had taken during pregnancy, he discovered that some 50 percent of them had been on Contergan, the brand name for thalidomide used by Grünenthal.

Lenz pursued this lead, and in November he informed the company of his suspicions. The same month the British firm Distillers, Ltd.—which was selling the drug under license from Grünenthal—received similar reports from Scotland and from their subsidiary in New South Wales, Australia.

By the end of November Grünenthal had withdrawn the

drug from the market and informed its licensees. On December 2, Distillers took similar action.

Merrell, however, appeared to be a good deal harder to convince of the dangers of thalidomide. It did not take its product off the Canadian market until March 2, and it was not until six days later that it withdrew its new drug application from the FDA in Washington.

By July 12, 1962—the day when the drug bill, successfully watered down by the PMA lobby and its supporters, was reported out by the Senate Judiciary Committee—the investigation that John Blair had instituted in April was complete. After studying the grim facts that had been accumulated in his office, it was apparent to him that Dr. Kelsey had saved America from the tragedy that was then being enacted in other countries.

This fact gave the story a dramatic personal angle that had been lacking in earlier press reports. It also revealed appallingly vividly the faults inherent in the whole control system. For Dr. Kelsey's resistance to the application had been inspired by little more than hunch plus a bit of information she happened to have picked up in her quinine research. What would have happened had the application been handled by another FDA official without her intuition? Clearly, in total, the story could give Kefauver a whole range of new leverage in his attempt to get effective new drug laws.

And it did. It completely transformed the situation in Congress. The drug lobby, which had been gaining ground daily, now began to lose the battle once more.

Blair tipped off the Washington *Post*. Morton Mintz, a vocal critic of the drug industry, covered the assignment. On Sunday, July 15, the *Post* front-paged Mintz's report under the headline HEROINE OF FDA KEEPS BAD DRUG OFF THE MARKET.

The next day Kefauver released the dossier on thalidomide that had been developed under Blair's direction, and two days later, in a speech in the Senate, he urged that Dr. Kelsey should be awarded the gold medal for distinguished federal civilian service—a suggestion on which the President acted quickly.

Day after day the story—now picked up by newspapers throughout the world—gathered momentum. In Phoenix, Mrs. Robert Finkbine, who had been taking thalidomide obtained abroad, announced that she would attempt to get a legal abortion of the baby she was expecting. She failed in America, so she flew to Sweden for the operation—and the obstetrician confirmed that her baby would, indeed, have been born deformed.

Two days after Mrs. Finkbine had stated publicly her intentions, George Larrick, head of the FDA, stated that Merrell had sent more than 2,000,000 tablets of thalidomide for clinical testing to no less than 1,200 doctors in the United States. Even though four months had elapsed since the company had withdrawn its FDA application, all supplies had not yet been returned to it. It was a terrifying revelation that so large a number of physicians could have been testing the drug on human patients before it had been cleared by the FDA—especially when it was now obvious that it was dangerous. What other unapproved compounds—the shocked American public began to ask—were being swallowed unknowingly by human guinea pigs?

Then, on August 1, President Kennedy stepped into the controversy, with its reflections on the entire system of drug development. At a press conference he said that the bill that was just about to be debated in the Senate did not go far enough. He pointed out that another bill, being promoted in the House by Representative Oren Harris, was better—notably in a clause, lacking in the Senate bill, that would cause immediate removal from the market of a new drug where hazard to the public health had been revealed. He added that the Harris bill had "other very essential safeguards which I hope the Congress will act on this year."

The following week HEW issued a string of new regulations about drug testing. Among other controls, they clamped down on the chaotic situation that the thalidomide scandal had revealed about clinical trials. Now the drug firms would have to supply the FDA with a whole range of information which would give the agency tight control. No testing of drugs could take place on humans until their safety had been proved in animals. Full details of the distribution to doctors of unapproved drugs for investigation were to be reported to Washington. Only qualified investigators were to be used. Products destined for children or pregnant women were to be subjected to special tests.

The new regulations posed this question: Since the government possessed the powers under existing laws to tighten up the testing system, why should a tragedy be needed to make them use them?

Today drug executives reflect wryly that although the thalidomide scandal enabled Kefauver to promote his bill effectively, there was very little in it that was designed to prevent another similar disaster. HEW had already taken most of the necessary steps. Kefauver's aims were far broader, and he did not hesitate to exploit the favorable climate to do his utmost to achieve them.

Meanwhile, following his statement to the press, the President asked the Senate Judiciary Committee to recall the drug bill that it had already approved and to strengthen it with his suggested amendments. These tightened up the FDA's approval system of new drug applications and gave HEW power to take a drug off the market immediately if evidence suggested it was injurious to health.

In addition, many of the teeth in the original bill that the drug lobby and Dirksen had drawn were reinserted—especially clauses controlling advertising, which the industry was fighting hard. But under the prevailing winds in Congress, its scope for action was greatly limited.

On August 20 the committee formally approved the revised bill. Two days later, as the PMA lobbyists watched anxiously from the gallery, it was debated in the Senate. Kefauver was still not satisfied with the bill. Although it represented an immense improvement in the area of control and safety and information to the physician, there was nothing in it that would bring down the prices—which was still the Senator's main purpose. So he planned some typical dramatics in a last-minute attempt to blast back into the bill a slightly altered version of his compulsory licensing proposals (under which patent holders, after three years, would have to license other firms that wanted to make the drug). He submitted them in the form of an amendment to the bill, and using John Blair's charts, which had been set up on the floor of the Senate, he repeated the attack on Schering with which he had opened the subcommittee hearings three years before. Again, he used the same formula for assessing profit that the drugmakers and, of course, Dirksen had argued was grossly unfair and misleading—namely, comparing the raw material cost of a single drug with the selling price. Citing case after case involving other companies, he jabbed at the industry the truly sound argument that its profits—its return on net worth—were nearly double the average of all manufacturing industries.

Senator after Senator appeared to be appalled by these revelations—giving the impression that Senators never read the newspapers which had now been reporting these allegations for a long time. "I say it's immoral," said Senator John O. Pastore indignantly.

"It is immoral," agreed Kefauver. "There is no doubt about it." His patent plan, he insisted, would redress the situation.

Although the shadow of the thalidomide tragedy hovered like smoke over the debate, the patent proposal struck deep into Senators' political attitudes. As before, it revealed the two basic viewpoints on the question that lay at the heart of the whole controversy: If Congress cut down the profits the drugmakers could make, would this remove their incentive to speculate in research? Would it result in fewer new drugs?

Emotionally, Senator Eastland, Democratic chairman of the Judiciary Committee, fought the amendment. "The issue," he declared, "is whether the great American drug industry shall be destroyed. . . . Millions of Americans are alive today because of the patent system of our country. . . . Sixty new drug breakthroughs have occurred in the United States since 1940 under our present system, as against 29 in Great Britain, France, West Germany and Switzerland combined. . . .

"The Senator from Tennessee would like to have the United States adopt the Italian system and destroy all incentive to make investments in research by limiting patents on drugs to 3 years. There has been no discovery in Italy since 1940. Why? Because Italy does not have a patent system. . . .

"I say, for God's sake let the drug industry continue," he demanded, ". . . so that it can develop the drugs to save the lives of the people of this country. . . . In my judgment, if the Senate concurs in such a proposal [to reduce exclusive rights to three years] it will be committing a crime against humanity. . . ."

If the drug lobbyists in the gallery were feeling unhappy, this must have cheered them up, for the Senator was drawing heavily on their reference material. Dirksen, too, took much the same line. "Mr. President," he said, "I am of mankind . . ."— an emotive lead-in to his use, as an argument, of the Fox case and other espionage actions involving drug firms that had now been exposed. "What a magnificent job the pharmaceutical industry of our country has done," he said. "So magnificent indeed is their work that our secrets are often times pilfered, then taken abroad, and in those countries in which there is no patent protection, frightful advantage is taken of the American pharmaceutical manufacturers."

In the prevailing mood, Kefauver made a great deal of ground despite these compelling defense actions. Other countries, he pointed out, seemed to manage without laws that were so protective as America's. Among the seventy-seven nations for which information was available, only twenty-eight granted product patents on drugs—as opposed to patents on manufacturing processes—and only three, including the United States, "do not have some special provision to protect the people against excessive prices."

Kefauver might well have achieved his aim if he had not been deliberately checked by Senator Mike Mansfield, who, on telephoned instructions from the White House, made a motion to table the amendment—a motion that, under Senate rules, is not subject to debate. The practical result of this technical move was that Kefauver's patent amendment—which presumably the President was against—would not be voted on.

If there were any signs of relief among the lobbyists following Senator Mansfield's action, they were not encouraged by the vote on the bill. In the roll call, there was not one vote against it—a situation that is so rare as to be unique.

Since the bill still had to pass the House of Representatives, the PMA had plenty of time to attack it. There were still technical stages at which they might be able to block it or, at least, blunt the cutting edge. Before making new plans, the association board sent a small committee to talk to Senator Eastland. He gave them blunt advice: They had better work to get a bill passed by the Congress in the present session. Otherwise, it would become the number one domestic issue in the coming election.

Either way the prospect for the drugmakers was poor. One Representative, who had sponsored an amendment to the Harris bill—which eventually was to be merged with Kefauver's Senate bill—had already gone so far as to vote against his own motion after learning that his electoral opponent at home was accusing him of being in favor of thalidomide. This was a measure of the hysterical public reaction to the wave of publicity.

"Our own private and informal polls of voters' views," Dr. Theodore Klumpp, president of Winthrop Laboratories and an active member of the PMA board, wrote later in a medical journal, "disclosed that the public equated the drug bill with thalidomide. If you were against the drug bill you were in favor of thalidomide and deformed babies. . . . In our industry councils, the debate on what course of action we should take was fierce . . . but the prevailing view was to support a bill and try to get the best one we could."

Shortly afterward the PMA lobbyists did, indeed, get a chance to kill the bill. The House Rules Committee—which decides what will be debated in the House of Representatives—met to consider it. The vote was six for allowing the bill to be debated and six against, which meant in practice that since the motion was not carried, it was dead in that session of Congress.

When the vote was announced, Representative Harris—playing a similar role in the House to that of Kefauver in the Senate—went before the committee and informed it that the PMA supported the bill. Could it be reconsidered?

The chairman, who had himself voted against the bill, was astonished. "I can't see why the industry should support a bill as bad as this," he commented, "but if it does, I'll change my vote." When the bill was voted again, it had a majority of eight to four.

As a result, the bill went to the floor of the House. But although it had made this possible, the drug lobby fought desperately hard to change its more damaging clauses while it still had a small chance. "The drug lobbyists had remained quite inconspicuous during the committee proceedings in the Senate," wrote Richard Harris in *The Real Voice*, "but it appeared that they considered members of the House more approachable, for when the Harris Committee members got to the door of the conference room on the morning of September 19, they found 20 industry men on hand. Among them were two former Congressmen. . . ."

It was a rearguard action in which they made a degree of progress. But in truth, it was a battle that was lost. The next month, in the White House—watched by a group that included Dr. Kelsey, the heroine of the hour—President Kennedy signed the bill, now officially designated Public Law 87-781.

In fact, despite all their complaining, the bill was not nearly as damaging to the drugmakers as they suggested. The reputable firms were already observing most of the requirements the new law demanded. The only aspect that the industry truly hated were the clauses controlling its advertising and promotion. Among these were new regulations that all side effects had to be printed in its literature and that the generic name of the drug had to be published every time the brand name was mentioned. But these clauses were still subject to FDA interpretation, leaving the PMA lawyers plenty of scope for argument.

By that October, as the drug bill that would affect the whole industry was going through the final agonizing stages of legislation, Lyman Duncan and the Cyanamid executives were once more deeply occupied by their own fight with the government.

The Justice Department showed no signs of beginning the trial of the three companies and their presidents following the indictment of the previous year. One probable reason for this inactivity was that the Attorney General had decided to hold his hand until the Federal Trade Commission had finished punching out its conflict with the antibiotics producers.

This fight had now moved to a new stage. Appeal hearings against the FTC examiner's opinion in 1961 that the companies had no case to answer had just opened in the FTC building on Pennsylvania Avenue. The 11,000 pages of evidence were under investigation by the full five-man commission that controlled the federal agency.

Although this had long been expected, there was a new factor in the situation that was disturbing to Cyanamid and its co-defendants. For a new chairman had recently been appointed to the FTC. He would be the senior man on the commission hearing the evidence. The facts that counsel would present in the hearings were not new to him, for—in his role as majority party counsel of the Kefauver Subcommittee—he had vigorously questioned executives in the three companies on the same issues. He was regarded by the industry as an enemy. His name was Paul Rand Dixon.

From Cyanamid's point of view, the situation in other parts of the world was not too encouraging either. In Britain, the company's biggest market outside America, Pfizer was locked in a conflict with the Ministry of Health that was just as fierce as its battle with the Defense Department—and for the same reason. The British government, too, was objecting to the high prices that it was being forced to pay for tetracycline. Like its counterparts in Washington, it also had exploited a clause in legislation designed for emergencies and was buying tetracycline for British hospitals—virtually all of which are owned by the state—from Italian sources. Pfizer had sued the government for patent infringement, but the Health Ministry was fighting the case with tenacity.

However, if the news from Washington that fall was not too encouraging, from Cyanamid's point of view, Lyman Duncan was not despondent. For his campaign to expose the Italians sparked into sudden progress.

11

I T was during that crisis-filled October in 1962 that Assistant U.S. Attorney Al Gaynor at last instituted the action that Walter Mansfield had been demanding with growing frustration since April. On the fourteenth floor of New York's Federal Courthouse, he stood before a grand jury, seated traditionally in a curved row, and presented his evidence in the industrial espionage case.

The foreman of the jury signed the indictment against eight men: John Cancelarich, Leonard Fine and Joe Gerace—who, between them, had supplied most of the evidence—Sidney Fox, Nathan Sharff, Caesar Bottone, Elio Salvetti and Count Niccolo Visconti.

Three days later, FBI agents in Suffern, East Paterson and Fort Lee formally seized Fox, Sharff and Bottone and took them before local U.S. commissioners. All three were released on bail.

At all ports of entry into the United States, the names of Salvetti and Visconti were registered. They would be arrested the moment they attempted to enter.

The moment that the news of the indictment was official, the Cyanamid public relations division went into uninhibited action. Within twenty-four hours, background stories to the indictment—which had long lain written by Paul Stessel's writers at Pearl River—were on the desks of news editors throughout the nation. Joe Calitri, in Wayne, sent long cables to the PR managers of all of Cyanamid's drug companies overseas. Several syndicated columnists wrote articles urging the government to stop the Defense Department from buying drugs in Italy and demanded that the laws that made industrial espionage so difficult a crime to prosecute be amended.

The indictment put Cyanamid's charges against the Defense Department and the Italians into a new category. They were now "respectable," brought by the government—albeit reluctantly—and not by the company.

Certainly, it placed Admiral Knickerbocker and the Defense Department in a delicate position, as Duncan had planned from the start that it should.

The Terramycin contract with Count Visconti's Pierrel had been signed in September. Soon supplies of the drug would be coming across the Atlantic. Even though Terramycin was not among the drugs involved in the Fox case, there was no question that the U.S. government was now dealing with a man who had been indicted by an American grand jury on charges alleging industrial espionage conspiracy. Was this the type of foreign contractor to which Knickerbocker should be handing out large bulk contracts for U.S.-patented drugs?

Ever since Mansfield had filed the Cancelarich affidavit, the admiral had known that he could find himself in this situation.

In August he had flown to Italy to talk to Count Visconti. His confused feelings were evident in his report on his return that although he would like to find a reason to declare the count "non-responsive as a potential supplier" because of possible embarrassment to the government, good business judgment dictated the award of the Terramycin contract to Pierrel.

Pierrel was not his only problem. Dr. Giovanni Auletta's Leo was providing bulk tetracycline for successful bids by Premo Laboratories of New Jersey. Auletta had made no effort to conceal that he had actually dealt with Fox, and even though there were no grounds for charges against him, he was named in the Cancelarich confession.

As the admiral saw it, this situation need not be too problematical. Auletta said he was not using the organisms Fox had supplied to him. All he had to do was to explain where he had obtained the bugs he *was* employing in his plant. Then Knickerbocker would have a perfect answer to the angry criticism from Cyanamid—and the industry as a whole—that would follow the indictment.

But Auletta was not much help. He refused to reveal the source of his organisms. He had promised, he said, to keep the information secret.

Knickerbocker warned him that this must inevitably cause difficulties. The U.S. government could not buy drugs whose origin was suspect. But the young tycoon was adamant. He had given his word. He could not break it.

So Knickerbocker blacklisted him. His procurement director called Premo and told Sol Silverang, the executive vice-president, that he must find himself a new supplier.

In January, however, Lyman Duncan's confidence that at last Cyanamid had the initiative in the international conflict was suddenly bruised by alarming news. Until that moment all the cut-price tetracycline had been made in Italy. Now he learned that new competition was imminent—this time on home ground, in California, in defiance of the patents and, most galling of all, with the expert guidance and organisms of an Italian company.

The catalyst that caused the spate of activity at Pearl River during those early days of 1963 was a telephone call to Bill Fulton from a Milan detective agency. Dr. Emilio Braun, he was informed, was scheduled to leave London for Los Angeles on January 18. Traveling with him would be a German technician.

Dr. Braun, as Fulton well knew, was managing director of an Italian drug firm called Fermentfarma. Los Angeles was the base of a newly formed company, Rachel Laboratories.

Back in June, 1962, information had come into the old farmhouse at Pearl River that Rachel might be planning to make a foray into tetracycline production in challenge of the patent. Since it was certain that none of the major U.S. companies would assist Rachel, it meant that it would almost certainly have to get its organisms and know-how from Europe. Lyman Duncan ordered Bill Fulton—who, since Frank Allen had retired, had now become chief of Lederle security—to find out everything he could about Rachel's advisers.

In fact, Duncan was way ahead of the Rachel board at that time. They did not have any advisers on antibiotic production, but they soon faced up to the fact that they were going to need them.

The parent corporation of Rachel Laboratories was International Rectifier—a company that made complex electronic equipment, some of which was used in spacecraft. The firm had been built from a very small base by Eric Lidow, a refugee from Nazi Germany.

During 1961 Lidow had decided that the market for semiconductors—a range of equipment in which International Rectifier did its biggest volume—was due for a shakedown. As a company they needed new fields, into which they could diversify. Then he read the press reports about the fight between the

FTC and the five big drug firms over the tetracycline issue that centered on the validity of the patent.

Lidow had attacked a patent before and emerged with overwhelming triumph. In 1957, when IR was only a $4,000,000 company, he had gone into the business of making controlled rectifiers—a vital component in spacecraft motors—challenging the patents held by Western Electric and by General Electric. Lidow won the battle that ensued and became the world's second biggest manufacturer of controlled rectifiers.

In the spring of 1962, only a few weeks before the Fox story broke in the press, the IR board decided to go into tetracycline —a decision that was not so strange as it might seem, for the company already maintained a substantial staff of chemists for its normal business.

An initial budget of $250,000 was authorized, and it was agreed that the new drug subsidiary would be called Rachel, which was Lidow's mother's name.

At first, according to a company spokesman, the Rachel microbiologists tried to use the bugs that Pfizer and Cyanamid had deposited in the public culture collections as part of the technical process of patenting. But when they failed to build the yields from these bugs up to economic levels, Lidow realized —as Duncan had known from the moment he had heard of its early plans—that Rachel would need help.

By this time the Fox case was in the newspapers, and it was clear that colored as the tetracycline business was by espionage, the company would have to move carefully. Dr. George Krsek, who had joined IR from Merck, was sent to Italy to find technical advisers with organisms that were not tainted in any way by the possibility that they had come from Pearl River.

The firm that Krsek selected—Fermentfarma of Milan—conformed with this specification. Ivan Villax, Fermentfarma's technical director, proved to Krsek's satisfaction that his bugs came from soil in the south of France.

All the same, Krsek could scarcely have chosen as consultants a company to which Cyanamid was more sensitive.

For at the time that John Cancelarich joined Ankermann in Milan, Herbert Wawretchek—the brother of the firm's managing director, Helmuth Wawretchek—was in charge of the fermentations in the plant. Herbert disliked the influx of Americans, and a few weeks after Cancelarich's appointment, he resigned from his brother's company, together with a girl who worked with him, Bridget Gratsch. Both of them joined Fermentfarma, which, like Ankermann, was a relatively new enterprise.

By the time news leaked to Pearl River about the negotiations in Italy of Rachel's Dr. George Krsek, John Cancelarich had made his confession. As a result, Duncan believed that Lederle's tetracycline organisms had been delivered to the Ankermann plant in Milan.

Under the circumstances, the fact that Herbert Wawretchek and Bridget Gratsch—the two people whose job at Ankermann was to work with the bugs—had moved to Fermentfarma had naturally caused the Lederle executives some anxiety about the company. Later Cynamid charged in a U.S. court that Fermentfarma's bugs were the same as those covered by the Lederle patent, but this was rejected by the judge.[27]

Meanwhile, any mention of Fermentfarma was enough to produce an apoplectic reaction in Lyman Duncan. That was why he pressed Bill Fulton hard to get him the information he needed to bring suit.

The security man did his best. He ordered a surveillance of the new Rachel plant that was then under construction, so that he was informed about what was being delivered and by whom. He initiated discreet inquiries among suppliers of chemicals and equipment that were inevitably needed by a new drug firm.

Gradually, a composite picture of Rachel's plans was pieced

together in the old farmhouse at Pearl River. Meanwhile, investigators had been briefed in Milan to report back any facts in the new association between the two firms that could be learned from Fermentfarma.

The phone call from Italy in January alerted Bill Fulton to the fact that the Fermentfarma president was leaving London for Los Angeles on January 18 with a German technician. There was a good chance that this man was Helmuth Wawretchek's brother, Herbert. If so, his presence in America gave Fulton a whole range of opportunity for action. For one thing, it was certain to interest Al Gaynor, who—even if he was not pressing the Fox case too hard—had obtained an indictment against men closely concerned with Ankermann.

From the moment Dr. Braun and his German technician left the Milan airport, they were under constant surveillance by Cyanamid's investigators. They were followed through London Airport to their hotel, where a detective also booked a room. This gave him an opportunity, by getting friendly with the desk clerk, to get a quick glimpse of the passport of the "German." The news that he was, indeed, Herbert Wawretchek, together with his passport number, was promptly phoned to Pearl River.

When the Pan Am jet—with the two men aboard—took off from London for Los Angeles, Walter Mansfield called the Federal Courthouse to inform Al Gaynor.

If Cyanamid's belief that Al Gaynor had dragged his heels over the whole Fox prosecution was justified, they certainly had no ground for complaint that day. When Wawretchek landed in California—under the alert gaze of four Cyanamid investigators, equipped with two cars—a grand jury subpoena was waiting for him. He was required to fly to New York for questioning.

The interrogation of Herbert Wawretchek did little to advance the case against the alleged espionage conspirators. But

Rachel's move into tetracycline production, with the help of Fermentfarma, was to prove very important when the fight between the FTC and Cyanamid and Company flared into bitter open conflict the next year.

Meanwhile, Lyman Duncan now had no doubt at all that the conflict had entered an anxious new phase. There were plenty of hospital purchasing authorities—who lacked the legal freedom of the Defense Department to buy in overseas countries drugs carrying U.S. patents—that were watching Admiral Knickerbocker's operations in Italy with envy. Rachel would have a range of big customers if, as it was clearly gambling, the legal barriers were removed by the FTC.

During this stormy period for Cyanamid and the drugmakers, life for most of the people who worked at Pearl River continued much as usual. The Fox indictment, the FTC case and even the drug bill caused only momentary interest. They all had been in progress for a long, long time, and they did not seem to have changed anything in the plant. Certainly, very few of the Lederle employees had ever heard of Walter Mansfield—whose shelves at 2 Wall Street were now thick with files marked "Cyanamid-Tallyho"—or of Fermentfarma or even of Rachel Laboratories.

The big fermentors were still producing tetracyclines in enormous quantities. Lederle's vans were still transporting thousands of cases of drugs every week from their ten regional depots to drugstores throughout the nation. In the research buildings, Lederle's force of 1,000 scientists was still striving to improve the production techniques of its 800 regular line products and searching for new drugs. In fact, that January, 1963, the teams of detail men were pushing their newest sulfa drug—one of a whole range of sulfas that were designed for new roles that had little to do with attacking bacteria. Quinethazone, Lederle's new product, was for example, a diuretic, whose purpose was to increase the excretion of body fluids.

However, it was a far more spectacular drug that was then

occupying much of Lyman Duncan's time—despite the demands made on him by the various conflicts that his corporation was waging at higher levels. The product was unquestionably sensational, and it had cost Lederle nearly $14,000,000 to develop. Work had, in fact, started on it only two years after Dr. Benjamin Duggar had begun his search for an antibiotic wonder bug.

The big difference between Duncan's new product and Aureomycin—or even Declomycin, for that matter—was that on this occasion Lederle's speculation, though massive, had not matured into a bonanza. This time the company had lost a contest that was international, highly publicized and watched closely by medical authorities throughout the world.

Now, ruefully, Lyman Duncan was doing his best to reap what commercial rewards remained in a drug licensed to him by an opponent—an opponent, furthermore, that had started working on similar lines to that of Lederle scientists long after the program at Pearl River had been set up. If a vivid example was needed to prove that speculation did not always put big profits into the pockets of the drugmakers—despite the high average earnings of the industry—Lederle's fight to develop a polio vaccine provided a perfect case in point.

Polio had been a scourge that—though relatively uncommon by comparison with other diseases—had been the source of a unique kind of fear for the best part of fifty years. It was often lethal. It maimed. Its main target was children. There was no cure, and no amount of money could buy protection. In fact, the disease was more prevalent in prosperous communities than in poorer districts.

When the first major epidemic of the disease struck America in 1916, it created panic. As newspapers in New York City—which bore the brunt of the attack—reported the rising daily figures of victims, polio bore all the appearance of a growing and terrifying plague. Parents stampeded railroads and ferries to get their children out of the city, and the authorities instituted frantic measures to limit the infected area. Health certificates were demanded from the hordes of escaping New Yorkers before they were allowed out of the city boundaries.

All kinds of conflicting theories on the cause of the disease were publicized through the columns of the press. Brooklyn police rounded up 215 cats on the theory that the animals were carriers of the scourge. The terror that gripped America reached its peak in August when, on a single day, 3,200 new cases were reported.

By the fall—the end of the polio season, as it came to be called—27,000 people in the United States had contracted the disease. Of these, 6,000 had died. A third of both totals were New Yorkers.

It was the beginning of a regular pattern that occurred every summer. Some years the epidemics were worse than others, but every spring inevitably marked the beginning of a terrible annual toll. Then, gradually, the disease broadened its range, attacking adults, as well as children. In 1921 it claimed Franklin D. Roosevelt, who, as his stature grew with his political career, remained an ever-present public symbol of the tragic results of polio and the courage that was demanded of its victims.

In 1938, when Roosevelt's prestige was still soaring, the National Foundation for Infantile Paralysis was founded in his name. Its president, one of Roosevelt's former law partners with a brilliant flair for public relations, was Basil O'Connor.

O'Connor's success in raising funds has probably been unequaled since. Between 1938 and 1962 he inspired the contribution of $630,000,000, much of which poured into the foundation HQ after O'Connor set up the March of Dimes and the later Mothers' March on Polio.

The sheer size of the foundation's resources produced a unique situation in the area of drug development. For in the long conflict that was about to begin—a conflict that centered on the best means of defeating polio—the main contestants were not, as was usual, commercial companies ranged against one another. Only one—Lederle—was in business. The other two were a privately financed foundation and a Communist government. Even though luck inevitably played a big part, the story provides an interesting case history for those studying the different methods available to society to obtain the drugs it needs.

Even before Cyanamid had purchased Lederle in the early 1930's, chemists at Pearl River had specialized in biological products, of which vaccines formed an important part.

In 1939, when the Cyanamid president had authorized the speculation for new drugs, virus research was one of the main areas in which Dr. Malcolm had ordered his fast-growing force of scientists to concentrate. To direct his program in the newly constructed virus research building, he had appointed a reserved, dedicated young man in his mid-thirties—bald and bespectacled, like so many scientists—named Dr. Harold Cox.

Cox—who, like Malcolm, came to Pearl River from the Public Health Service—had behind him an outstanding record that included the development of vaccines against both typhus and Rocky Mountain spotted fever. He was one of America's leading young virologists and was ideally suited to head an important arm of Lederle's new aggressive research effort.

In the summer of 1946—while Dr. Benjamin Duggar, in a neighboring block, was working on his new antibiotic-producing bug, *Streptomyces aureofaciens*—America was in the midst of one of the worst polio epidemics it had yet experienced. Cox asked Dr. Malcolm for permission to set up a polio research program, and in the prevailing mood of that summer, this was enthusiastically granted.

Although science had provided physicians with medicines—such as antibiotics—to cure diseases caused by bacteria, they had not discovered any techniques for treating illnesses caused by the much smaller virus organisms. The one weapon available to doctors—and one that they had used with great effect against many scourges—was prevention by vaccination.

When faced with an invasion of harmful germs, the human body has a defense system. It manufactures in the bloodstream an army of antibodies that fight off the attack by attaching themselves to the viruses in an attempt to prevent them from entering its cells. Normally, they are successful. When they fail, illness follows. But the viruses often become an enemy that the body remembers because, once they are made, the antibodies remain in the bloodstream. If a repeat assault is made, they can normally present an adequate resistance. The body has then developed immunity—at least for a time—against that particular disease. The sheer size of this internal struggle is indicated by the single fact that 25,000,000 polio viruses would fit on the head of a pin.

The principle of vaccination is to introduce into the body disease germs that are strong enough to create antibodies but so weak that they do not cause the illness.

This precise balance is very hard to attain; that is why the development of a live vaccine inevitably takes a long time. The corners can be cut to some extent by using viruses that have been killed, for even then they will create an antibody reaction. But normally the immunity they produce is neither as complete nor as long-lasting as that of live viruses. As a result, booster doses are often needed.

From the start, Cox and his team at Pearl River programmed the whole weight of their effort to developing a live polio vaccine on the theory that only by this method could they stamp out the disease effectively.

The problems faced by Cox and his assistant, Dr. Hilary Koprowski, who was in direct charge of the project, were enormous, largely because relatively little was known about polio.

They started with a virus, taken from a human patient, that they tried systematically to render harmless. Pasteur, searching for his rabies vaccine, had discovered that a virus could be weakened by growing it from generation to generation in an unnatural host—in other words, by infecting animals that were not normally vulnerable to the disease, recovering the virus from them, and using this to infect yet other animals.

This was what Cox and Koprowski did with their human strain of virus. The "unnatural host" animals they used were cotton rats.

It was a long and cumbersome technique, revolutionized in 1949—three years after they started—when a team at Harvard Medical School under Dr. John Enders won a Nobel Prize in Medicine for discovering that it was possible to grow the polio virus in the chopped-up kidney tissue of a monkey. This meant that the virus could be developed in a test tube—vitally important for the mass production that would follow the basic research period.

There was a certain irony in the fact that while, in one research building at Pearl River, the scientists were breeding up antibiotic-producing bugs to develop better and better strains, there were other men in another building, breeding down polio bugs in an effort to weaken the family.

However, by January, 1950, there was at Pearl River a polio vaccine that, after repeated tests in the brains and nervous systems of monkeys, was regarded as a possibility for human use. To prove their confidence, both Cox and Koprowski adopted the role of human guinea pigs and swallowed their new product. They were the first men to be orally immunized against polio. The following month they set up a controlled trial on twenty people who were not Lederle employees. Proudly, Koprowski reported in the *American Journal of Hygiene* that "all non-immune volunteers promptly developed antibodies in their blood. In not a single instance were there any signs of illness noted."

To Dr. Malcolm, happily watching the soaring sales of Aureomycin, it must have seemed as though another wonder drug, with a tremendous potential both for prestige and for profit, was on the stocks. Lederle's reputation, as a result of the research program that Malcolm had fathered some twelve years earlier, was already greatly enhanced by the progress of his scientists. The new vaccine, it seemed, would push it to even higher pinnacles.

Had Malcolm known that even ten years later his vaccine would not have been in general use in America, he would have been appalled. But all kinds of trouble lay ahead of his virologists. For one thing, polio was caused by more than 100 types of virus, and immunity against one kind did not necessarily mean that there was no danger from another.

In 1951 a group of scientists from several universities discovered that despite the number of different strains, they all stemmed from three main types of virus. Cox and Koprowski replanned their campaign, aiming to develop three different types of vaccine that would, together, be effective against each category of polio.

Moving cautiously, testing the vaccines repeatedly on monkeys that were then slaughtered so that the effects on their nervous system could be scientifically assessed, they began a series of human tests on a bigger scale. In 1952 they gave vaccines against two of the three types of polio to a group of eighty-five children at Sonoma State Hospital, in California, with their parents' permission.

In the case of polio, clinical trials raised even greater ethical problems than those involved in the testing of some other drugs —an issue that was to move into the public spotlight after the thalidomide scandal in a few years' time. Even monkeys, the nearest animals to man after the apes, did not contract the disease in the same way or as easily as humans. "This meant," comments John Rowan Wilson in *Margin of Safety*, his book on the vaccine story, "that for Koprowski's live virus vaccine, there was really no suitable experimental animal at all. The trial had to begin with man."

Meanwhile, Basil O'Connor, with millions of dollars at his disposal in the national foundation, had taken the opposite view to Lederle. Every year polio was claiming thousands of victims. The chances were that a killed vaccine—regarded by many virologists as safer—could be developed more quickly than a live one. O'Connor put the main weight of his support behind Dr. Jonas Salk, professor of biology at the University of Pittsburgh—in an operation that involved the import and slaughter of 30,000 monkeys.

In 1952 Salk conducted his first test with killed vaccine on a group of children in Pennsylvania, and after two more years of sustained work on the vaccine, a mass nationwide trial was organized in which 200,000 children took part.

The foundation was highly pleased with the results. The vaccine did not provide 100 percent immunity, but clearly it could provide a formidable weapon in the fight against the disease.

O'Connor made plans for it to be manufactured for national distribution in the early months of 1955 before the polio season started. The foundation placed orders amounting to $9,-000,000. In the full glare of coast-to-coast publicity—which naturally attracted even more funds—a massive vaccination program was instituted. Since Lederle was one of the best-equipped firms in America for making vaccines, the foundation invited it, together with others, to manufacture the Salk killed product. But Dr. Malcolm was backing his virologists' policy of aiming for a live vaccine. He wrote that Lederle would produce the vaccine if called on to help out, but that "it wished to pursue the concept that a live vaccine would confer longer immunity."

So other companies made the vaccine under the care of the Laboratory of Biologics Control in Bethesda, Maryland, which, directed by HEW, was responsible for the standard of biological products—as opposed to other drugs, for which the FDA was responsible—made in America.

In April the first signs of trouble began to mark the program which had been launched with a speed that, like the resources behind it, was quite exceptional. From California came a report that five children who had just been immunized had been paralyzed by polio. This followed an isolated case in Chicago.

The mass trial had shown that the vaccine was not 100 percent effective. There was always the possibility, too, that the child had already contracted the disease before immunization. The only disturbing aspect was that all six of these children had been given vaccine made by the same company—Cutter Laboratories.

Reports of other cases of the disease appearing in vaccinated children flowed into the Laboratory of Biologics Control from states all over the continent—especially from Idaho, where twenty-two children who had been immunized, were struck down by the disease.

On May 6 the Surgeon General, the government official who had the powers to ban further production of the Salk vaccine, stopped distribution. Although Cutter had made its vaccine to the specification laid down by the government, the danger inherent in a killed vaccine—at least in those early days—had materialized. Somehow, in the massacre of the viruses in the production process, an organism had escaped death and remained undetected in the testing process.

In fact, all the companies had experienced great technical problems while manufacturing the vaccine.

Coming after the sustained blast of publicity, the news inspired an anticlimax that was awful in the literal sense of the word. Polio had not been beaten after all.

By the end of the year, however, the technical difficulties had been overcome, and the vaccine was once more available, with official approval, to American children.

Although Lederle had not been involved in the making of the killed vaccine, the experience of that year greatly affected its program for the development of a live product. For the government, having at last survived the ordeal and obtained a vaccine that seemed safe, was very nervous about any new variety that, even if it might be more effective in the long run, was still unproved.

The result was that major clinical trials in America for the Lederle product were impossible to organize. Cox and his team, if they were going to be able to develop their vaccine, would clearly have to look abroad for human subjects.

The next year, in 1956, they were given their opportunity. Dr. George Dick, professor of microbiology at Queen's University, Belfast, was impressed by one of Koprowski's papers in an American medical journal and arranged with public health officials in Northern Ireland to mount a trial of the Lederle strains of vaccine against two of the three polio types.

The result of Dick's investigation was a disaster. In some of the cases he investigated, the virus changed and grew stronger while it was within the children on whom he tested it. Although it successfully built up the antibodies, the virus, when excreted, was shown to be capable of causing paralytic polio—even though it had not been when it was swallowed. Furthermore, in the case of one strain, two people who had been living with vaccinated subjects were actually infected with the disease.

"Thus," as an old Lederle press release puts it, treating the unpleasant incident as briefly as possible, "more than eight years of research went out of the window."

It created a management crisis at Pearl River. Should Lederle cut its losses? Or should it pour even more millions into the gamble that it could develop new strains that were not virulent or would not change their characteristics? Koprowski resigned to join the Wistar Research Institute in Philadelphia, taking with him several of the Lederle research staff. Cox remained and persuaded Lyman Duncan, who was now running Pearl River, and Malcolm, now president of the corporation, to allow him to continue.

It could be said, with the advantage of hindsight, that it was possibly the wrong decision. For by now there was a new contender for the live vaccine laurels—Dr. Albert Sabin, a white-haired Polish-born immigrant, who was often compared in appearance with Groucho Marx. Sabin, professor of research pediatrics at the University of Cincinnati College of Medicine, was also working on a live strain of polio vaccine.

At one time there was a faint possibility that he might combine his efforts with those of Dr. Cox at Pearl River, but this never materialized, and the two scientists became fierce competitors. While Cox had the big resources available to a major American corporation, Sabin sought his backing from a far wealthier patron—the Russian government, which, apart from all the other advantages, was in a position to offer him massive clinical trial facilities.

Cox, with his reorganized team, developed strains of virus that lacked the character faults of the vaccine tested in Belfast. But this failure in Ireland had only made American authorities, already highly nervous, even more resistant. A small trial was eventually arranged in Minnesota, but mainly Lederle looked to Latin America for its field experiments.

There they were more welcome. In April, 1958, the town of Andes in Colombia was struck by a serious outbreak of polio. The Colombian government approached the Pan American Health Organization with a request for the Salk vaccine. PAHO officials considered that a live vaccine had a better chance of stopping the epidemic. Nearly 7,000 children were inoculated with vaccines developed by Cox's team against all three types of polio. The outbreak was halted.

At Pearl River, Lyman Duncan began to feel that after all, the decision to continue the fight for a live vaccine would pay off. Another vaccination program was mounted in Colombia, this time with 130,000 children, followed by others in Nicaragua, Costa Rica and Haiti.

Meanwhile, Dr. Sabin with his Russian sponsors, was also mounting enormous trials with his live vaccine. Among others, he stopped an epidemic in Singapore, though most of his field testing was conducted with vast numbers of subjects in the Communist countries.

Hilary Koprowski, Cox's former assistant, was also pushing ahead with trials with a vaccine, but ultimately a head-on clash occurred between Cox and Sabin.

In 1959—the year of the start of the Kefauver hearings, of Admiral Knickerbocker's first contracts in Italy, of Sidney Fox's resignation from Pearl River, and of the FTC's courtroom fight over tetracycline with Cyanamid and the other companies— the International Scientific Congress on Live Virus Vaccines was held in Washington. It was at this that Sabin, who had published no recent reports on his work in medical journals, made the sensational announcement that he had now tested his vaccine on 4,500,000 people with good antibody response and, more important, no ill effects.

The results that Cox had achieved in Latin America—and in bigger, more recent trials in Minnesota—were impressive, but against Sabin's millions, he could only claim that his vaccine had been tested in hundreds of thousands.

The Russians asserted that with the help of the Sabin vaccine, polio would soon be an illness of history. It would no longer be a contemporary disease.

The Salk killed vaccine, which had clearly made a big contribution to the fight against polio, had certainly not eradicated it. In 1957 the number of cases of the disease in America had fallen to a new low of 2,499, but they had risen sharply in 1958. The figure for 1959 was to be 6,289. Clearly, there was a strong case for licensing a live vaccine, but memories of 1955 were still unpleasantly fresh.

Throughout the second half of 1959 the conflict between Sabin and Cox—each hoping that the Laboratory of Biologics Control would license his vaccine for use in America—grew fiercer. Eventually the two scientists agreed to submit their strains to arbitration by an independent investigator. The man chosen was one of America's most famous virologists, Dr. Joseph Melnick of Houston, Texas.

Melnick reported in favor of Sabin's strains, ruling that Cox's were more virulent. However, he also commented that "if caution was called for in 1954 and 1955 when the Salk vaccine was introduced into large-scale field use, then caution should also be the watchword now." So the Surgeon General played safe and advised everyone to continue using the Salk killed product, pending further investigation of the live vaccines.

The arbitration was yet another severe blow for the Pearl River team, but worse setbacks lay ahead.

During 1959 Lyman Duncan ordered an all-out effort to overcome the remaining problems. For Lederle—despite the result of the arbitration—had one advantage over its competitors. Cox had found a way of combining his strains so that one pill could be taken in defense against the three varieties of polio. Sabin's three vaccines could only be taken separately.

In the spring of 1960, for all practical purposes, the contest came to an end. Cyanamid was given two new opportunities to display its product. The health authorities in Dade County, Miami, Florida, were growing disturbed about the Salk vaccine. In 1959 there had been forty-six cases of paralytic polio. Of these, seven had received three Salk injections. Two of them had died. As a result, the Dade County authorities were prepared to mount a trial of Cox's three-in-one oral vaccine.

By then the Sabin vaccine had been used in national vaccination programs in Russia and the Iron Curtain countries. This left West Berlin, an island in East Germany, exposed.

Politically, an epidemic of the disease in this small non-Communist territory would have compared badly with Socialist polio-free areas on the other side of its boundaries. The city authorities appealed for supplies of live vaccine, which Cox, at Pearl River, was only too delighted to provide.

The results of these operations in both areas doomed the Cox product. Dade County reported several cases of the disease, but in West Berlin, thirty-four people fell ill with polio. Of these, twenty-three had taken Cox's combined three-strain pill.

Even today, after careful investigation, no one knows exactly what went wrong in Berlin. It was, however, the last throw. Lyman Duncan ordered the end of the program, and Lederle announced that it had stopped work on the Cox strains. Instead, it negotiated a license with Sabin—together, of course, with other applicants. Both Pfizer and Wyeth were given the same facilities.

In August, 1961, two of the Sabin strains were licensed by the National Institutes of Health for use in the United States. Approval for the third was granted the following March.

Cox's team, making the best of an unhappy situation, went to work to incorporate the three Sabin strains into a single product—something about which some scientists were openly skeptical because they believed that the strains interfered with one another when given simultaneously.

Throughout 1962 Cox worked on his new program with his rival's product. By the spring of 1963 Lederle was ready to launch its Sabin-based trivalent vaccine under the brand name of Orimune—and the Surgeon General was pressing it to do so before the start of the polio season.

But Cyanamid's fingers had been badly burned in Berlin. It faced civil suits from polio victims that were hard to defend. Since the human body takes three weeks to acquire immunity after vaccination, some of the litigants could well have contracted the disease before they were given Cox's product. But this was an impossible fact to prove. Almost always, the courts ruled against the manufacturer.

For this reason, the thought of introducing the vaccine to a U.S. population of 200,000,000 at a time of the year when some people were almost sure to have already contracted the disease was formidable. The alternative was to postpone marketing the drug until the fall, when the polio season would have ended —when, too, thousands more Americans would have been crippled for life by the disease.

Once again, the Cyanamid management faced the crucial conflict—human lives against big financial risks.

It was a hard decision. Lyman Duncan tried to make it easier by flying to Washington to ask the Surgeon General to indemnify Cyanamid against suit. But the principle was clearly too dangerous. The administration, he was told, would never agree.

The meeting, held in the Cyanamid HQ at Wayne to decide what action it should take, was tense. "I remember," Duncan recalls, "that someone came out hard against it. 'Good God,' he said, 'we can't afford to take this kind of risk.' Weed Malcolm turned to me and asked: 'Are you completely convinced you can stop polio with this vaccine?' "

There was no doubt in Duncan's mind. The trials had been exhaustive. "All right," answered Malcolm, "in that case we'll take a chance. We're just going to have to gamble that it'll be a light polio year."

Fortunately, it was. Pfizer and Wyeth—the two companies who had also acquired licenses from Sabin—made the same decision. The fact that the total effort was successful is proved by the steep drop in annual cases. Today, with U.S. yearly figures hovering around the 100 mark, polio is no longer a disease of consequence.

During that spring, when Malcolm made the decision that— after seventeen years of struggle and controversy—made the polio vaccine just another of Lederle's line products, the appeal hearings in the tetracycline case in the FTC building in Washington were making their slow but steady progress. They would soon develop into violent activity.

Walter Mansfield, commuting between New York and the capital, was also pressing on hard with Cyanamid's case against Sidney Fox with the aim of forcing him into jail, in the hope that he would confess to his role in the espionage conspiracy. For more than a year, the chemist's attorneys had been exploiting the appeal tactics that were open to them to protect their client against Mansfield. But by July they had exhausted everything that they could do—at least for the time being. A final appeal was rejected by a state judge.

The chemist was arrested in the courtroom by a deputy sheriff, and later that day the big doors of the red-brick civil prison on New York's West Thirty-seventh Street closed behind him.

12

WALTER Mansfield's strategy to make Fox talk by keeping him in prison was challenged very fast. Within a month, on the urging of the chemist's lawyers, a judge in the New York State Courthouse in Foley Square ordered Cyanamid to prove its case fully in a civil trial. Otherwise, he ruled, he would release him from jail.

This ruling occurred in court on a sultry August morning. Mansfield was certain that he could persuade the judge to change his mind if he could return that afternoon and announce a date for the criminal trial, mounted by the government, of the espionage conspirators. For this, he needed Al Gaynor's cooperation.

With this aim, he left the State Courthouse and hurried into the tall Federal Building next door. Apart from the confessions of Fox's partners and his other evidence, Mansfield had now handed Gaynor a new and vital witness. After a stormy meeting with Cyanamid's attorney in Montreal, Helmuth Wawretchek, managing director of Ankermann, had agreed to testify for the government. His purpose—now that his former business partners had been indicted—was to clear his name. Since he had actually bought organisms from Nat Sharff [19]—and signed a formal contract which he had now handed over—his evidence would clearly be most important.

But the meeting on that August morning between the two attorneys was just as abortive as all the others. Al Gaynor insisted that he could not yet mount the Fox trial. The department was busy, and the case had to take its turn.

"All I needed," Mansfield recalls, "was a date, but Gaynor wouldn't give me one. I tried hard to persuade him. I pointed out that if I had to try the case in the civil courts, it'd mean revealing most of my evidence to the other side. I'd have to put John Cancelarich on the stand as my main witness. I'd hold back what I could, but naturally I'd have to be sure of winning."

But Gaynor—handsome, polished, amiably polite, even apologetic—would not be moved.

Angrily, believing that the antitrust case against Cyanamid was the cause of the government's inertia, Mansfield took a cab back to his office and called Lyman Duncan.

Cyanamid had two alternatives: Either it could let Fox out of jail and wait until eventually the government got around to organizing his trial in the federal criminal court, or it could hold him in prison and stage in the civil courts its own trial, which would virtually be a dress rehearsal for Al Gaynor. If it won—as Mansfield was certain it would—it would give the drug company an even closer hold on Fox.

Duncan was in no doubt what Cyanamid should do. The drugmakers' public image—spoiled by the Kefauver hearings and shattered by the thalidomide disaster—was still very clouded. The Defense Department, although it had blacklisted Pierrel and Leo, was still buying tetracycline in vast quantities from Italian companies. In California, Rachel Laboratories was still pressing on, with Italian help, with their plans to challenge the U.S. tetracycline patent. The Cyanamid vice-president wanted action. "Walter," he said, "we've horsed around long enough. We're going to trial."

Mansfield had only four weeks to prepare for the trial, which started on September 11 and continued for nearly three months. It was a strange case because the broad implications were more important than the issues in dispute. It was, in effect, a trial within a trial. If the judge ruled against Cyanamid, with the corporation's confessor witnesses—and in addition to Cancelarich and Fine, they included a man who had actually bought bugs and know-how from Fox—it would support the contention of the chemist's lawyers that the whole affair was fabricated: a Machiavellian scheme, it was inferred, built on bribed or at least pressured testimony, for political ends. These were not specified in detail, but Cyanamid's campaign to portray the Italian drug executives as men who preferred to buy from industrial spies as a quicker and surer way to success than research was no secret. Nor was its hope that it could force the Defense Department to stop buying Italian-sourced products and to give its contracts once more to American companies.

Clearly, however, if the judge found Fox not guilty, it would place a question mark over Cyanamid's motives and, in view of the background, could erupt into a big scandal, with political repercussions.

The overt issues were simple enough. Cyanamid charged that Fox had stolen its bugs and process secrets and sold them to American and Italian companies. Fox's answer was that this was untrue. He had acted as a consultant, offering nothing more than his experience. He agreed that most of the alleged meetings with Italians had occurred but insisted that this conformed with his role as a professional chemical expert.

For five weeks, John Cancelarich was on the stand under constant pressure by Theodore Wolkoff, Fox's counsel, whose dramatic courtroom tactics were aimed at exposing Cyanamid's key witness as a liar. Quietly, Cancelarich told the story that he had already described in detail in his sworn confession.

Hundreds of the microfilms that Fox and Cancelarich had made of Lederle process documents were projected in the courtroom, as Wolkoff questioned Cancelarich in detail about each one.

On one occasion, the judge asked suddenly, "Mr. Wolkoff, are you going to dispute that this man [Cancelarich] stole the stuff?"

"I think that the story is a figment of his imagination," answered the defense attorney. "I don't think he ever stole it. I think it's an apocryphal story . . . to nail Dr. Fox to the cross."

Week after week the case continued, pitched on this issue: Who was lying—Fox or the others?

At last, on December 5, the trial came to an end.

Five weeks later, in January, 1964, the judge handed down his ruling. He found that John Cancelarich and Leonard Fine had told the truth. "The testimony of Fox . . . is not accepted as credible," he said. The documents and reports that Fox had sold were not in the public domain—as the defense had tried to show at one stage of the trial—but contained confidential and secret information. The signatures on the microfilm process slips were not forgeries but were written by Dr. Fox. The chemist, the judge concluded, had masterminded the conspiracy, and Cyanamid was entitled to judgment.

The joy at Wayne and Pearl River was unrestrained. At a lunch at the plant Lyman Duncan made a formal, though light-hearted, presentation to their attorney that was cynical but apt: a fox's tail mounted on a plaque that bore the words "They said it couldn't be done—Tallyho!"

But for Fox who heard the news in jail, it spelled out a bleak future. It seemed unlikely that the jury in the criminal case against him would reach a different decision from a judge who had listened to the evidence for three months. Worse, as a result of the trial, Cyanamid could hold him in jail indefinitely.

It was the end of the road. In February he broke. He offered formally to talk. Cyanamid dropped all suits against him and agreed to his release from the civil jail.

In Mansfield's office the fox's tail was removed tactfully from the wall, and for days, the chemist sat there with him, relating the true story as he knew it.

The Fox confession—coupled with a similar statement he made to the FBI—gave Mansfield more ammunition to press Al Gaynor and Robert Morgenthau, the U.S. Attorney for New York's Southern District, to bring the criminal case to trial.

On July 14, 1964, Gaynor appeared once more before a grand jury in the Federal Courthouse and asked it to vote a new indictment. Two new names were added to the list—Seymour Salb and Maurice Rosenblatt, consultant to the large and prestigious Italian drug firm Le Petit.

Robert Morgenthau issued a statement to the press claiming that "it was one of the first indictments in the field of industrial espionage," for it charged the defendants with transporting, not only organisms, which were unquestionably tangible property, but also documents containing secret research information.

This time Sidney Fox pleaded guilty to the charges. The case did not go to trial for nearly two years, and when it did, Al Gaynor had temporarily left the U.S. Attorney's staff, leaving it in the hands of another prosecutor. Fox was a key witness in the government's case, and despite repeated attempts by defense lawyers to use his lies on oath in the civil case to make his testimony in the criminal trial seem suspect, the jury believed he was telling the truth.

Nat Sharff, Seymour Salb and Caesar Bottone all were found guilty and sentenced to two years in jail. Fox, Cancelarich and Fine—despite intervention by Cyanamid's lawyers and the prosecution attorneys—were given six months each. Count Visconti, Elio Salvetti and Maurice Rosenblatt remained in Italy outside the jurisdiction of the court. Joe Gerace—praised by the judge for his voluntary confession of the tiny part he had played—got a suspended sentence.

Meanwhile, Cyanamid continued with its campaign against Italian drug firms. Back in July, 1963, Mansfield had filed part of Fox's affidavit and brought suit against Maurice Rosenblatt, who, although he was consultant to Le Petit in Milan, was an American citizen. The company claimed the astronomical damages of $5,000,000.

It inspired a spirited reaction from the penthouse executive suite at the Le Petit head office block in Milan. Edward Gottlieb & Associates, the New York PR firm, issued a statement on behalf of Le Petit. Fox's statement, it said, was untrue and "inconsistent with depositions he was reported to have made previously under oath in another suit." Le Petit had been making and selling tetracycline since 1954—five years before the alleged thefts—and had been doing so since 1956 under a license from Pfizer. The company had never planned to make Declomycin.

Maurice Rosenblatt, Le Petit's consultant, whom Fox swore had engineered the deal, asserted that the action had "been brought by the American Cyanamid Company in New York for the real purpose of furthering its design, in concert with other American pharmaceutical companies, to deprive American consumers of the benefits of competition by excluding the products of the Italian pharmaceutical industry from the American market."

But Cyanamid was given judgment in its case against Rosenblatt—tried in his absence.

Technically, the verdicts at the end of the Fox case were a triumph for Lyman Duncan. Walter Mansfield had given him precisely what he had been demanding since the fall of 1961. He had got justice against the men who had robbed his plant and the foreigners who had financed them by providing a market.

He had branded Italian firms as crooks exploiting American brains. He had got in some hard punches against the government—proved, in fact, that it had been promoting industrial espionage, which was now accepted as a serious commercial risk for U.S. drug firms.

When the dust cleared, however, it became evident that most of the achievement, in terms of results beyond the courtroom, had been in the intangible area of public relations—which, without question, the drugmakers needed. But in the major power struggle, nothing was changed. The case had not even stopped the Defense Department from buying drugs in Italy, even if it had to be a lot more careful whom it dealt with. Rachel Laboratories, with Italian help, was still proceeding with its tetracycline plans in California. Premo was still importing bulk drugs from Italy.

There is some evidence that the Fox case helped achieve one of Duncan's aims: It proved that Cyanamid's scientists were working to good effect. After the trial, there was a lessening tendency for the enemies of the industry to mock research as useless. It became rarer for them to suggest, as Kefauver tried to show, that the invention of the American drug industry was pathetically small.

The change was one of direction, rather than substance, but at least it was more fairly based. For now the criticism was pitched on the premise that the discoveries of the drugmakers did not justify the price barriers that were responsible for excessive profits.

(Today Duncan claims that these limited results were all he ever sought. It is hard to accept this when the background that existed in 1961 is considered—with Cyanamid smarting under recent indictment and the drugmakers as a whole under searing attack. Apart from the obvious need to stop espionage—Merck, after all, prosecuted its espionage cases vigorously even though it was not under assault by the Justice Department—all the indications suggest that Duncan hoped the case would give him ammunition in the bigger battles. There is no doubt that it did this. What is more, Walter Mansfield continued to use it in conflicts that lay ahead. But—in the opinion of this writer— it never truly fulfilled its promise.)

At any rate, the Cyanamid management had little time to savor its moment of triumph. It was, in fact, going to need every particle of ammunition that the case had given it. For in December, 1963, only twelve days after the civil trial of Fox had ended, the tetracycline companies were fighting against the biggest attack they had yet encountered from a government agency.

13

THE drug bill promoted by Senator Kefauver, who died only a few months after it had become law in 1962, had not satisfied the political enemies of the industry. They wanted far stronger controls. They wanted to break the whole system of brand names under which doctors were forced to rely on the drug firms for much of their information. They wanted to weaken the rigid effect of patents. But most of all, they wanted to smash the high price barriers and the big profit levels that these sustained. For this was an area that the Kefauver bill had barely affected.

For the time being, however, there was little that the anti-industry pressure groups could do. Congress was still digesting its last dose of drug legislation and opposing the social aid programs that President Kennedy had initiated.

However, the opponents of the drugmakers were to derive

some consolation in the limited area of the tetracyclines. In December, 1963, the antitrust conflict between Cyanamid and Company and the government, which had lain dormant since 1961 while the FTC held further hearings, erupted once more. The FTC reversed the earlier decision of its examiner in favor of the companies. Formally, it ordered Pfizer, as holder of the patent, to license all domestic applicants to make tetracycline on at least the same terms that it had granted to other companies named in the conspiracy charges.

In short, apart from allowing royalty payments, the FTC was removing the protection provided by the tetracycline patent.

Promptly, Pfizer mounted an appeal, but the order opened the legal gates to companies and authorities that had been watching Admiral Knickerbocker's operations in Italy with care.

Back in August the FTC had published the opinion that the patent was invalid. Since then, Herman Nolen, president of McKesson & Robbins, America's biggest drug wholesaler, had twice approached Pfizer for a license to sell unbranded tetracycline.

In April, 1964, he made the request a third time, offering to pay a higher royalty than the 2½ percent suggested by the Federal Trade Commission. Pfizer flatly refused.

In August, McKesson, deciding to challenge Pfizer, began to sell to drugstores a generic tetracycline—with no trade name—at a third of the price charged for the branded products of the five main companies. This would have concerned Lyman Duncan in any case, but there was one salient fact about the situation that infuriated him. McKesson made no secret of its supplier. It was Rachel Laboratories in California—the firm that had obtained their bugs and know-how from the Milan company, Fermentfarma, that employed Helmuth Wawretchek's brother, Herbert.

When Lyman Duncan, breakfasting at 7 A.M. in Hastings, read the news in the New York *Times,* he flung the paper to the ground and stalked out of the house. As he entered his office that day, he snapped at his secretary to get him the legal department on the phone.

Within days, a letter was on Herman Nolen's desk in the McKesson building on East Forty-fourth Street in New York City. Lederle Laboratories was canceling all its distribution contracts with the firm. McKesson would no longer be able to offer pharmacists throughout the nation Lederle's 800 products. This represented an enormous loss of business.

Immediately, McKesson went to court to ask a judge to issue an injunction preventing Cyanamid from taking this action.[27] The shadow of Sidney Fox reached across the whole trial, for the hard core of Walter Mansfield's case was that McKesson came into court with "unclean hands." Fermentfarma's bugs and process, he claimed, had been stolen from Lederle and sold to Ankermann Italiana. Herbert Wawretchek and Bridget Gratsch had joined Fermentfarma from Ankermann. He called independent expert witnesses who stated that the Fermentfarma bug that Rachel was using—*Streptomyces lusitanus*—was exactly the same as Cyanamid's *Streptomyces aureofaciens*.

But the judge ruled against Cyanamid. Lederle was ordered to continue supplying McKesson.

Meanwhile, another assault had been launched—this time from a very big buyer indeed: New York City.

Major General Roger Brown—a short, dark-eyed Air Force commander who had controlled a force of fighter bombers in the Allied invasion of Europe—was the city's commissioner of purchases. He controlled a budget of $100,000,000 a year, which included the purchase of drugs for twenty-one municipal hospitals. Already Brown had fought out a price battle with one big pharmaceutical firm. When the salesman for Parke, Davis had refused to cut the price of Chloromycetin for bulk orders— "you pay the same for one bottle as you do for five thousand," he insisted—Brown retorted: "Right, from now on, we'll buy one bottle at a time."

And that—according to Brown—was what the city did. For the next few days, it sent Parke, Davis hundreds of orders, each for only one bottle of the drug. The tactic caused such confusion in the Parke, Davis offices that Brown was asked to meet the company's president in Detroit. The two men worked out a deal over a game of golf. New York City got a discount of 15 percent.

Even though the new Federal Trade Commission decision was being appealed by Pfizer, Brown was advised that there was now nothing to prevent the city from buying from Italian sources. In March he was publicly pressured. William Haddad, onetime political assistant to both Kefauver and Robert Kennedy, was running for Congress. From his campaign headquarters on Seventy-second Street, he charged that the city was losing millions of dollars by paying far more than it needed to for tetracycline for its hospitals. Haddad had long been a vigorous opponent of the big drug firms.

Pfizer countered Haddad's charges by issuing a warning in a press statement that the company would sue the city if it proceeded with its plans to buy from Premo. By this time Premo had got the contract.

And where was Premo getting its supplies, now that it could not buy from Leo? From two firms, one of which was Fermentfarma. By then, too, Premo—like McKesson & Robbins—had launched its own generic tetracycline at a price that was nearly a third of that of the big companies.

By August, 1964, the maze of conflicts reached their peak. Pfizer sued New York City and Premo, both of which filed countersuits charging the five tetracycline companies with illegal price-fixing. New York demanded triple damages of $39,-000,000. Premo was more modest. It claimed $30,000,000.

None of these actions was formally fought out in court. Eventually Pfizer—operating presumably on a principle of "if you can't beat them, join them"—settled its quarrel with Premo and became its main supplier of bulk tetracycline. New York

City decided to await the result of the government criminal antitrust case. Cyanamid patched up its quarrel with Rachel Laboratories in a secret deal on which both companies have refused to divulge any details. What was certain was that Rachel continued to produce and sell tetracycline in America.

Meanwhile, the attacks had broken the price barrier of the old tetracycline producers. In May, 1964—a few weeks before McKesson and Premo moved into the market—the prices dropped by 20 percent. Two years later, in April, 1966, they fell a further 15 percent.

In January, 1967, following yet another cut, a bottle of sixteen capsules cost the drugstore only $1.84—some twenty years, millions of dollars of litigation cost, and many many months of executives' time since Weed Malcolm first decreed that the pharmacist should pay $15 for a bottle of Aureomycin.

By then the pressure in Washington on the drugmakers was growing once more. This time it was not so spectacular as Kefauver's attacks. The public had now grown so accustomed to strident criticism of the men who produced their medication that these events did not often rate front-page news. It was, however, to be a lot more damaging than the sensational tactics of the late Senator from Tennessee eight years before.

To some extent, this was probably due to a gradual acceptance of some of the ideas that Kefauver had aired, a growing belief that—important though incentive was in a country that had been developed by individual enterprise—drugs could possibly be in a special category.

However, the main reason for this changing climate of opinion in Washington—which enabled the enemies of the drugmakers to make quiet but steady progress—lay in the fact that America was taking its first painful steps toward government-sponsored medicine. In 1965 Congress had at last approved the Amendments to the Social Security Act, cornerstone of the Great Society. In the first half of 1966 the Medicare program—entitling patients over sixty-five to free hospital treatment—and Medicaid legislation, which provided for federal grants to states to help finance treatment for the needy, came into effect.

These programs transformed social aid into a major charge on the taxpayer. By the end of that year total payments under Medicaid for drugs amounted to an estimated $55,000,000. Under Medicare they totaled a dizzy $776,000,000.

But these figures were small by comparison with the future liabilities inherent in the principles of social aid. If it was morally just for an affluent society to pay for the hospital treatment of its old people, the provision of drugs and medical care to those who were not actually institutionalized was a consequence that, though it might be fought in Congress, was almost certainly inevitable. This alone would increase the number of *annual* applications for aid under Medicare from 30,000,000 to 300,000,000 and boost the size of the federal government's purchases to a point at which it would be buying an estimated 46 percent of the drugmakers' total output by 1975. And this took no account of probable extensions of the Medicare program, such as Kiddie-care, covering free medication for children, or a lowering of the age limits at which elderly people became eligible for free treatment.

This fast-changing picture put the practices of the drugmakers into a different category. Kefauver had attacked them in the main for the prices patients had to pay in the drugstores either from their own resources or from sickness plans such as Blue Cross. Now, with the prospect of billions of dollars being paid annually to the industry from public funds, the whole issue of prices and profits came under keener scrutiny.

Although several hearings into various aspects of drugs had been conducted by Congressional subcommittees since Kefauver's bill in 1962, these, for the most part, had been fairly mild in their potential for damage. Early in 1967, however, several Senators moved to pick up the ball that Kefauver had dropped, but two of them, in particular, actually got their hands on it: Louisiana's Russell Long, chairman of the power-ful Senate Committee on Finance, and Wisconsin's Gaylord Nelson, who occupied the senior chair on the Monopoly Subcommittee of the Select Committee on Small Business. The main target for both of them was the trade name system of marketing because they believed that it was this, coupled with the patent situation, that was the key to the high prices of drugs.

Once more the pace began to heat up in the political area, for the drugmakers and the now highly experienced PMA lobby were just as determined to fight off the attack on their right to sell drugs under their own brand names as they were to defend the patent system against Kefauver's onslaught at the beginning of the decade.

The Nelson hearings bore much the same pattern as Kefauver's—with the same emphasis on price differentials between the big firms and the small companies, with the same strident complaints from the drugmakers about distortion of the evidence. It was a replay of 1959—but without the same level of publicity.

Senator Russell Long, however, took direct legislative action that, though the idea had been aired from time to time, was plowing new ground.

In a bill that he proposed should be attached to the Social Security Amendments Act, he called for a drug formulary, compiled and published by a committee of federal officials.

This would list by generic name all "qualified" drugs—those, in other words, that government agencies would buy—together with "reasonable" sales prices. In other words, the formulary would dictate the drugs used in the mammoth Medicare and Medicaid purchases and establish a form of price control.

To the concern of the PMA lobbyists, inevitably opposed to any attempt to control them, the Senate approved Long's bill. It was, however, killed in the Senate-House conference—where the two houses thrash out their differences—when another proposal was adopted in its place that, warmly backed by the drug men in the Capitol, seemed to put off the evil hour effectively. This urged that HEW should make a special study of quality and cost standards of drugs financed under Social Security before considering further legislation.

As a defense tactic, the drugmakers' support of this move was to backlash. In June, 1967, at the direction of the President, HEW set up a special task force—made up mainly of government experts—to study the problems.

The report of the task force a year later came as yet another unpleasant shock to the PMA. For it went way beyond its limited brief. It handed out a few bouquets. Commenting on the industry's research and development program, the report conceded that—based on percentage of sales—the drugmakers spent three times more on this area than any other major industry. It noted the "impressive" number of new products that had resulted and commented on the fact that "virtually all the important new drugs of recent years have come from countries providing patent protection"—a view, of course, that was the exact opposite of the arguments that Kefauver had used so vigorously in support of his attempts to get a patents clause into his bill.

Nevertheless, despite this concession, the task force did not believe that the existing laws should remain. In fact, its recommendations turned out to be the biggest clobbering the drugmakers had yet experienced. It was handed out, furthermore, not by a lobby or a campaigning Senator, but by the administration itself.

It criticized the number of "me too" drugs the industry issued as new products, which were, in fact, merely modifications of existing lines. More important, among the drastic changes proposed for "study" in the report were that the life of patents should be cut to seven years, that compulsory licensing should apply after three years, that brand names should be replaced by generic titles followed by the name of the maker, that the mailing of free samples to physicians should be restricted only to those who requested it, and that the government should issue a compendium of all available drugs, including side effects and prices, to guide doctors—a proposal that shared some ground with Long's idea for a formulary except that it had no element of actual price control.

"The Task Force," said the report, "has been unable to find sufficient evidence to support the concept of the drug industry as a particularly risky enterprise. . . ." Although it conceded that "the development of an individual drug may be associated with a high degree of risk . . . and is an economic as well as a scientific gamble," the record showed that "painful losses" of this kind were generally covered "by substantial profits on other drugs."

The task force had ample material to support its views. Kefauver's anguished comment in the Senate in 1962 that his bill would have no effect on drug firm profits had been proved correct. In that year, according to PMA figures, the industry earned 16.8 percent, after taxes, on its net worth. By 1966 rising profits had boosted this return to 20.3 percent.

By 1967 Americans, in one way or another, spent close to $3.5 billion on prescription medication—nearly $1.5 billion more than they had in 1959, the year when Kefauver opened his controversial hearings.

Certainly, nothing in the legislation so far had deterred the drugmakers from research. It had soared to a peak figure of $500,000,000 annually—more than double the annual total in the days of Kefauver—and, according to the HEW task force, had spawned 311 "important new single entities which . . . represent significant advances that had been introduced onto the market between 1957 and 1958." A peak year had been 1958, after which the figures "decreased steadily until 1967, when the number started to rise again."

With the increasing role of the federal and state authorities as enormous buyers of drugs, these figures could afford only temporary satisfaction to the drugmakers. For they supplied their opponents with a wide range of ammunition. In 1959, Kefauver had represented a dramatic threat, but now, ten years later, the industry was backing away nervously from a far more powerful assault. The presidential election, that fall—won, as it was, by a Republican—would possibly give them a little more time, but the writing was on the wall.

However, while the drugmakers as a whole were under this new pressure, the battle on the narrower front between the government and the tetracycline companies was moving gradually to its climax.

By February, 1966, the Antitrust Division of the Justice Department had still made no move to bring its case to trial—even though the indictment was now more than four years old. In fact, some of the defense lawyers, still confident that the government had no case, began to believe that the U.S. Attorney was looking around for a good reason to avoid going to trial at all.

If he were, then Senator Russell Long may well have helped to change his mind. From the floor of the Senate, he launched a violent assault on Cyanamid, Pfizer, Bristol and the other two companies that were selling tetracycline. "For more than a dozen years," he declared, "American drug manufacturers have been involved in a world-wide cartel to fix the price of wonder drugs at identical, grossly inflated and unconscionably high prices. . . . Although children, the elderly and the poor have been and are still unable to afford such drugs, and although the existence of at least one aspect of this conspiracy has been known to federal agencies since at least 1958, the cartel continues to operate in all its vigor."

The Senator not only was demanding action over the alleged conspiracy in America, but was laying charges that the companies were operating a cartel abroad—especially in Latin America. His evidence, mainly internal company correspondence, memorandums and cables, sounded like features in a spy novel: secret meetings where prices were fixed; elaborate codes; letters marked "Confidential—Please destroy"; and concerted action against any representative of the cartel that sold at a discount—what Long described as "the effective working of an industrial Gestapo."

In one graphic account of the supply of tetracycline to the New Orleans Charity Hospital—in which, the Senator said, the bids of the five companies and of three dealers were all identical—the issue of who was to be awarded the contract was decided by a game of crap. "Cyanamid won the award on a roll of the dice," asserted Long and placed in the Senate record an internal company letter of the Upjohn staff on which a comment had been penciled: "Too bad our boy isn't a better crap shooter. . . ."

If this is what happened, it was a variation of the system of drawing lots to decide who should get the contract when more than one company bid the lowest price.

"Since 1954," ended the Senator, "these conspirators have been victimizing us all! It is high time that we stop them!"

As an attack, supported by what appeared to be hard confidential evidence, the speech seemed lethal and made a big impact. Yet another grand jury, this time in Washington, assembled to hear charges against the companies presented by an Assistant U.S. Attorney. These were concerned purely with the companies' activities abroad, mainly in Latin America—but, on closer inspection of the facts, the jurymen were evidently unimpressed, for they refused to vote an indictment.

Meanwhile, the FTC case was still pursuing its long and complex journey through the appeal procedures of the U.S. courts. The companies gained certain ground. The appeals court ruled, for example, that the commission should rehear certain evidence without its chairman, Paul Rand Dixon. His previous role as counsel for the Kefauver Subcommittee could raise the possibility of conflict of interest.

Another decision of the court was that the commission should hear the evidence of the patent examiner who, back in 1955, had issued the tetracycline patent. Did *he* think he had been misled by Pfizer, as the FTC alleged? For technical reasons, throughout all the lengthy hearings, he had never been called to testify even though this aspect was central to the whole conspiracy charge.

In the end, these final twists in the ten-year story made little practical difference to the result. The FTC dropped its price-fixing charges against the companies, but its decision that Pfizer must license all applicants was supported by the court. By that time the company had already begun to do so.

The attorneys for the companies believed that the jury would take the same view of the price-fixing charges as the appeals court in the FTC case but they were due for a shock.

At last, in December, 1967, the Justice Department put the companies on trial on the criminal charges. The corporations were now the sole defendants. The personal indictments against Malcolm, McKeen and Schwartz had been quashed as the result of careful strategy by Pfizer's attorneys.

A witness, called by the government in an antitrust action, is automatically immune from subsequent prosecution for anything he may say on the stand—a regulation designed primarily to permit officials working in the government to testify without claiming the Fifth Amendment, which might otherwise make inquiry impossible.

Technically, the three presidents had not testified in an antitrust action, but they all had been witnesses in an inquiry into the sparetime activities of Dr. Henry Welch, onetime head of the FDA's Antibiotics Division.

In addition to his job at the FDA, Welch had been editor of two medical journals that relied heavily on advertising from pharmaceutical firms. Since the Antibiotics Division of the agency had to approve new drug applications submitted by the antibiotic manufacturers, who were also important advertisers in the journals he edited, there was an obvious possibility of a conflict of interest.

The purpose of the inquiry—following revelations in the Kefauver hearings—was to examine this situation. The testimony of the three drug firms' presidents included areas of fact that overlapped the events in the government's monopoly charges against Cyanamid and the other companies.

In 1965 it had occurred to Jud Parsons, a young attorney acting for Pfizer, that although the inquiry had not in itself been an antitrust matter, it *had* been conducted by the government, and the evidence had included antitrust issues. Surely, he suggested, this brought it into the category covered by the immunity rule. In September of that year a New York federal judge had taken the same view and ordered the withdrawal of the personal indictments.

But although the three men no longer faced the possibility of jail, their companies were still vulnerable to liabilities of millions of dollars—not only from fines, but also from the civil suits to which a guilty verdict would open them. All the buyers of the drug—including the big state and city purchasers that spent enormous sums every year on tetracyclines for hospitals —would be able to claim that, owing to the conspiracy, they had paid too much and could demand triple damages as recompense.

On a cold morning in December, 1967, after days of wrangling over technicalities, the trial of the corporations opened. Harry Sklarsky, the prosecutor, stood up before the jury in the same courthouse in which the Fox case had been heard two years before and related the complex story of the fight for the tetracycline patent and the events that followed it—a conspiracy, he charged, that had monopolized the market in one of the world's most important drugs, as well as fixed the prices of Terramycin and Aureomycin at levels that were "substantially identical and non-competitive" and "unreasonably high."

Graphically, he described how the five companies—for Squibb[28] and Upjohn, though not defendants, were named as co-conspirators—controlled a dominant share of the market in broad-spectrum antibiotics. In the peak year of 1957 this amounted to 80 percent of total market sales of $170,000,000.

There was, in fact, only a relatively small area of dispute between the two sides over the basic evidence in the case. The cross-licensing deals between Pfizer and Cyanamid, the story of the desperate struggle by Frederic Schwartz to chip out a place for Bristol in the tetracycline picture, and the vital dependence at that time in the early 1950's by all three companies on the new drug were all described—without challenge since they were supported by signed agreements and public documents. The prices of the three drugs, too, were a matter of incontestable fact.

But—so Sklarsky charged—it was in the private agreements that lay behind these formal contracts that the true conspiracy had taken place, especially in bids for big contracts such as those of Admiral Knickerbocker at the Defense Department. Here, he charged, they had carved up the market between them. An example was the time in 1957 when the three companies bid for a government award of 454,000,000 bottles of tetracycline oil. Both Pfizer and Cyanamid bid $1.83 a bottle. Bristol went in at $1.82.8 cents—two-tenths of a cent below the other two.

"But there was a snafu in the specification," declared the prosecutor. "Pfizer complained and it was re-bid. Once more, however, the tenders of all three companies were the same as before." Bristol got the contract for $803,642 and made a net profit of $562,329. "Now significantly enough in that year, 1957," Sklarsky went on ominously, "Bristol's total sales to the Federal Government amount to only a few thousand dollars more than this bid. In other words, it was found business. . . ."

Witness after witness from the companies was grilled on

the common price the three companies charged to druggists. The prosecutor was on weaker ground here because it was shown that every time one of them had dropped its price, the others had followed suit. The only advantage to the firm that initiated the move was the short period that existed before the others were physically able to counter the competition —which was why on one occasion Pfizer had announced a price drop on a Saturday by sending telegrams to druggists and wholesalers.

But, even if his proof of price-fixing was more limited in this area, Sklarsky had available to him the same emotional arguments to impress the jury that Kefauver had employed to influence the American public. The defense lawyers fought hard to stop the government from introducing evidence on profit differentials. This, they argued, had nothing to do with the alleged conspiracy which the prosecutor was required to prove.

But the judge ruled against them. He allowed Sklarsky to demonstrate the fact that in 1954, for example, Cyanamid's cost of making 100 capsules of tetracycline was only $2.55. These were sold for $30.60 to the drugstores, which charged their customers $51.

As always, it sounded terrible—a selling price of more than ten times the cost, a profit of more than 1,000 percent. As they had done so often before, the companies defended themselves by arguing that this whole basis of estimating profit was completely fallacious. Cyanamid aimed at an overall profit after research, promotion and overhead—of 15 percent on sales. Sometimes this figure was exceeded, and sometimes it was not.

Both McKeen and Schwartz took the stand to answer the prosecutor's probing questions. Because he was seriously ill, Malcolm was not present in person in the courtroom, but the judge gave permission for testimony he had given in other hearings to be read into the court record.

The trial was long and dull—this was why the press gave it

barely a passing mention—and the only moment of surprise came when Sklarsky ended the case for the government. For the counsel for the three companies declared that they would present no evidence for the defense. The government, they claimed, had not proved its charges of conspiracy. There was, therefore, no case to answer.

The jury did not agree. It brought in a verdict of guilty. The judge sentenced the companies to fines of $150,000 each, but as they well knew, this was only a small part of the price that they would now have to pay.

It was in the civil suits that would now follow the convictions that the real potential for damage truly lay. The three companies filed appeals, but it was not long before the civil suits from the big buyers of their drugs, who could now claim that they had paid too much owing to the artificially high prices supported by the conspiracy, began to roll into the attorneys' offices.

Within a year, forty-three states and thirteen cities as well as private hospitals and insurance companies which had paid for drugs under sickness plans, had brought suit.

Eventually, in February, 1969, the drug firms offered a deal to all their suitors. Even though "convinced that they had not violated the anti-trust laws" but had "contributed greatly to the public health," they were, they announced, prepared to make a total settlement payment of $120,000,000. It was the biggest damages proposal in the history of the antitrust laws.

Of this figure, $5,600,000 was to go to New York City. New York State was to get $4,000,000, while the State of California, with the biggest claim, was to be entitled to $10,000,000.

There were unique aspects about the settlement, which was described by J. Lee Rankin, counsel to the New York City Corporation, as "a milestone in consumer protection." For built into it was an attempt to reimburse individual consumers— people, in other words, like Walton Hamilton, the Washington attorney who had possibly started the whole series of events back in 1951 when he was angered by the fact that the prices, regarded by him as exorbitant, of all the broad-spectrum antibiotics were the same—$8 for a four-day course.

The states could sue as *parens patriae* on behalf of their citizens, who would then be able to make claims against consumer funds that would be set up—provided, of course, that they could prove that they had bought the drugs.

Under the settlement, Cyanamid—which, with Aureomycin and with its high sales of tetracycline, had benefited most—was to pay more than $48,000,000.[29]

However, even at this final stage in the long conflict, the shadow of Wall Street loomed over the events—as it had, in truth, ever since 1939. In their announcement, the drug firms gave the reason for their action. It was, they declared, in the best interest of their stockholders to offer a program in settlement. Failure to do so "would mean that the companies would be burdened for many years with numerous . . . suits involving very large claims." It would not, however, they assured investors, materially affect current earnings but would be charged against earnings retained from prior years.

It was an ironic ending to the story of wonder drugs that had cured the diseases and saved the lives of millions of people throughout the world. Men—who without question were benefactors of mankind—had been condemned by the society they had aided.

In essence, their crime was that they had profited too much from the good they had done. They had rigged the market in miracles—at least in what, at the time when they were invented, had seemed like miracles.

As a climax, it underlined with special poignancy all those issues, argued in Washington, about an industry that is subjected to the same pressures and motivations as other industries that are not, as it is, concerned with the material of life and death, or senility, or the quality of human existence. It posed once more—but this time in far more dramatic terms—the same old questions: It is not hard to calculate the value of an automobile or a television set, but what should a man crippled by polio pay for the use of his limbs? What is the cash worth of twenty years of life to someone who would have died of pneumonia? And what, too, is a fair reward to the man or company that gave him that extra time?

This is the argument that the drugmakers have put forward repeatedly, and it is one that has been labeled specious by their critics who—in common presumably with the jury in the antitrust trial—believe that there is a limit to the price of miracles and that their makers have already exceeded it.

Time and events, in the view of this writer, are on the side of the opposition. The drugmakers are fighting what over the long term must be a losing battle in the sense that they will be forced to relinquish ground that they are now fighting desperately to retain. The main reason for this view is the fast-growing role of public funds as the industry's main source of income. Within a decade, it is probable that federal and state authorities will be providing well over half the drugmakers' earnings. It is highly unlikely that under these conditions, politicians will permit profit levels that are substantially and regularly above the averages earned by other industries.

If this prediction is correct, one result is certain. The days of the really big killing, of the profits bonanza—resulting from a new breakthrough drug like Aureomycin in 1948—are numbered. Many operators will stay in business content with a good average return bridging the peak years and the bad years. But the gamblers—who, in return for playing with high stakes, insist on the chance of fat winnings—will probably have to look elsewhere.

If they do—despite the other advantages, such as lower prices, that society will almost certainly derive from the

changed system—the intriguing questions will still remain:
Without the big speculators will the rate of new drug discovery be higher or lower? Will the human race fare better—or
worse?

Acknowledgments

The many people I have talked to in the process of gathering material for this book represent very different viewpoints. For this reason, it is clearly important that they should be named and that my gratitude to them for giving me their time—in some cases a great deal of time—should be recorded. Although most of the men and women from whom I have sought interviews have granted them and spoken very freely, there are a very few who, for legal or personal reasons, have declined to see me.

At the government level, I would like to record my thanks to: Earl Kintner, general counsel and later chairman of the Federal Trade Commission; Dr. John Blair, chief economist to the Senate Subcommittee on Antitrust and Monopoly under the chairmanship of the late Senator Estes Kefauver; Herman Gelfand, Assistant U.S. Attorney in the Antitrust Division of the Justice Department; Albert Gaynor, John Martin and Daniel Murdoch, Assistant U.S. Attorneys for the Southern District of New York, who prosecuted the Fox case; Joseph Marcheso, Assistant U.S. Attorney for the Eastern District of New York, who was in charge of an action against Constantino Peretti, in which certain people indicted in the Fox case were also named; Admiral William Knickerbocker, who, as head of the Military Medical Supply Agency (now incorporated in the Defense Supply Agency), pioneered the government purchases of Italian drugs; Joseph Lucca, FBI agent in the Fox investigation; John Riley, Athanasius Christides and Adam Olszewski of the U.S. Customs Service; and Major General Roger Brown, commissioner of purchases for New York City.

Among the people concerned with drug companies in Italy, I am extremely grateful to Count Niccolo Visconti di Madrone —and also to Frank Delaney, his attorney in New York—Dr. Giovanni Auletta, and Dr. and Mrs. Helmuth Wawretchek. I was also glad of the long talks on the telephone I enjoyed with Elio Salvetti and Dr. Caesar Bottone, even though in neither case would their attorneys consent to their meeting me personally.

I have received cooperation, which I have much appreciated, from the management, staff and attorneys of Merck, including executive vice-president Frederick Bartenstein, general counsel James Fulton, Edward Stiffler, Orville Schell of Hughes, Hubbard, Blair & Reed in New York and Frank Bate of Shanley & Fisher in Newark, New Jersey. I also had useful meetings with Paul Bosted of International Rectifier, in Los Angeles, and Sol Silverang of Premo Laboratories in Hackensack.

Others who have been most helpful were John Cancelarich, Joseph Gerace, John Kelly, head of a New Jersey investigation company, Edward Ricciutti, reporter on the Bergen *Record,* and William Haddad.

Among the many books that I have studied, four have been of particular help to me: *The Real Voice* by Richard Harris, *Margin of Safety* by John Rowan Wilson, *Merchants of Life* by Tom Mahoney and *The Lobbyists* by James Deakin.

Finally, I wish to record my appreciation to the American Cyanamid Company. What led me to its door was the publication in England of newspaper reports about the litigation with Dr. Sidney Fox.

The case intrigued me, not merely because it was a very big industrial espionage operation, involving major companies on both sides of the Atlantic, but because it was obvious from the few facts that were then available that the Justice Department had not provided the main dynamic in the prosecution. Clearly, this had been supplied by American Cyanamid.

What made this situation additionally interesting to me was that although any company would clearly take strong action to bring industrial spies to justice, the background was unusual. Cyanamid itself at that time was under indictment concerning one of the drugs whose secrets Fox had admitted selling. The drug industry as a whole was under attack following the Kefauver Senate investigations. The government was buying U.S.-patented drugs from Italy, which had supplied Fox with his main market.

Here seemed to be a unique crime story with an intriguing political background. I wrote from London to the American Cyanamid Company and asked for its cooperation. When I received no reply, I followed this approach with a personal visit.

For a year, during which there were discussions and correspondence, the company refused to cooperate, but at the end of this period (by which time the criminal trial of Fox's associates had taken place) its executives reconsidered my approach.

If there was an earlier reluctance, this cooperation, once the decision was made, was wholehearted. At all levels the corporation's executives and scientists in America, Britain and Italy have given me all the time I needed. In fact—as Walter Minton, president of G. P. Putnam's Sons, has pointed out to me—the book, as it is now, has developed far beyond my original subject about which I approached Cyanamid. The Fox case, on which I had intended to concentrate the main focus of the book, is now merely one of several elements of a volume that purports to tell the much larger story of a major industry at bay—a story that, of necessity, describes in detail the events that led to Cyanamid's indictment and conviction under the Sherman Act.

I must record, however, that the degree of frankness and help I have received from men who worked for Cyanamid has been exceptional, even to making available to me full transcripts of the several trials involved and other formal legal documents, thus saving me a great deal of trouble obtaining them elsewhere. Many of the scientists and executives of the corporation have gone well beyond their brief to give me what facts I needed, often supporting these with off-the-record impressions and anecdotes.

The list of these men, who gave me many hours of time, is long but includes, in particular, Lyman Duncan, Dr. Robert Parker, Jack Stewart, Dr. Robert Winterbottom, William Fulton, Dr. Edward Scholz, Austin Phillips, Ralph Schreiner, Robert Bogan, Edward Candee, Joseph C. Calitri, Paul Stessel, Dr. John Growich, Dr. James Boothe, and many others in the research division. W. E. "Ted" McAlister of Cyanamid of Great Britain, Dr. Franco Gorgone, managing director of Cyanamid Italiana, Vittorio Crainz, his public relations adviser, and members of the partners and staff of American Cyanamid's attorneys were also extremely helpful.

I would like, too, to express my thanks to Mrs. Sylvia Voller, who has typed the book in its various stages of production with a patience that I found remarkable.

Notes

1. The indictment of Dr. Malcolm, John McKeen and Frederic Schwartz was quashed in 1965, although it remained against their companies. This trial of the three corporations on charges under the antitrust laws took place in New York in 1967. They were convicted.

2. There are, in fact, four basic drugs in the tetracycline family: chlortetracycline (Aureomycin), tetracycline (sold by Cyanamid as Achromycin and by other companies under other names), dimethylchlortetracycline (Declomycin) and oxytetracycline (Terramycin). To avoid confusion, I normally refer to all, except tetracycline itself, by the trade names by which they are commonly known.

3. The account in this chapter of the battle for the tetracycline patent is based on testimony given at the trial of Cyanamid, Pfizer and Bristol-Myers that took place in New York in 1967. References to charges that the patent examiner who issued the tetracycline patent was misled are also based on charges made by the Federal Trade Commission in lengthy hearings and stated in its final order (d7211) made on October 4, 1967, as well as in other documents.

4. Although Cyanamid proceeded with Heyden's application for a *process* patent, it withdrew Heyden's application for a *product* patent on tetracycline— a fact that was cited in the grand jury indictment as one of the events in the alleged conspiracy. The implied motive behind the purchase of Heyden was to remove competition from Pfizer's application for the patent.

This situation is complex, but it should be stated that the patent examiner had rejected the Heyden product claim because the application had been submitted after Pfizer's scientists had published a paper about tetracycline. He would require proof that the Heyden team had actually made their discovery before Pfizer's chemists.

The question that is posed is, therefore: If Cyanamid had not made its cross-licensing deal with Pfizer, would it have pressed Heyden's product claim more aggressively? The government has suggested that this was one more piece in the mosaic of evidence of a conspiracy. On the other hand, it is hard to believe that Cyanamid would not have preferred to own the tetracycline product patent—if it had any chance of obtaining it—instead of relinquishing it to Pfizer.

5. Although the prices of Chloromycetin tended normally to be the same as those of the tetracycline drugs, Parke, Davis was *not* charged by the government with price-fixing, as were the makers of the other drugs mentioned.

6. The FTC charged Pfizer with making "false, misleading and incorrect statements" to the Patent Office to obtain a patent in tetracycline and alleged that Cyanamid and Bristol had aided it by witholding from the Patent Office "material information." The complaint alleged that Cyanamid, Bristol, Squibb and Upjohn had accepted licenses from Pfizer "knowing that material information had been withheld" and that all five companies had fixed the prices of broad-spectrum antibiotics including tetracycline.

7. Dr. Sidney Fox pleaded guilty to a grand jury indictment in 1964 charging him with theft of Lederle drugs, organisms and trade secrets. Nathan Sharff and Seymour Salb, owners of Biorganic Laboratories, were indicted with him on related charges. The trial took place in New York in 1965. Both Sharff and Salb, who pleaded not guilty, were convicted. The events revealed by the investigation by Cyanamid—and described in this and following chapters—were revealed in testimony during this trial.

8. All the companies selling tetracycline have hotly denied collusion on prices, asserting that their similarity resulted from natural market laws, as did many other prices in other fields, such as gasoline. Bids for government contracts, they have emphasized, are calculated on the basis of historical facts—*i.e.,* the pattern of previous bids—and guesswork on competitors' plans.

9. In the trial of Cyanamid, Pfizer and Bristol in New York in 1967—when the three companies were found guilty under the antitrust laws—carving up of the market in MMSA contracts was charged by the prosecution.

10. It should be noted that *all* Italian drug companies did not exploit the patent-free situation in their country. Even though they did not have to, some of the reputable firms signed agreements with patent owners in America and even obtained licenses to make drugs. These usually provided for the provision of technical know-how.

11. In the trial of Nathan Sharff in 1965 his brother-in-law testified that he had allowed his address to be used for the "Dr. Mancuso" advertisement at Sharff's request.

12. Dr. Bottone was also one of the defendants in the criminal trial in New York in 1956 on charges of conspiracy related to Sidney Fox's thefts of organisms and secret data from Lederle Laboratories—and was ultimately convicted. Apart from Lederle's suits for patent infringement, Merck also mounted actions against Dr. Bottone for infringement of its vitamin B_{12} patents.

13. Austin Phillips testified about Bottone's revelations, which are described on these pages, in the criminal trial of Bottone, Sharff and Salb in New York.

14. The names Irving Rosenblatt and John Casei were, in fact, errors. It was never formally alleged that anyone with these names was involved, and it is probable that Bottone had misheard them.

15. Lyman Duncan assumed that this product resulted from the theft of Declomycin organisms from his plant, and Count Visconti was later indicted for this. It should be stated, however, that Visconti has always claimed that his organisms came from a sample of Italian soil—a statement that Pearl River experts have disputed because their organism was developed by mutation and they have never to this day seen or heard of another Declo bug in a natural environment.

16. For a time Siegfried Muller was under suspicion, and Cyanamid actually named him as a co-conspirator in its civil suit against Sharff and Salb in 1962. However, when all the facts came out, Muller was found to be innocent and gave evidence as a witness for the government in the subsequent federal criminal trial.

17. The events described in Chapter 9—and referred to briefly in earlier parts of the book—not only formed the main part of an affidavit sworn out by John Cancelarich and were used in evidence in an action against Fox brought by Cyanamid in 1962, but were also testified to by Fox and Cancelarich in the federal trial in 1965.

In a memorandum submitted by his lawyer to the U.S. Attorney in an attempt to suppress the indictment that was later brought against him, Count Visconti admitted meeting Fox and receiving from him technical information about dimethylchlortetracycline (Declomycin) but asserted that it was only public information. He denied receiving organisms.

18. Neither Le Petit nor the company's chemical consultant, Maurice Rosenblatt, has testified in court about the allegations that either was involved in dealings with Fox. Le Petit has issued a denial through a New York PR firm. However, Rosenblatt was indicted by a federal grand jury after Fox had sworn statements—which he later repeated in court—that he had negotiated with Rosenblatt to sell to Le Petit organisms and know-how. On the basis of Fox's sworn statements, Cyanamid was awarded $5,000,000 in damages in a civil suit when Rosenblatt defaulted. The transactions with Le Petit were testified to by Fox in the federal criminal trial of Sharff, Salb and Bottone—he himself pleading guilty—in New York in 1965 and in affidavits introduced in Cyanamid's action against Rosenblatt.

19. The testimony of Halmuth Wawretchek, president of Ankermann Italiana and its sister company in Germany, about the connection between the company and the alleged espionage conspirators was given as part of the government's case in the federal criminal trial of Sharff and Company in New York. He also assisted Cyanamid and Merck with their investigations.

20. Sharff and Salb were later found guilty in the federal criminal trial in 1965 of selling Lederle organisms to Ankermann.

21. The story of the deal between Auletta of Leo and Salvetti and Fox was also testified to by Fox and Cancelarich in the federal trial in New York.

22. Although the government charged that the cross-licensing deal between Pfizer and Cyanamid was the *start* of the conspiracy for which they were later indicted, there was, of course, nothing illegal about the arrangement itself.

23. According to Fox's testimony in the federal trial in New York in 1965.

24. During the trial of an action brought against Fox in New York by American Cyanamid in 1963, Dr. Phillip Berke of Formet Laboratories testified to these transactions with Fox.

25. Senator Cremisini has publicly denied this transaction.

26. At the time of writing, this trial had not ended, and the results were, therefore, not known.

27. Fermentfarma was named in a lawsuit brought by McKesson & Robbins, America's biggest drug wholesaler, against Cyanamid in 1963. McKesson was selling tetracycline made by Rachel Laboratories of California. Cyanamid charged that Rachel's management had obtained its organism and processes from Fermentfarma; that Fermentfarma was a drug company operating in a country that, having no patent protection, became a haven for bugs and information stolen from U.S. drug companies; and that the culture acquired by Rachel from Fermentfarma had been pronounced, in a Canadian action, the same as those organisms covered by a Cyanamid patent. The lawsuit has since been settled.

28. By this time Squibb had been acquired by Olin Mathieson.

29. The repercussions of the trial of the companies and of the decision in the FTC case will almost certainly continue. A suit was brought by the government in July, 1969, claiming damages estimated at more than $25,000,000 because it had had to pay uncompetitive prices for tetracycline.

Index

Achromycin
 as Lederle's trade name of tetracycline, 51
 spectacular success in sales of, 53, 55,
  66
 stepped-up promotion of, 52–53
Advertising
 of drugs, exaggerated claims in, and
  Kefauver investigation, 107, 124
 of drugs, regulations of new drug
  law on, 215
 of tranquilizers, Congressional hearings on, 75
Albrecht, William A., 24
Allen, Frank, security chief at Lederle
 plant, 82, 83, 86, 98, 134, 137, 220
American Cyanamid Company. See
 Cyanamid Company
American Journal of Hygiene, 229
Ankermann Italians of Milan, 130,
  138–39, 149, 151, 179, 183, 190, 194
 production of tetracycline by, 139,
  195
Anselmi, Joseph, agent of Farmochimica Cutolo-Calosi, 105
Antibiotics
 continuing rise in domestic market
  for, 37
 cut in death rate of diseases responsive to, 15
 demand for, in Korean War, 37
 development of, 15, 21
 discovery of Aureomycin by Duggar
  of Lederle, 24–28, 205
 discovery of Dectomycin at Lederle,
  93–95, 133–34

discovery of Terramycin by Pfizer,
 34–37
FTC 1958 report on business of,
 72–74
problem of side effects, 43–44
and race of drugmakers for development of new kinds of, 22, 23
Antibiotics Symposium, Mayflower
 Hotel, Washington, D.C., 46, 47,
 133
Antihistamines, development of, 15
Antitrust case against drug firms. See
 Government criminal case against
 tetracycline producers.
Aristocort, Lederle's trade name of triamcinalone, 84, 188
Association of the British Pharmaceutical Industry, 199
Auletta, Giovanni of Leo in Rome
 information obtained from, on espionage conspirators, 149–55, 180
 refusal to reveal source of his organisms, 219
 refusal to testify in espionage ring
  case, 180
Aureomycin
 competition from Terramycin, 36
 discovery and development by Duggar of Lederle, 24–28, 205
 effectiveness against broad spectrum
  of diseases, 27, 28, 29
 gastrointestinal complaints as possible side effects, 44
 importance in earnings of Lederle, 39
 lag in sales of, with success of Achromycin, 55

launching of, and acceptance by doctors, 28–29
as patented product of Lederle, 27
price, 29, 30, 31–32, 36
sales (1950), 37
testing on human beings, 27–28
as trade name of chlortetracycline,
41

Bambach, Karl, assistant director of
AMA, 178
Bayer plant in Elberfield, Germany, 12
Bell, William B., of American Cyan-
amid, 16, 17, 20
Bergen *Record,* 159–60
Biorganic Laboratories, 84, 88, 89, 92,
95, 119–20, 159, 188
Blackman, Seymour, executive secretary
of Premo Laboratories, 115
Blackman, Theodore, president of
Premo Laboratories, 106–7
Blair, John, of FTC
as chief economist for Kefauver committee, 74, 75, 102, 110, 114, 120,
122, 177
quoted on antitrust cases, 71
reaction to FTC's quarterly report
listing profit figures for drugs, 76
Blatnik, John A., 75
Bliss, Eleanor, 13
Bogan, Bob, executive director of Cyanamid International, 148–54, 155
Boothe, Jim, research chemist at
Lederle, 41–43, 44, 47
Bottone, Caesar, International Pharmaceuticals, 128–29
as co-owner of Kasal Trading Company, 129–30, 191
found quilty in industrial espionage
case and sentenced to two years,
245
indictment in industrial espionage
case, 217
as shareholder in Ankermann Italiana, 139, 195
tells Cyanamid patent attorney of
ring selling Lederle's organisms
and process in Italy, 130, 139
Bowman, Philip, Bristol Laboratories,
123–24
Bradley, Thomas G., general sales manager of Pfizer, 53

Braun, Emilio, managing director of
Fermentfarma of Milan, 220, 223
Bristol Laboratories
and break into tetracycline business,
58, 60
and development of bug for making
of tetracycline directly, 58
dropping of Pfizer suit and licensing
of Bristol to make and sell tetracycline, 65
as ethical drug division of Bristol-
Myers Company, 37–38
indictment under Sherman Act, 140
and penicillin production, 37–38, 58
suit of Cyanamid against, for infringing Aureomycin patent, 61
suit of Pfizer against, for infringing
tetracycline patent, 62, 63
tapping of wires of, 64–65
unsuccessful efforts to effect deal with
Cyanamid, 58
unsuccessful efforts to effect deal with
Pfizer, 59–60
Bristol-Myers Company, 10. *See also*
Bristol Laboratories
Britain
and buying of tetracycline in Italy,
216
effects of Kefauver drug investigation
in, 124
British Medical Journal, 12
Broady, tapping of Bristol's wires by,
64–65
Brown, Francis, Schering Corporation,
108–13
Brown, Roger, N.Y. City commissioner
of purchases
and battle with Pfizer over cut-price
purchases of tetracycline, 252–53
and price battle with Parke, Davis,
251–52

California, amount to be paid to, following drug antitrust convictions,
264
Calitri, Joe, PR manager of Cyanamid
International, 198–99, 218
Cancelarich, John
confrontation with Mansfield, Joe
Gerace, and Bill Fulton, 182–86
contacts with Leo of Rome, 152, 154,
180

given six months in industrial espionage case, 245

indictment in industrial espionage case, 217

John Jane as alias used by, 152, 184

makes full confession to Mansfield and Fulton, 186

named co-conspirator in suit against Sharff, 159, 181

as process engineer at Lederle, resignation of, 136

as production manager at Ankermann Italiana, 139, 179, 183

role in espionage conspiracy, 187, 191–94

and sample of tetracycline mash furnished to, 161–62, 180

as suspected espionage conspirator, 149

swears out lengthy affidavit on espionage conspiracy, 195

as target of Mansfield strategy in espionage ring case, 179

as witness in civil case against Sidney Fox, 243–44

Candee, Ned, PR director of Cyanamid International, 197, 198

Carey, Benjamin, medical chief at Lederle, 44

Carroll, Senator John, 173

Cater, Douglass, Washington correspondent of *Reporter*, 109

Chain, Ernest, 21

Chemical & Engineering News, 119, 122–23, 190

Cheplin Biological Laboratories, purchase of, by Bristol-Myers, 37

Chloromycetin

aplastic anemia as possible side effect of, 43–44

competition from Terramycin, 36

development by Parke, Davis, 32, 36

price, 36, 274

Walton Hamilton, and cost of, 70–71

Chlortetracycline, generic name for Aureomycin, 41

Chumbris, Peter, counsel for minority party of Kefauver Committee, 110

Citric acid, as specialist line of Pfizer, 32–33

Civil suits following drug antitrust convictions, 264

deal offered by drug firms, 264

reimbursement of individual consumers built into settlement, 264–65

settlement as biggest damages proposal in history of antitrust laws, 264

Colebrook, Leonard, 12–13

Contergan, brand name of Grünenthal, for thalidomide, 207

Cooney, Tom, Pfizer sales force, 104

Cortical steroids, investigation of, 108

Cox, Harold, director of virus research at Lederle, 227, 229, 233, 234, 235

Cutler, Lloyd N., special counsel of PMA, 171, 175

Cutler Laboratories, and Salk vaccine manufactured by, 232

Cyanamid Company

activity of public relations division on indictments in industrial espionage case, 218

amount to be paid under settlement after drug antitrust convictions, 265

concedes patent priority to Pfizer in tetracycline battle, and accepts cross-licensing for Lederle, 52

and counterattack against effects on public of Kefauver hearings, 168–69, 197

Cyanamid International, 148–49

emotional conflicts of, in summer of 1961, 144–45

indictment, under Sherman Act, 140

and maneuvering of PMA lobby in Washington, 178

purchase of Heyden Chemical Corporation by, 57

purchase of Lederle Laboratories by, 16–17

story of, 11, 16

suits against Sidney Fox and Nathan Sharff by, 157–60

testimony of executives in Kefauver hearings, 120–24

"Cyanamid-Tallyho" file of Mansfield, 149, 224

Dansby, Doris, lab researcher at Lederle, 23

Declomycin
    discovery and development at Led-
        erle, 93–95, 133–34
    Demetetra, as chemically identical to,
        133, 138
    organisms and know-how of, sold in
        Italy, 130
Defense Department, buying of drugs
    abroad. *See* Knickerbocker Wil-
    liam, and buying of drugs for
    MMSA abroad
Demetetra, production of, by Pierrel
    Company of Italy, 133, 138
Dick, George, 233
Dirksen, Everett
    in debate in Senate on drug bill, 212
    and Kefauver hearings, 172
    as Kefauver's main political adver-
        sary over drug bill, 172, 173, 174,
        175, 176
Diseases
    effectiveness of Aureomycin against
        broad spectrum of, 27, 28, 29
    effectiveness of Chloromycetin in
        treatment of, 32
    responsive to new wonder drugs, 15,
        26, 27
Distillers, Ltd. of Britain
    sales of thalidomide under license
        from Grünenthal, 207
    withdraws thalidomide from market,
        208
Dixon, Paul Rand
    as chairman of FTC, 216
    quoted on drug lobby in Washing-
        ton, 165
    as top counsel for Kefauver Commit-
        tee, 74, 109, 110, 112–13, 120, 122
Domagk, Gerhard, 12
Drug industry. *See also* Kefauver in-
    vestigation into drug industry
    attitude of public as result of Kefau-
        ver investigation, 113
    beginning of reaction against, 69
    complacency on eve of Kefauver in-
        vestigation, 100
    counterattack against effects on pub-
        lic of Kefauver hearings, 165–66,
        168–70
    detailed exploration by Irene Till of
        Kefauver committee, 76, 101
    effect of wonder drugs on, 14–15

emotional conflicts of, in summer of
    1961, 144–45
excesses in, as objects of Kefauver
    investigation, 107, 166–67
and questions of price and profit, 30–
    31
racked between conflicting forces of
    human welfare and profit motive,
    10
and regulations of new drug law, 215
soaring profits, as result of wonder
    drugs, 15–16, 38–39
Drug lobby in Washington, 119, 165,
    168, 170, 171–73, 174, 175, 214, 255
Drug Trade News, 59
Drugs
    bad publicity from withdrawal of
        product from market, 205–6
    increasing role of federal and state
        authorities as buyers of, 257–58
    marketing after too-limited clinical
        testing, 75, 107, 203
    and paradox of system under which
        produced, 30
    price, under generic name and under
        trade name, 101–2, 115
    regulation of new law of publishing
        generic name along with brand
        name, 215
    regulations concerning development
        before submitting to FDA, 204, 205
Duggar, Benjamin, 22–28
Duncan, Lyman
    and assessment of results of industrial
        espionage verdicts, 246–48
    and counterattack against effects on
        public of Kefauver hearings, 168–
        69
    as Cyanamid vice-president in charge
        of medical affairs, 131, 134, 136–37
    and espionage conspirators, 143–45,
        146–48, 149, 156
    and FTC 1958 report on antibiotics
        business, 73–74
    as general manager of Lederle, 66,
        90–92, 98, 100, 119
    and Kefauver investigation, 107, 110–
        11, 113, 124
    and Lederle's development of polio
        vaccine, 225
    as witness in Kefauver hearings, 120–
        24, 131, 190

Eastland, James O.
in debate in Senate on drug bill, 212
and Kefauver drug bill, 174, 175, 176–77, 213
Edelblute, Harvey, attorney of Cyanamid, 40, 54
Enders, John, 229
Espionage conspirators
complete story of, 186–95
confession of Sidney Fox, 245
confessions of Cancelarich and Leonard Fine become public documents, 196
criminal trial on industrial espionage, 245–46
and "Cyanamid-Tallyho" file, 149, 224
expenditure of nearly $1,000,000 by Cyanamid to get evidence on, 136–37
indictment by grand jury, 217, 245
information secured from Auletta of Leo, 149 55
publicity after conspirators' confessions, 197–99
securing of evidence by Bogan 148–54
suits filed against Fox and Sharff by Cyanamid, 157–60
work of Bill Fulton on, 137–38, 139, 148, 149, 155, 161, 162, 180, 183–84, 186
Evans, Dorothy, lab researcher at Lederle, 23

Farmitalia, supplier of bulk tetracycline powder to Farmochimica, 106
Farmochimica Cutolo-Calosi
production of tetracycline by, 105
purchase of tetracycline by MMSA from, 105–6
FDA. See Food and Drug Administration
Federal Bureau of Investigation, 137, 140, 143
Federal Trade Commission (FTC)
and accusations against Pfizer in tests on Aureomycin fermentation, 62
announces formal charges of market rigging against five companies selling tetracycline, 74, 274
appeal hearings on examiner's opinion, 215–16
drops price-fixing charges against drug companies, 260
exoneration of tetracycline companies by examiner of, 145–46
hearings in New York on market-rigging charges, 99–100
1958 report on cut in death rate from diseases responsive to antibiotics, 15
report on antibiotics business, 72–74
reverses decision of examiner, 250
and ruling of judges on indirect evidence in conspiracy cases, 71–72
and testimony on Cyanamid's reply to Patent Office on bugs that produce Aureomycin, 54
Fermentfarma
and Rachel Laboratories, 220, 221, 223, 224, 250
and source of organisms used by, 221, 222
Fine, Leonard
given six months in industrial espionage case, 245
indictment in industrial espionage case, 217
role in espionage conspiracy, 161, 187, 192, 193, 194
swears out affidavit on espionage conspiracy, 195
Finkbine, Mrs. Robert, 209
Finland, Maxwell, 44
Fleming, Alexander, 21, 23
Florey, Howard, 21, 25
Foley, Edward H., legislative strategist of PMA, 171, 175
Food and Drug Administration (FDA), 27, 35, 43, 46
functions and powers of, 204
implications against, in Kefauver hearings, 115–16
and Kefauver drug bill, 175
Fortune magazine
and charts used in Kefauver hearings, 110
on "The Terramycin Blitz," 36
Fox, Sidney
access to secret valuable information and material, 85, 87

access to top-yielding pedigree micro-organisms, 87
arrest and imprisonment, in Cyanamid's suit, 239
and Biorganic Laboratories, 84, 96–98
as chemist at Lederle, 84
confession on espionage conspiracy, 245
as "consultant" for Leo of Rome under alias of Joseph Martin, 130, 138, 152–54
Cyanamid files suit against, 157–59
given six months in industrial espionage case, 245
indictment in industrial espionage case, 217
interest in Declomycin, 92, 93, 119
as key government witness in industrial espionage trial, 245
named co-conspirator in suit against Sharff, 159
named in ring selling Lederle organisms and processes in Italy, 130
notes in handwriting of, and organisms bought from, obtained from Leo, 155, 180
as operator of Kim Laboratories, 132, 152, 159, 188, 189
personal background, 88–89
resigns from Lederle, 98, 189
role in espionage conspiracy, 187–94, 196
ruled against in Cyanamid's suit against, 244
surveillance by security department and internal contacts, 86, 88–90, 92–93
suspicious actions noted by Lederle personnel, 84–87, 119
tailing to Biorganic Laboratories, 96–97
takes Fifth Amendment and refuses to answer Mansfield's questions at pretrial examination, 163
Free drugs given by drug firms in securing contracts, 56
FTC. See Federal Trade Commission
Fulton, Bill
as assistant security chief at Lederle plant, 81–82, 83, 134
as chief of Lederle security, 220
and confrontation with Cancelarich, 183–84, 186
and getting information on Rachel Laboratories, 220–23
and leads tying Fox into espionage network, 132
and linking of Fox to Biorganic Laboratories and Italian drug industry, 119–20
surveillance of Sidney Fox by, 88–90
tailing of Fox to Biorganic Laboratories by, 96–97
and work on uncovering espionage conspiracy ring, 137–38, 139, 148, 149, 155, 161, 162, 180, 183–84, 186
Furman, Gerald, George Uhe Company, 132, 153, 154

Gaynor, Al, Assistant U.S. Attorney
begins action in industrial espionage case, 217
and Cyanamid's case against Fox, 181–82
delays in pressing case against espionage conspirators, 201
relationship with attorney Mansfield, 181, 242
Gerace, Joe, of Lederle plant
confession of, 161–62, 180
confrontation of Cancelarich, 182–84
given suspended sentence in industrial espionage case, 246
indictment in industrial espionage case, 217
Gilmore, Donald S., Upjohn drug firm, 63
Gorman, Mike, 114–15
Gottlieb, Edward, & Associates, 246
Government criminal antitrust case against tetracycline producers
indictment of firms and presidents, 11, 140, 143
jury brings in verdict of guilty, and judge fines each company $150,000, 264
personal indictments against presidents quashed, 260–61
trial of companies, 260, 261–64
Government-sponsored medicine, beginning of steps toward, 253–54
Gratsch, Bridget, 222

Growich, John, Lederle microbiologist, 93
Grünenthal of Germany
as producers of thalidomide, 206
withdraws thalidomide from market, 207–8
Gwynne, John, 72, 73

Haddad, William, 252
Hamilton, Walton, 69, 71, 101, 264–65
Harris, Oren, drug bill of, 209, 213, 214
Harris, Richard
quoted on Kefauver as genius for publicity creation, 116
and The Real Voice, 69, 109, 175, 176, 214
Health, Education, and Welfare, Department of (HEW) and Kefauver drug bill, 175, 176
new regulations about drug testing issued after thalidomide crisis, 210
study by task force into drug problems, 256–57
Heyden Chemical Corporation
and development of bug for making of tetracycline directly, 57
purchase by Cyanamid, 57, 273–74
Hill and Knowlton, 117, 168
Hirsch, Ursula, microbiologist at Lederle, 93, 133
Howrey, Edward F., 72
Hruska, Roman, 172, 176
Human welfare and profit motive, as conflicting forces in drug industry, 10–11
Hutz, Werner H., Pfizer's patent attorney, 62

IBI. See Istituto Biochemico Italiano
Individual consumers, reimbursement by drug firms in settlement of antitrust convictions, 264–65
Industrial espionage. See also Espionage conspirators
and advertisement in Chemical & Engineering News, 119, 123
becomes element in political arena, 123
International Pharmaceuticals, infringement of Cyanamid patent in sulfadiazine by, 128–29
International Rectifier (IR), 220–21

International Scientific Congress on Live Virus Vaccines, 1959 meeting of, 235
Irvine, Ralstone R., director of Cyanamid, 76–77
Istituto Biochemico Italiano (IBI), deal with Salvetti and Cancelarich to supply Declomycin processes and bugs, 194, 200
Italy
and absence of patent laws protecting pharmaceuticals, 78, 274
Cyanamid's attack on government buying of drugs in, 122–23
development of drug market in, 78–79
Knickerbocker's buying of drugs for MMSA from, 105–7

Jane, John, alias used by John Cancelarich, 152, 184
Journal of American Chemical Society, 48
Journal of the American Medical Association, 35

Kasal Trading Company, selling of sulfadiazine by, 129
Kavanaugh, Bill, Cyanamid's man in Washington, 107, 110–11
Kefauver, Estes
as chairman of Senate Subcommittee on Antitrust and Monopoly, 74–75
death of, 249
in debate on drug bill, 211, 213
as exploiter of public opinion, 116, 166, 167–68
skill as tactical politician, 107–8, 166
Kefauver drug bill, 145, 167, 170, 197
battles over, 173–77
debate in Senate, 211–13
formal approval by Senate Judiciary Committee in revised form, 177
in House of Representatives, 214–15
Kefauver amendment to, 211
Kefauver amendment tabled, 213
PMA lobby against, 171–73, 197, 214–15
revised in secret meeting of Senate Judiciary Committee, 175–77
second revision, after thalidomide crisis, 210–11

signed into law by President Kennedy, 215
unanimous passage by Senate, 213
Kefauver investigation into drug industry, 16, 69, 99, 107–17, 120–25, 166–67
attitude of public resulting from, 113, 197
counterattack of drugmakers against effects on public by, 165–66, 168–70
impression of drugmakers as imparted by, 116
worldwide effects, 124
Kelsey, Frances
as heroine of the hour, 208–9, 215
holds up clearance of Merrell's thalidomide, 206–7
Kennedy, John F.
and drug bill of Representative Oren Harris, 209
and Kefauver drug bill, 174–75, 176, 215
Kennedy, Robert, 141
Kevadon, Merrell's trade name for thalidomide, 206
Kim Laboratories, 131, 192
inquiries about, made by Leo, 132, 153
report by Furman on, to Auletta of Leo, 153, 192
Sidney Fox as operator of, 132, 152, 159, 188, 189
Kintner, Earl, 72–73
Klumpp, Theodore, Winthrop Laboratories, 214
Knickerbocker, William
apprehension over possible criminal indictment of espionage conspirators, 200
and buying of drugs for MMSA abroad, 105–7, 190, 194, 197, 200, 242, 247
criticism of drugmakers by, 75–76, 102
delicate position after indictments in industrial espionage case, 218
as witness in Kefauver hearings, 123
Koprowski, Hilary, assistant in Lederle's polio research program, 228, 229, 233, 235
Korean War, and increased demands for antibiotics, 37

Kraemer, Terry, secretary at Lederle plant, 82, 83, 88
Krsek, George, International Rectifier, 221–22

Laboratory of Biologics Control in Bethesda, Maryland, 231, 232
Lancet, The, 207
Larrick, George, 209
Lasagna, Louis, 205
Le Petit drug firm in Milan
statement of PR firm in behalf of, 246
use of Lederle organisms and processes, 130, 138, 189–90
Lederle Laboratories
amount of research investment, 91
and breeding up of production microorganisms to pedigree bugs, 39
change into research-orientated organization, 17–18
development of new sulfa drugs, 18, 19
discovery and development of Aureomycin, 24–28, 205
discovery and development of Declomycin, 93–95, 133–34
early research projects, 19–20, 27
earnings (1951), 39
and fight to develop a polio vaccine, 225–37
negotiates license with Sabin for production of polio live vaccine, 237
produces Sabin-based polio vaccine under brand name Orimune, 237–38
purchase by Cyanamid, 16–17
scavenging global investigation of microscopic bugs, 22–24
status in Cyanamid complex, 66
value of annual drug production of, 91
Lenz, Widikund, 207
Leo drug firm in Rome
activities of espionage conspirators with, 149–55
bulk tetracycline powder supplied to Premo Laboratories, 200, 219
Sidney Fox's work for, under alias of Joseph Martin, 130, 138
use of Lederle organisms and processes by, 130

Lidoff, H. J., 54, 61
Lidow, Eric, 220–21
Long, Perrin H., 13
Long, Russell
    attack on Cyanamid, Pfizer, and Bristol on Senate floor, 258–59
    and fight over trade name system of marketing drugs, 255
Loss lines in drug industry, 30–31, 112
Lucca, Joe, 137, 140, 143, 161, 162

Magnuson, Warren G., 72
Malcolm, Wilbur, American Cyanamid Company, 100, 107, 227
    and efforts of Bristol Laboratories to effect deal on tetracycline, 57–58
    and improved methods at Lederle, 39
    indictment in antitrust case, 9–10, 11
    and patent battle over tetracycline, 50–52
    personal indictment in antitrust case quashed, 260–61
    and plans for promotion and production of tetracycline, 45–46
    as president of Cyanamid, 66, 136
    and price of Aureomycin, 29, 30, 31–32, 36
    and reorganization of Lederle Laboratories as research-orientated organization, 17–18
    as witness in Kefauver hearings, 120–24
Mancuso, Angelo, 119, 122, 190, 191, 274
Mansfield, Mike, 213
Mansfield, Walter, 76–77
    as attorney for Cyanamid in court battle with McKesson & Robbins, 251
    as attorney for Cyanamid in espionage conspiracy, 147–49, 154–63, 178, 179, 246, 248
    as attorney for Cyanamid in FTC hearings on market-rigging charges, 100
    as attorney for Cyanamid in Kefauver hearings, 120, 121
    gives evidence on espionage conspiracy case to Morgenthau and Gaynor, 195–96
    relationship with U.S. Attorney's office, 181, 242

and strategy of Justice Department in indictments of tetracycline producers, 141
March of Dimes, 226
Margin of Safety (Wilson), 230
Market factors in price of new drugs, 31
Markup in drug industry, and Kefauver investigation, 110, 113, 118
Martin, George, Cyanamid's general counsel, 136
Martin, Joseph, alias used by Sidney Fox, 130, 152
McAlister, Ted, Cyanamid's PR man in Britain, 198, 199
M & B 693 (sulfapyridine), 19
McClellan, John, 174
McCormick, Jerry, 94–95
McKeen, John, Charles Pfizer & Company, 32–33, 105, 107
    and development and promotion of Terramycin, 34–37, 44
    indictment in antitrust case, 10, 11
    and Kefauver investigation, 117
    and patent battle over tetracycline, 48–52
    personal indictment in antitrust case quashed, 260–61
    as witness in antitrust trial of tetracycline producers, 263
McKesson & Robbins
    Lederle attempt to cancel all distribution contracts with prevented by court ruling, 251
    sale of unbranded tetracycline by, 250
McNey, Harry, Cyanamid sales, 169
Medicaid, payments for drugs under, 254
Medicare program, payments for drugs under, 254
Melnick, Joseph, 236
Merck drug firm
    and development of streptomycin, 26
    and patent rights to streptomycin, 33
    prosecution of espionage cases by, 247
    vitamin B_{12} patented by, 138
Merrell, William S. Company
    delay in approval of Kevadon by FDA, 206–7
    distribution of thalidomide tablets for clinical testing before with-

drawal of application from FDA, 209

granted permission to market thalidomide in Canada, 207

production of thalidomide under license from Grünenthal of Germany, 206

withdraws thalidomide application from FDA and takes product off Canadian market, 208

Meyers, Frederick H., 115

Mintz, Morton, 208

Miracle drugs. See Wonder drugs

MMSA (Military Medical Supply Agency). See Knickerbocker, William

Morgenthau, Robert

relationship with attorney Mansfield, 181

statement on industrial espionage indictments, 245

Morton, John, research chemist at Lederle, 46

Mothers' March on Polio, 226

Muller, Siegfried

as chemist at Lederle, resignation of and suspicions about, 135–36, 137

employed by Ankermann Italiana, 139, 195

named co-conspirator in suit against Sharff, 159, 275

as suspected espionage conspirator, 149

National Foundation for Infantile Paralysis, 226–27

National Research Council, 43

Nelson, Gaylord, 255

New York City, amount to be paid under settlement following drug antitrust convictions, 264

New York State, amount to be paid under settlement following drug antitrust convictions, 264

New York Times, 76–77

Nolen, Herman, president of McKesson & Robbins, 250, 251

Obsolescence in drug industry, 29–30

O'Connor, Basil, 226, 230–31

Operation Sphinx of Bristol Laboratories, 60

Orimune, brand name of Lederle's Sabin-based polio vaccine, 237

Oxytetracycline, trade name of Terramycin, 41

Parke, Davis & Co.

development of Chloromycetin by, 32

refusal to cut price for New York City bulk orders of Chloromycetin, 251–52

Parker, Bob, general manager of Lederle, 131–32, 160

Parsons, Jud, attorney for Pfizer, 261

Pasteur Institute in Paris, 13

Pastore, John O., 211

Patent laws protecting pharmaceuticals

absence in Italy, 78

Kefauver drug bill aimed at, 145, 170, 173, 197

in United States, criticisms of, 113–14

Patent Office. See U.S. Patent Office

Payout time in drug industry, 29

Pearson, Drew, 174

Penicillin

declared not patentable by U.S. Patent Office, 21–22

developing as practical usable product, 21, 24–25

discovery by Fleming, 21, 23

history as unpatented and therefore unprotected, 33

increased demands in Korean War, 37, 38

Lederle's research project into, 19, 20–21, 24

making by Pfizer, 33

overproduction and falling prices, 33

production by Bristol Laboratories, 37–38

as wonder drug, 15

Pfizer, Charles, & Company, 10, 32–33

battle orders for selling of Terramycin and Tetracyn issued to salesmen, 55–56

discovery and development of Terramycin, 34–35

dropping of lawsuits by, 65

FTC's accusations against, in Aureomycin fermentation tests, 62

gross annual sales (1953), 49–50
indictment under Sherman Act,
140
licensed to produce Sabin live polio
vaccine, 237, 238
ordered by FTC to license all domestic applicants to make tetracycline,
250, 260
promotion campaign for Terramycin,
35–37
settles quarrel with Premo and becomes its main supplier of bulk
tetracycline, 252
sues British government for patent
infringement of tetracycline, 216
suit for infringement of tetracycline
patent against Bristol, Squibb, and
Upjohn, 62, 63
suits and countersuits of New York
City and Premo Laboratories over
infringement of tetracycline patent, 252
tapping of Bristol wires, 64–65
Pharmaceutical Manufacturers' Association (PMA)
aim in lobby against Kefauver drug
bill, 171–72, 174, 175
and compromises agreed on, in Kefauver drug bill, 175
conference in New York (December,
1959), 117–19
lobbying organization, 119, 171–73,
174, 175, 214, 255
refurbishing to promote public image, 117–18
and regulations of new drug law,
215
Phelps, Dr., head of chemical production section of Lederle, 83,
84
Phillips, Austin, patent attorney for
Cyanamid, 52, 128–31, 139, 274
Pierrel drug firm in Capua
Terramycin contract of MMSA with,
200, 218–19
tetracycline produced under trade
name Demetetra, 133, 138
use of Lederle organisms and processes by, 130
Pink Sheet, 174
PMA. See Pharmaceutical Manufacturers' Association

Polio vaccine, 225–38
development of Sabin live vaccine,
233–37
development and introduction of
Salk killed vaccine, 231–32, 235
failures of Lederle's live virus, 236–
37
field experiments with Lederle's live
vaccine, 234, 235
Lederle ends program on Cox strains,
and negotiates license with Sabin,
237
live polio vaccine as objective of
Lederle's research program, 228,
230, 231, 232, 234
massive clinical trial facilities offered
by Russian government for Sabin
live vaccine, 234–35, 236
polio research program of Lederle,
227–30
rivalry between Lederle and Sabin
for acceptance of their live vaccines, 235–36
Sabin strains licensed by National Institutes of Health, 237
testing of Lederle's live vaccine by
Dr. Dick, 233
Polycyclin, Bristol's trade name of tetracycline, 60
Powers, John, Charles Pfizer & Company, 60–61
Prednisolone, production of, by Schering Corporation, 108, 112
Prednisone
investigation by Kefauver committee,
108–13
price, under generic name and under
trade names, 101
production by Premo Laboratories,
101
production by Schering Corporation,
101, 108
Premo Laboratories, 101, 105, 106, 154,
197, 200, 219, 247
Pfizer settles quarrel and becomes its
main supplier of bulk tetracycline,
252
sale of own generic tetracycline at
greatly reduced price, 252
Prescriptions
amount spent by Americans on medication in form of (1967), 257

using generic names of drugs as against trade names, 102, 115, 205

Press
and antitrust case against tetracycline producers, 263–64
and Kefauver investigation, 100, 107, 110, 113, 116–17, 120

Prices of drugs
break in price barrier of old tetracycline producers, 253
and Kefauver investigation, 107, 124, 166, 167, 170, 197
under generic name and under trade name, 101–2, 115

Procaine penicillin, patent conflict over, 60

Profit motive and human welfare, as conflicting forces in drug industry, 10–11

Profits in drug industry
and Kefauver investigation, 167, 170, 197
listing of, in FTC quarterly report, 76
and wonder drugs, 15–16, 38–39

Progynon, production by Schering Corporation, 112–13

Promethazine, development of, 38

Prontosil, experimentation with, 12–13

Quinethazone, sulfa drug of Lederle, 224

Rachel Laboratories
continues as producer and seller of tetracycline in America, 253
Cyanamid patches up quarrel over tetracycline, 253
and Fermentfarma of Milan, 220, 221, 223, 224
Italy as source of organisms and know-how of, 220, 221–23
organization and objectives, 220–21
production of tetracycline, 219–20, 221, 224, 243, 247
as suppliers of tetracycline to McKesson & Robbins, 250

Rankin, J. Lee, 264

Real Voice, The (Harris)
and Kefauver investigation of drug industry, 69, 109

quoted on drug lobbyists in House, 214
quoted on special interests operating in revisions of Kefauver bill, 175

Remensnyder, John P., Heyden Chemical Corporation, 57

Research
criticism of Kefauver Committee on use of word as a smokescreen by drug industry, 114
in drug industry, Mike Gorman quoted on, 114–15
by drug manufacturers, Seymour Blackman quoted on, 115
and exploitation of Patent Office, Dr. Frederick H. Meyers quoted on, 115
investment of drug firms in, and development of wonder drugs, 12, 14–15

Reutter, Caroline, secretary at Lederle, 90–91, 92

Roerig, J. B., & Co., 53

Rogers, Donald I., 123

Rosenblatt, Maurice
as chemist consultant to Le Petit, 189–90
Cyanamid wins suit against in absentia, 246
indictment in industrial espionage case, 245
remained outside jurisdiction of court in industrial espionage case trial, 246

Rubinstein, Ben
as lawyer for Cancelarich, 185–86, 195
as lawyer for Leonard Fine, 195

Sabin, Albert, 233–37

Salb, Seymour
found guilty in industrial espionage case and sentenced to two years, 245
indictment in industrial espionage case, 245
as officer of Biorganic Laboratories, 89–90, 95, 97
role in espionage conspiracy, 187, 188, 190, 194, 196
as stockholder in Ankermann Italiana, 139, 151, 194–95

Salk, Jonas, 231–32
Salvetti, Elio
  contacts with Leo, 150–51, 152–54, 193
  indictment in industrial espionage case, 217
  as partner of Bottone in Kasal Trading Company, 129, 151, 191
  remained outside jurisdiction of court in industrial espionage case trial, 246
  role in espionage conspiracy, 191–95, 196
  as stockholder in Ankermann Italiana, 151, 195
Schering Corporation
  and Kefauver investigation, 108–9
  production of prednisone, 101, 108
Scholz, Ted
  as head of process improvement department of Lederle, 83, 84, 155
  and suspicious actions of Fox in his department, 84–86, 88, 89, 92–93
Schwartz, Frederic, Bristol Laboratories, 38, 57–66
  indictment in antitrust case, 10, 11
  personal indictment in antitrust case quashed, 260–61
  as witness in antitrust trial of tetracycline producers, 263
Senate Subcommittee on Antitrust and Monopoly, 74–75. See also Kefauver investigation into drug industry
Sharff, Nathan
  Cyanamid files suit against, 157–60
  found guilty in industrial espionage case and sentenced to two years, 245
  indictment in industrial espionage case, 217
  as officer of Biorganic Laboratories, 89, 95, 119
  role in espionage conspiracy, 187–91, 194, 196
  as stockholder in Ankermann Italiana, 139, 151, 194–95
Side effects
  of antibiotics, 43–44
  bad publicity from, 205
  minimizing of, and Kefauver investigation, 107, 167
  regulation by new drug law, 215

Silverang, Sol, executive vice-president of Premo Laboratories, 219
Sjolander, Newell, 94–95
Sklarsky, Harry
  as Assistant U.S. Attorney from Justice Department's Antitrust Division, 140
  as prosecutor in government antitrust case against tetracycline producers, 261–64
Smith, Austin, 117, 118
Smith, Stewart, sales director of Lederle, 18
Social Security Act, 1965 Amendments to, 253
Squibb drug firm
  Bristol as supplier of bulk tetracycline to, 60, 63
  as co-conspirator in antitrust case against tetracycline producers, 262
  and development of streptomycin, 26
  licensed by Pfizer to sell tetracycline, 65
Steele, J. Murray, 75
Steroids, development of, 15
Stessel, Paul, Lederle's public relations manager, 100, 169, 197, 218
Stevenson, Ian, 75
Stewart, Jack, head of Lederle industrial and community relations, 83, 92, 98, 119, 134, 137, 143, 159
Stichter, Jack, 157–58
Streptomyces aureofaciens. See Aureomycin
Streptomycin
  development by Dr. Waksman, 26
  overproduction and falling prices, 33
  as wonder drug, 15, 26
Sulfa drugs
  first experiments in United States, 13
  as opener for big stakes of drug firms in research investment, 14–15
Sulfadiazine
  development by Lederle, 19
  infringement of Cyanamid patent by International Pharmaceuticals, 128–29
  infringement of Cyanamid patent by Kasal Trading Company, 129–30
Sulfaguanidine, development by Lederle, 19, 20

Sulfanilamide
Lederle's work on, 19
production by Cyanamid, 17
Sulfapyridine, production by Lederle, 18–19
Sulfonamide, as anti-strep-infection agent, 13
Supertranquilizers, promethazine as first of new school of, 38
Synthetic cortisone, development of, 38
Synthetic vitamins, development of, 15

Taussig, Helen B., 177–78
Television, and Kefauver drug investigation, 107, 110
Terramycin
annual sales (1953), 49
and claim of few side effects, 44
as competition in broad-spectrum antibiotics market, 36
discovery and development by Pfizer, 34–37
as Pfizer's "seventy million dollar baby," 53
plus values, over Aureomycin, 34
price, 36
promotion campaign by McKeen of Pfizer, 35–37
as trade name of oxytetracycline, 41
Tetracycline. See also Government criminal antitrust case against tetracycline producers
Achromycin as Lederle's trade name, 51
and battle for control, 48–52, 273
break in price barrier of old tetracycline producers, 253
civil suits following convictions in antitrust trial, 264
competitors for patent, 46
criticism of producers by Knickerbocker, 75–76, 102
deal worked out between Pfizer and Cyanamid, 51–52
declared unpatentable by patent examiner, 61
discovery by Pfizer scientists simultaneously with that of Lederle, 48
discovery and development at Lederle, 42–43, 44–46
discovery and development of Declomycin at Lederle, 93–95, 133–34

exoneration of companies involved in FTC charges of market rigging, 145–46
four basic drugs in tetracycline family, 273
FTC announces formal charges of market rigging against five companies, 74
FTC reverses ruling in favor of tetracycline companies, and orders Pfizer to license all domestic applicants, 250
generic, production and sale by Premo Laboratories, 252
generic, sale by McKesson & Robbins, 250
Operation Sphinx of Bristol in production, 60
plans of Lederle for production and promotion, 45–46, 51
Polycyclin as Bristol's trade name of, 60
production by Rachel Laboratories, 219–20, 221, 224, 243, 250, 253
production of Demetetra by Pierrel Company, 133, 138
purchase from Italy by MMSA, 105–7
reversal of decision of patent examiner and issuance of patent to Pfizer, 62
rising price, 103
suits and countersuits of Pfizer, New York City, and Premo Laboratories over patent infringement, 252
superiority to other antibiotics, 43, 45
Tetracyn, as Pfizer's trade name, 53
Tetracyn
Pfizer's sales promotion, 53
as Pfizer's trade name of tetracycline, 53
Thalidomide
administered in United States during clinical trials, as unapproved and uncontrolled drug, 204
and births of deformed infants, 177–78, 207
hysterical public reaction to publicity on, 213–14
report in New York Times on Dr. Taussig's speech about, 177–78
story in Time magazine, 178

warning of PMA to staff about, 178
Till, Irene
  detailed exploration of U.S. drug
    business, 76, 101
  as economist with FTC, 70, 71
  on staff of Kefauver Committee, 74
Trade name distribution of drugs
  attacked in Kefauver investigation,
    115
  fight on, by Senator Long, 255
  fight on, by Senator Nelson, 255
Tranquilizers
  Congressional hearings on advertis-
    ing, 75
  development, 15
Triamcinalone
  Aristocort, Lederle's trade name, 84,
    188
  production by Lederle, 84, 93, 187
  sale by Fox to Biorganic Laboratories
    for resale in Italy, 188

U.S. Patent Office. See also Patent laws
    protecting pharmaceuticals
  examiner at, raises question about
    patentability of tetracycline, 54, 61,
    62
  implications against in Kefauver
    hearings, 115–16
  penicillin declared not patentable by,
    21–22
Untold Story of the Drug Hearings,
    The, 168
Upjohn drug firm
  Bristol as supplier of bulk tetra-
    cycline to, 60, 63
  as co-conspirator in antitrust case
    against tetracycline producers, 262
  licensed by Pfizer to sell tetracycline,
    65

Vaccines, development of new and
    miraculous, 15. See also Polio vac-
    cine
Virus research at Lederle, 227
Visconti, Count Niccolo
  as head of Pierrel Company, 133, 187,
    193, 194, 200, 219, 275
  indictment in industrial espionage
    case, 217
  remained outside jurisdiction of
    court in industrial espionage case
    trial, 245–46

Vitamin B$_{12}$
  development, 38
  as postwar wonder drug, patented by
    Merck, 138
Vitamin C, making by Pfizer, 33

Waksman, Selman A., 26
Washburn, Frank Sherman, founder of
    Cyanamid Company, 16
Wawretchek, Helmuth
  agrees to testify for government in
    industrial espionage case, 242, 275
  in charge of fermentations at Anker-
    mann, 222
  joins Rachel Laboratories, 223–24,
    250
  move from Ankermann to Ferment-
    farma, 222
  as president of Ankermann Italiana,
    133, 138–39, 155, 156, 190, 194, 222
Weiss, Arnold, 103, 104, 105
Welch, Henry
  as head of Antibiotics Division of
    FDA, 105
  inquiry into sparetime activities of,
    260–61
Wendt, Henry, sales director of Lederle,
    28, 45, 52
Whitney, Simon, 72, 73
Whittlesey, Granville, 158, 159
Williams, H., research director at
    Lederle, 44
Wilson, John Rowan, 230
Wolkoff, Theodore, 243–44
Wonder drugs
  appearance of additional, in late
    1940's, 38
  beginning of age of, 12
  development of sulfas, 13–14
  and expansion of drug firms in re-
    search, 14–15
  medical practice revolutionized by,
    15
  pioneering of Cyanamid in, 11
  and soaring profits in drug industry,
    15–16, 38–39
Wyeth drug firm licensed to produce
    Sabin live polio vaccine, 237, 238
Wynn, Thomas J., Pfizer general man-
    ager, 55

Yuncker, Barbara, 120, 122, 123